phie Tucker Arrested

Censors insisted that a sketch bout a blind man and a omosexual, from the Steve uttenberg show, be removed or the rerun, despite the fact it ad already aired with their pproval. They also demanded hat a sketch called "What's My ddiction?" be deleted from a how hosted by Paul Shaffer.

Wednesday, December 7, 1949

Comedy Cycle Due for a Change
— By JOE LAURIE, JR. —

Toronto Hotel Bans Religious, Political Spoofs

A YOUNG comedian and impressionist, Rich Little, has been banned om presenting religious and political oofs at Toronto's Royal York Hotel.

rson: *Meant* o *Disrespect* o *Morticians*

Dice Clay gets cheers, jeers
TTERS TO THE EDITOR

Minstrel Show Demeaning?

omen's Lib Want Prostitutes, sbians OK'd, Dean Martin Axed

omedian s Slapped

COMEDIAN SLAPPED.
WANSEA, England — A woman in the audience slapped Ossie orris, Welsh comedian, because let slip two swear words during a variety show here. The ac-

Cit C

American "Sick" Act

M.D." have in common?

They share the wrath o Virginia - based organiza called STOP IMMORAL ON TV, which wants to cl up television.

Can't Be Clean Anymore, Sez Oldtime Scot Comic In Rapping Today's 'Filth'

'Frito Bandito' is subject of protest
Milt Josefsberg

reprises some the kookie Mad A and intramural concepts on w vis-a-vis ethnic groups an homebody sensitivities, on certain teleprograms

KOTTER UNWELCOME

Boston Bans ABC Comedy

You have no right to make fun of Reagan. He's doing the best he can for the country.

Michael Dobes, 9
Canyon Country

You Mustn't Say That
Smothers Brother Police Feud Reviv

Are Comedians Too Bras or Public Too Sensitive?

6 arrested for protest at 'Saturday Night Live

Gay groups to picket Kinison

Smothers Brothe Pro-Marijuana Sk Irks Police Chief

OUTRAGEOUS

Also by the author

*The Comedians: Drunks, Thieves, Scoundrels
and the History of American Comedy*

*We Had a Little Real Estate Problem: The Unheralded
Story of Native Americans and Comedy*

OUTRAGEOUS

A HISTORY OF SHOWBIZ AND THE CULTURE WARS

KLIPH NESTEROFF

ABRAMS PRESS
NEW YORK, NY

If you want to get comedians . . . allow them freedom of speech. They haven't got any . . . That's why I think there's no more comedy.
—Groucho Marx, April 1962

We have created a marketplace out there in which it is no longer a marketplace of ideas—it is a marketplace of opinions. It is a marketplace of lying and calumny. It is a marketplace in which, tragically, the most outrageous views get the greatest attention.
—Ted Koppel, November 2019

CONTENTS

Note to the Reader

Please be aware that some of the material quoted within this book includes archaic terminology that might be considered wildly offensive by modern standards.

INTRODUCTION

The modern news cycle presents us with a new controversy every week. If social media is any indication, comedians, actors, musicians, and filmmakers are continually under attack and on the defensive. Americans are no longer civil or respectful. We are engaged in a battle for the soul of the nation. These are unprecedented times. The country is polarized like never before.

These are common beliefs. But do they hold up to scrutiny?

In the old days of newspapers, one could read disturbing articles, distressing editorials, and horrific headlines—but readers looked at them only once, and then threw them away. Today we scroll through the same horrific headlines over and over again, all day long. The headlines are repeatedly reinforced, but much of what is reinforced is opinion, much of it is doomsday prophecy about what *might* happen. And a good deal of it is intentionally composed to incite and manipulate the reader, placing it in the category of "Culture War."

The Culture War can be defined by a simplistic philosophy: "*We* are good. *They* are evil." Historian Richard Hofstadter described this philosophy long before the term "Culture War" existed, in his 1965 book, *The Paranoid Style in American Politics*:

"The central image is that of a vast and sinister conspiracy, a gigantic and yet subtle machinery of influence set in motion to undermine and destroy a way of life . . . and what is felt to be needed [is] an all-out crusade. The paranoid spokesman sees the fate of this conspiracy in apocalyptic terms—he traffics in the birth and death of whole worlds, whole political orders, whole systems of human values . . . He constantly lives at a turning point: it is now or never in organizing resistance . . . Time is forever running out . . . Since the enemy is thought of as being totally evil and totally unappeasable, he must be totally eliminated."

Show business was dragged into the Culture War and used as a scape-goat. Jazz music, rock music, hip hop. The tango, the jitterbug, the twist. Radio comedy, stand-up comedy, television comedy. All have been blamed for the downfall of America at one time or another—and all have been subject to censorship and suppression as a result. The end is near, we are warned, unless we do something to stop the madness right now.

Author Fritz Stern observed in his 1961 book, *The Politics of Cultural Despair,* that societies often "mistook change for decline, and, consistent with their conception of history, attributed the decline to a moral failing."

"Nothing short of a great Civil War of Values rages today throughout North America," said evangelical leader James Dobson. "Two sides with vastly differing and incompatible worldviews are locked in a bitter conflict that permeates every level of society. Bloody battles are being fought on a thousand fronts, both inside and outside of government."

James Dobson followed the game plan of Paul Weyrich, a political strategist who turned the evangelical movement into a political force. Weyrich's specialty was Culture War hysteria—which he relentlessly amplified for the purpose of consolidating political power.

Paul Weyrich began as a lecturer with the John Birch Society in the early 1960s. Founded by Junior Mints manufacturer Robert Welch and Fred C. Koch, father of the infamous Koch brothers, the John Birch Society despised Dr. Martin Luther King Jr. and the Civil Rights Movement. They accused Dr. King of implementing a Soviet conspiracy and warned that the Civil Rights Act of 1964 would be a step toward tyranny.

Throughout the 1960s, the John Birch Society was routinely mocked by showbiz personalities like George Carlin, Bob Dylan, and Johnny Carson.

Weyrich was savvy enough to realize he was affiliated with a laughingstock, one that could hamper his political ambitions. After campaigning for Alabama segregationist George Wallace in 1968, Weyrich distanced himself from the John Birch Society, but he retained their political philosophy. With a massive handout from Joseph Coors of the Coors beer dynasty, Weyrich developed an elaborate Culture War infrastructure. He founded the Heritage Foundation with Coors in 1973, the Moral Majority with Jerry Falwell in 1979, and helped establish the Christian Coalition with Pat Robertson in 1989. Each organization crafted a series of bogeymen meant to divide and conquer the body politic. The Culture War gave traction to unpopular policies that the public would not otherwise support. Weyrich had taken the discredited John Birch Society philosophies and rebranded them for the mainstream—with remarkable success.

★

Today comedy has been drafted into the Culture War. People with no relation to comedy—and who are the political opposites of Lenny Bruce, Richard Pryor, and George Carlin—have become self-proclaimed experts. One of the main talking points is that you can't joke about *anything* anymore, and one need only look at the taboos placed on certain slurs as proof. Yes, there *are* new taboos, the defamation of transgendered people being an obvious example. However, there's also more freedom of expression on television today than ever before. One can repeatedly hear the word "shit" in commercials, talk shows, and on awards programs when it's in reference to the sitcom *Schitt's Creek*. A mainstream program with such a title would have been an unthinkable scandal just twenty years ago. One need only look at the HBO series *Euphoria*, with its explicit drug use and full-frontal nudity, to see that taboos have been shattered even as new ones are established. Yet, through the daily reinforcement of social media—and orchestrated Culture War talking points—we are told precisely the opposite.

Talking heads on cable news, radio, and social media have received substantial handouts from "think tanks" to shape their coverage. As multiple talking heads from multiple outlets conform to the same think tank talking points, the result is a convincing illusion that thousands of people are in agreement. In exchange for massive cash payments, media personalities have included the talking points provided by the Heritage Foundation, the Heartland Institute, the Olin Foundation, the Scaife Foundation, and a handful of other "foundations." Most receive substantial financial support from Charles Koch of Koch brothers fame, in exchange for furthering his political interests. Koch ran a John Birch Society bookstore in Wichita, Kansas, in the late 1960s.

★

"I think the people today in the humor field—their limits are much greater than Will Rogers," said *Tonight Show* host Steve Allen in the year 1955. "Today we have a great many pressure groups and a great many self-appointed people who are ready to criticize . . . These are very touchy times."

For generations, comedians were censored if they joked about sex, politics, or religion. Today these are among comedy's most commonly discussed topics. But not long ago, if a comic insisted on covering any of those three categories, the result was not just censorship, but potential arrest. Lenny Bruce was arrested for saying the word "schmuck" onstage in Los Angeles in 1962. George Carlin was arrested for vulgarity in Milwaukee in 1972. Richard Pryor was arrested for swearing in Alexandria, Virginia, in 1974. Andrew Dice Clay was threatened with arrest in Dallas, Texas, in 1990. The harassment of comedians was far more serious when they were up against the law.

Obscenity laws changed and societal taboos shifted in the late 1960s, allowing for criticism of politicians, police, and foreign policy. As a result, accusations of political bias were directed at comedians. Joseph Keeley, an editor at *TV Guide*, wrote in 1971:

"If you want to ascertain the liberal or liberal-left position on almost any issue, you can quickly find out from a certain type of run-of-the-mill comedian. The targets of such comedians . . . tie in with the headlines, but for months Spiro Agnew has been a favorite . . . Others who are currently unpopular are Governor [Ronald] Reagan, [Chicago] Mayor Daley, FBI and CIA agents, policemen, Southerners and those silly people they call flag wavers . . . Military people are also prime targets of the comedians, and there seems to be a standing rule that the higher the rank the more stupid and ridiculous the officer must be made to appear."

Meanwhile, students opposing the Vietnam War or marching in favor of equal rights were classified as humorless. "The fact that Americans are losing their sense of humor is especially evident in the college classroom," reported the *Boston Globe* in 1968. Speakers were "increasingly running up against walls of stone-faced students who appear disenchanted and unenlightened."

In recent history, the college campus has been cast as a villain in the Culture War. Colleges not operating solely in the interest of big business have been accused of brainwashing or suppressing free speech. One of the organizations created by Paul Weyrich now has a subsidiary called the Center to Protect Free Speech (funded by Charles Koch). According to one study, the Center to Protect Free Speech specializes in "the manufacturing of culture war narratives" about "snowflakes" and "social justice warriors" for the purpose of "spreading a moral panic." The Center to Protect Free Speech pays Culture War provocateurs to speak on college campuses for the purpose of incitement. When protests erupt, such objection is used as proof that the campus is opposed to free speech. Demonized in the body politic, funding is threatened—and legal action undertaken—until the campus is made hospitable to think tank interests.

Jerry Seinfeld announced in 2015 that he was no longer interested in performing stand-up at colleges because the modern generation was far too sensitive. Think tank strategists seized on the statement. A member of the Olin Foundation, the chemical company think tank that helped create the Federalist Society, explained the strategy: "The PC movement is really the first issue that has split the left on campus. This opportunity should be exploited: the more of a wedge we can drive between heretofore closely aligned leftist constituencies, the better."

Soon a talking point about how "you can't joke about anything any-more" was spread by think tank operatives on cable news, talk radio, and social media. The same John Birch Society and Moral Majority elements that had previously opposed free speech in comedy now claimed to be its savior.

The hysteria mystified some comedians, even those who generated occasional controversy. "You can joke about whatever the fuck you like," insisted comedian Ricky Gervais. "And some people won't like it and they will tell you they don't like it. And then it's up to you whether you give a fuck or not. And so on. It's a good system."

The haters and complainers of social media are used as evidence that "you can't joke about anything anymore," but the same argument existed in the 1950s and '60s when the majority of complaints came through the mail.

"This atmosphere of fear which can be produced by a few letters is a serious problem in our country today," said Groucho Marx in 1954.

"There's this wild lunatic fringe of letter writers that greatly affect what the sponsor has in mind," complained *Twilight Zone* creator Rod Serling in 1959.

For most of the twentieth century, hostile grievances were published as letters to the editor in newspapers, magazines, and *TV Guide*. The complaints were often irrational and outrageous. They were also moderated and filtered by a newspaper editor. In those days, perhaps one out of every one hundred complaints would be published and the rest discarded. But today, social media has removed the editor from the equation and every hostile expression is published automatically. It gives the impression that people are more irrational, humorless, and overly sensitive than in the past. But the vitriol found in vintage letters to the editor is remarkably similar to sentiments found on social media today.

The Smothers Brothers Comedy Hour was a classic example of how letter-writing pressure could affect popular comedy. Stand-up comedian David Steinberg delivered mock sermons in front of a stained-glass backdrop on *The Smothers Brothers Comedy Hour* during the program's 1968–69 season. Just mentioning the Bible in a comedy routine was largely taboo at the time.

"My husband and I were shocked and amazed to hear the comedian on the Smothers Brothers show," wrote a viewer. "We could not believe our ears when he uttered the blasphemous material he called humor. The idea of making jokes about God is beyond belief."

"The CBS switchboards all over the nation lit up," said CBS executive Robert Metz. "The mail was overwhelmingly condemning and several letters mailed directly to the Smothers Brothers' Hollywood offices contained razor blades."

The hate mail sent to the Smothers Brothers was as venomous as any modern internet comment section. "Am surprised you lousy stinkers have lasted so long," wrote an angry viewer. "I hope you get the [N-word] shit kicked out of you. Will come down and Butter your Motzahs [sic] with Arab shit."

CBS received a letter addressed to the "Gay Smothers Brothers." It said, "Why do you queers continually show this so-called new generation? I for one am fed up with looking at [N-word]s, [N-word]-lovers and long-haired fruits on your and every other show on TV."

One of the producers of *The Smothers Brothers Comedy Hour* was Ernest Chambers, a comedy writer who wrote material for nearly every major comedian in the business. CBS forced Chambers and his fellow writers to delete "offensive" phrases like "sex education" and "freak out" from their scripts. Network executives, corporate sponsors, and Washington allies all concluded that *The Smothers Brothers Comedy Hour* was too blasphemous and that its star, Tommy Smothers, was too antagonizing to the White House and their foreign policy. The show was essentially removed from the air so as not to inflame the already tense relationship between CBS Television and the Nixon-Agnew administration.

Now ninety-one years old, Ernest Chambers is surprised to hear current complaints about a lack of freedom in comedy. "There's no question there's now more freedom of expression in comedy today," says Chambers. "I mean, having been through the Smothers Brothers situation—what we could and could not say fifty years ago compared to now? It's no comparison. People just don't know their history."

This book covers that history. *Outrageous: A History of Showbiz and the Culture Wars* will not chronicle every modern showbiz controversy nor every current internet hysteria. Controversies from the social media age—Michael

Richards to Daniel Tosh, Kathy Griffin to Dave Chappelle—will not be recounted here. The purpose of this book is to provide context for showbiz controversies as they arise—and how to make sense of them. And while the showbiz of a hundred years ago may seem remote, it is remarkable how similar the issues of the past are to the concerns of today.

1

THE 1800S: PROTEST.
CENSORSHIP. CONTROL.

American show business essentially begins in the 1830s with the blackface minstrel show. Ever since that time, audiences have complained.

For two hundred years, performers were subjected to criticism, protest, and outrage. Long before modern catchphrases like "PC police," "cancel culture," and "woke mob," popular artists were threatened, blacklisted, fired, and publicly shamed. Sometimes the grievances were thoughtful and logical. Just as often they were impulsive and irrational.

Religious patrons objected to performances considered insulting to their faith. Ethnic minorities protested that which they found bigoted. The political class attempted to censor that which criticized their rule and expressions of sexuality were against the law.

The notion of a "cancel culture" was already present in the colonial era. "Public amusements were criticized, and acting was considered sinful," explained showbiz historian Armond Fields. "The stalwarts of the Continental Congress passed a law decreeing the closure of all places of public entertainment."

The original blackface craze began in the 1830s. It was Thomas Rice as his enslaved character Jim Crow that made blackface a national phenomenon. The comic was described as a "scrambling-looking man with a sepulchral falsetto voice" and he inspired hundreds of performers to alter their skin tone, speak in dialect, and sing about the plantation.

Blackface troupes were soon pilfering material from one another, and as the same material was repeated over and over in the early 1840s, blackface minstrel songs became American standards. The *New York Tribune* was surprised by its popularity: "It seemed as though the entire population had been bitten . . . In the kitchen, in the shop and in the street, Jim Crow monopolized public attention."

To white Americans, blackface was just another form of stage makeup, used by the same actors who previously wore pancake powder or spirit gum. You were scarcely considered a thespian unless you applied burnt cork to darken your face. But not everyone considered it acceptable. As early as 1848, abolitionist Frederick Douglass referred to blackface comedians as the "filthy scum of white society, who have stolen from us a complexion denied to them by nature, in which to make money, and to pander to the corrupt taste of their white fellow citizens."

The formerly enslaved Douglass was touring the country at the time. His antislavery speeches were often interrupted by hecklers armed with "brickbats, fire-crackers and other missiles."

Minstrel shows presented takeoff versions of *Uncle Tom's Cabin*. The popular novel by Harriet Beecher Stowe was antislavery in theme but stereotypical in nature. Detractors said it was racist. Fans said it was anti-racist. A believer in phrenology, the pseudoscience that equates the shape of the head with the size of the mind, Stowe claimed *Uncle Tom's Cabin* had come to her "in a vision," and had been written by God.

In a 1956 study of her work, author J. C. Furnas said Stowe sent "her readers into deepening their belief in the half-baked racism of that time . . . Her books are the only racist propaganda known to have been read favorably by very many at that time, and their effect must always have been to instill or to strengthen racist ideas."

And yet the success of *Uncle Tom's Cabin* galvanized abolitionist sentiment. It was credited with bringing the antislavery movement mainstream. It also solidified stereotypes for a new generation of blackface performance.

Minstrels used blackface to further both progressive and regressive points of view. Historian Eric Lott said a blackface show might contain "proslavery and antislavery views, depending on who was doing the writing and performing."

Many blackface acts advocated for abolition, but as the Civil War approached, they were outnumbered. Historian Mel Watkins explained, "From about 1853 to the Civil War . . . nearly all vestiges of black humanity were excised from minstrel performances. During this period the portrait of the plantation was made even more idyllic, and the stereotype of black males as childlike, shiftless, irresponsible dolts was heightened . . . distorted comic stereotypes intended to 'prove' that slavery and black subordination were justified."

It remained that way after the Civil War. According to historian Jim Haskins, "White southerners had no sympathy for former slaves, and so the caricatures became cruel."

Vaudeville shows in the post–Civil War era were informed by the old minstrel shows. For that reason, comedians were criticized as old fashioned and unoriginal. The *Brooklyn Daily Eagle* wrote in October 1877, "Hitherto . . . the form of amusement we call comedy has not changed much. We meet the same types every day played by the same men who pictured them twenty years ago. Indeed, the traditions of the stage have preserved the old men and maidens of the earliest times."

Immigration would change it. Jewish immigrants, Irish immigrants, Italian immigrants, and formerly enslaved African Americans took to the stage and established the roots of modern American showbiz. They did so because there was nowhere else to go. Xenophobia shut them out of the traditional workforce.

Samuel Morse, the man for whom the Morse Code was named, was convinced immigrants were destroying America. "A conspiracy exists . . . its plans are already in operation," he wrote. "The serpent has already commenced his coil about our limbs, and the lethargy of his poison is creeping over us . . . We must awake, or we are lost."

Business owners deflected labor discontent in the direction of immigrants. Newspapers blamed an economic slump on "long-haired, wild-eyed, bad-smelling, atheistic, reckless foreign wretches, who never did an honest hour's work in their lives." The president of the American Iron and Steel

Association said the country's economic depression was due to "thousands of idle and vicious foreigners who have not come here to work for a living but to stir up strife and to commit crime."

Newly arrived Jewish, Irish, and Italian immigrants joined the formerly enslaved in a scramble for employment. Medicine and law were "restricted" professions. In order to survive, immigrants sold scrap metal or did hard labor under perilous conditions. Most found it difficult to secure a living wage.

Meanwhile, show business was considered a disreputable genre comparable to prostitution or drug dealing. Actors were considered ne'er-do-wells, bums, liars, perverts, reprobates, and thieves. Among the upper class, it was an embarrassment if your daughter dated an actor. Showbiz historian Arthur Frank Wertheim said these "traditional animosities" could be traced to the Puritan era. "The more conservative religious groups viewed actors as the devil's advocates. The low pay of the average performer, frequent unemployment, and a reputation as alcoholics and philanderers only served to intensify the stereotype."

In the town of Bethel, Connecticut, show business was "rigorously forbidden by law, and even those found playing a social game of cards were arrested and fined."

Accused of spreading immorality and crime, performers were often assaulted and run out of town. Vaudevillian Sam Devere fought an attacker and beat him to death with his banjo. Vaudeville comic Eddie Foy was tied to a horse, dragged through town until his limbs were raw, and dumped face-first into a water trough.

The material of vaudeville comedians was subject to criticism. Comics who had done the same shtick for years found themselves doing damage control as societal attitudes changed. A vaudevillian named Nat Goodwin walked to the footlights in 1895 and apologized for some unspecified stand-up material:

"Ladies and Gentlemen, during a professional career of over twenty-two years, this is the first time I have appeared before the curtain with a heavy heart. I assure you what occurred last night was the fault of the head and not of the heart. I endeavored to hold a mirror up to nature and failed. If you will forgive me you will make me very happy . . . Forget this, my first offense, and I promise it will never happen again."

Vaudeville reporter Grant Dixon observed, "It is not unusual for comedians to go a little bit too far. One example of the license taken by comedians engaging in what Broadway calls 'ad libbing' is brought to my attention. The comedian, during the middle of his act . . . pointed to the pit orchestra . . . describing the musicians as 'five men and two other people.' Pointing to the bass player, the actor added there was one he couldn't vouch for. The musician, infuriated, leaped over the footlights, grabbed the actor and dragged him in front of the curtain, forcing him to apologize to the house for his bad taste."

The *Topeka Daily Capital* argued that vaudeville's greatest sin was not insult comedy nor blackface caricature, but references to unwed mothers. "If there is one objectionable, unwarranted and discreditable feature of up-to-date farce-comedy it is not caricature, but such false and immoral depictions of contemporary life . . . a disgrace to the theatrical business. Compared to rank indecency, the grossest mere caricature is harmless."

★

Rank indecency in the 1870s, 1880s, and 1890s focused on sexuality and ignored bigotry. Dance shows were raided if too much leg was shown. Medical literature was seized for providing clinical information about pregnancy.

Anthony J. Comstock was the king of such anti-sex campaigns. He founded the New York Society for the Suppression of Vice in 1873 and started rounding up anyone involved in sex. Comstock said masturbation was "dangerous" and "embracing" was pornographic. "If almost all of America's young men are addicted to this lethal practice," wrote Comstock, "what hope remains for America?"

Comstock was skeptical of reading. "It breeds lust," he claimed. "Lust defiles the body, debauches the imagination, corrupts the mind, deadens the will, destroys the memory, sears the conscience, hardens the heart, and damns the soul." He bragged of the books he confiscated and the authors he hounded. "I have destroyed 160 tons of obscene literature [and] convicted persons enough to fill a passenger train of sixty-one coaches, containing sixty passengers each."

Juries convicted authors without even hearing the offending passages as they were considered "too obscene to be placed upon the records of the courts." Police reports *about* obscenity were deemed obscene. A document prepared for an anti-obscenity crusade in Chicago was banned from the mail because it was pornographic. Even the Bible was too salacious. Noah Webster of *Webster's Dictionary* published a new abridged version of the Bible, explaining, "Many passages are expressed in language which decency forbids to be repeated in families and the pulpit."

George Bernard Shaw coined a new phrase, "Comstockery," and the defensive Comstock responded by dismissing Shaw as "an Irish smut dealer."

"Inevitably Comstock was the chief object of animosity and ridicule," said his biographer Heywood Broun. "No other person connected with the cause of purity was so forthright, so colorful, so extravagant and fanatical . . . To him the liberals and the freethinkers were always 'smut-dealers' and 'ex-convicts.'"

Comstock had poor grammar and seldom patronized the theaters he condemned. He attended vaudeville only once "to investigate a complaint that one of the dances was obscene" and his notes were full of misspellings like "gass," "yeild," and "smutt."

Ruining the lives of authors and artists, Comstock was targeted for revenge. While escorting an arrest, he was stabbed in the head. The *Brooklyn Daily Eagle* reported, "The blow was instantly repeated, the dirk this time cutting a fearful gash in Comstock's face, extending from the temple to the chin, and laying the flesh completely open to the bone. Four of the facial arteries were severed. With the blood spurting from his wound, Comstock seized the prisoner . . . and presenting a revolver, threatened to shoot him if he resisted."

Comstock survived, and his crusade inspired others. The Western Society for the Suppression of Vice began in 1876 to stop the "contamination of the youth of the country." Others sprang up throughout the Midwest and New England, but even in a puritanical era, they were accused of totalitarian lunacy.

"Do these people need to be informed at this late day in the world's history that words and ideas are not crimes?" asked a newspaper editorial in 1891. "Do they not know that it was a difference of opinion as to words and ideas that all or nearly all the religious persecutions of the past have arisen?"

Some of the world's most famous authors were included in the purge. *The Kreutzer Sonata* by Leo Tolstoy was banned for questioning the logic of marriage, leading Theodore Roosevelt to declare Tolstoy a "sexual and moral pervert." Mark Twain's *Adventures of Huckleberry Finn* was banned on the grounds that it was "suitable only for slums." The federal government banned Walt Whitman's *Leaves of Grass,* but controversy was good for business. It increased demand and earned Whitman enough in royalties to buy a new house.

Anthony Comstock, his face covered in gruesome scars, raided a New York gallery and seized 117 French photographs. "The morals of the youth of this country are endangered by obscenity and indecency in the shape of photographs of lewd French art," said Comstock. He attended a dance pavilion at the world's fair in Chicago in 1893 and declared, "The whole World's Fair must be razed to the ground."

To the Pure, an early book about American censorship, argued that people like Comstock didn't give a shit about morality—merely control: "During many centuries the great moral drive was to protect women. They were restricted in dress, limited as to hours when they could walk the thoroughfares and even discouraged from entering into serious discussions. When the stage became a transmitter of public thought, women were barred for years from the audience . . . Knowledge was kept from the poor. They weren't ready for it . . . Our poor brothers were to be kept poor in knowledge, for knowledge is power and we wanted to retain the power . . . Censorship became synonymous with subjection."

★

And so it was in vaudeville comedy. Throughout the 1890s, comedians were accused of "lowering the standards of thinking and in consequence of living." Lighthearted references to the Bible were completely forbidden.

The *Maysville Evening Bulletin* reported in April 1894, "A sacrilegious comedian in a Cincinnati beer hall made light of the Bible and referred to preachers in an offensive way last Saturday evening. This raised a storm of protests and he was hissed off the stage."

In an attempt to prevent "sacrilegious" comedy, the towns of Red Bank, New Jersey, and Madison, Indiana, forced comedians to attain a license. If they performed "sacrilegious" material, their license was revoked. The First Baptist Church said the licenses were necessary to ensure "the morals of the young people." The McKay Opera Company was "ordered out of town" for presenting "an obscene show" in Chambersburg, Pennsylvania, in January 1898. The *Chambersburg Valley Spirit* observed, "Some of the jokes, especially those by the black faced comedian were indecent and obscene."

Vaudeville comedians were frequently busted for obscenity, but the definition of obscenity was broad and arbitrary. References to birth control or demonstrations of "race mixing" were enough to get a vaudevillian arrested.

At the turn of the century, objections to ethnic and racial stereotyping on the vaudeville stage turned into a movement. Vaudeville comedy frequently ridiculed immigrants. The most common stereotypes portrayed the immigrant "as a lawless creature, given over to violence and disorder."

With each new round of immigration, comedians perfected ethnic dialect at their expense. The mockery of immigrants using mangled English gave comedy one of its most effective devices: malapropisms. Ironically, vaudeville largely consisted of assimilated immigrants who held contempt for newer arrivals. And yet, the more established the immigrant group, the less patience they had for being insulted. By the end of the 1890s, Irish and Italian immigrants were objecting to portrayals of intoxicated leprechauns and moronic organ-grinders. And when their children came of age, they organized sustained protest movements to end ethnic stereotyping on the stage. Vaudevillian Walter Kelly received "a letter threatening his life if he did not immediately cut out several Italian stories in his act," and a group called the Clan na Gael sabotaged shows wherever Irish stereotypes were presented.

Meeting with vaudeville impresario Oscar Hammerstein, the Clan na Gael informed him that any "act ridiculing the Irish, or in any way calling attention to the pronounced characteristics of the race, would be met by stern objection." They threatened "means of the most stringent sort" if their demands were ignored. The *Washington Evening Star* reported, "Hammerstein had agreed with the committee that if any act in which the Irish were portrayed proved objectionable to the Irish themselves it should not be presented . . . however . . . a contract had already been signed with the Russell Brothers, and since their act had proved unobjectionable for many years, he had no legal right to break the contract with them."

The Russell Brothers dressed in drag in an act called "The Irish Servant Girls." Performing as scheduled, the newspapers explained what happened next:

HISSED OFF THE STAGE
Remarkable Demonstration at Theater in Gotham

MUST RESPECT THE IRISH
Three Hundred Irishmen Resent the Ridicule of Their
Country

CLAN-NA-GAEL ARE INVOLVED
Theater Audience Thought a Riot Was in Progress
Curtain Had to Be Rung Down

The Victoria Theater was the scene of a remarkable demonstration last night in which nearly 300 persons in the audience joined. Hardly had the curtain gone up on the sketch of the Russell Brothers, who portray comic Irish servant girls, when screams and catcalls arose from the orchestra and galleries. In all parts of the house men arose, shouting, 'Take 'em off,' 'Get the hook,' 'Away with 'em,' 'They're rotten.' Others contented themselves with whistling and hooting . . . The Russells, on the stage, struggled to make themselves heard and the uproar became louder. The orchestra and the sound of the actors' voices were drowned in the general racket. Finally the curtain was rung down on the struggling brothers. Then almost

instantly the house became quiet . . . the audience slowly
settled back in their seats.

The *Brooklyn Daily Eagle* concluded, "Sensitiveness under such conditions may very easily be carried to extremes. The stage abounds in racial
types of which a multitude are frankly caricatures. The violent objection . . .
is a spirit that reveals a regrettable absence of the sense of humor." In their
opinion, ethnic minorities were selfish for wanting to eliminate stereotype
comedy when it was enjoyed by so many: "A few may seriously object,
from rooted prejudice to racial caricature. But more enjoy and applaud,
and they have rights that are at least worthy of consideration."

An editorial published in the *Topeka Daily Capital* in 1903 cautioned
vaudeville comedians not to succumb to pressure groups because it might
inspire others: "This may well worry the playwrights and players, for racial
caricature . . . has been regarded as legitimate ever since Shakespeare. If
the well-known and almost indispensable Irish policeman is to be abol-
ished from the stage by decree of the Clan-na-gael, what is to hinder the
'Afro-American' societies from following suit and threatening dire consequences on the heads of players who represent the stage type of negro?" The
writer predicted it would lead to the death of comedy. "The final upshot
[would be] to strip comedy of its most engaging and popular features. If
the raid should extend to all sorts of people caricatured in the theater and
in print, then good-bye to comedy."

Black stereotypes were seldom objected to in the white newspapers,
but complaints were common in the Black press. The *Indianapolis Freeman*
reviewed a minstrel show in 1901: "As a whole the show was one that the
citizens of this place care not to see repeated. It is a slander on the Negro
of America . . . Every flag was displayed with honor, then a rag with a
chicken and watermelon on it was displayed . . . The white people enjoyed
this flag business . . . but for us, we say shame, shame!"

As the *Topeka Daily Capital* had feared, minority protests proliferated
once Irish and Italian protests prevailed. In 1910, the *Placer Herald* wrote
of a rabbi who "protested against cheap and vulgar misrepresentation of
Jews on the stage and in the comic press, and advises a campaign against

it, pointing to the good results of a similar movement among Irish leaders against the stale and witless caricatures of alleged Irish types."

Jewish Americans, African Americans, Asian Americans, and Native Americans organized against stereotypes while actors, comedians, and lyricists specializing in racial and ethnic caricature scrambled to defend themselves.

The *Pittsburgh Daily Post* reported in 1910, "The hue and cry that is being raised all over America against racial caricatures on the vaudeville stage, particularly those of Hebrews and Irish types, has provoked a defense of the stage from Ben Welch, a caricaturist, representing types of Hebrew and Italian characters. He is, therefore, qualified for such a defense. He cites the case of a young Hebrew of the Eastside, New York, who, through the impersonation of his own parent's manners and customs, lifted his family from poverty to affluence." The new argument was that racial stereotyping wasn't racist, but a helpful way for impoverished minorities to climb the social ladder—and everyone else should gain a sense of humor. "No person should be so thin skinned as to find fault with an innocent caricature," concluded the *Daily Post*. "We ought to be broad enough to recognize our own racial eccentricities, however, and to laugh with other people."

The *Pittsburgh Post-Gazette* defended blackface in November 1910 by noting that many Black performers also did minstrel routines, therefore those routines could not be racist. Furthermore, they claimed "critics of acting contend that the white man can portray the negro character far more accurately than can the negro himself, and perhaps the contention is true."

The *American Israelite* in Cincinnati strongly disagreed. In an editorial from 1910 titled "Racial Caricature Out of Date," the paper argued, "It is high time racial caricature on the stage or in the press should be reformed altogether. Everything about such caricatures is so ancient, so pointless, so devoid of reason, art, legitimate fun, that their complete retirement would please all. Including the manufacturers of the ghostly jokes." The *Tonopah Daily Bonanza* agreed: "The stage loses nothing by the removal of racial caricatures. In fact, their removal clears the way for some realism that is sadly needed."

After years of agitation, theater owners and vaudeville chains buckled to the demands of protest and altered their policies. The *New York Herald Tribune* ran the headline "NO RACIAL CARICATURES—William Hammerstein Explains That His Order Forestalls Probable Protest."

Hammerstein, recalling the aggressive nature of the Clan na Gael, said, "A number of years ago the Irish people made several demonstrations. There was one right here in this theatre, while the Russell Brothers were on the stage, and another in a theatre in Greenpoint, when an audience took umbrage at an act. I have taken the initiative now because I feel it will only be a matter of time before the Jewish people will take up the situation . . . It may take the form of letters or petitions, but I have forestalled protest here." Asked if he expected other vaudeville theaters to follow suit, Hammerstein answered, "Without a doubt: it will only be a question of time . . . Vaudeville actors who portray Hebrew characters are too apt to overdo the thing, thereby making the impersonation repulsive, both in make-up and dialect, not only to Hebrews, but to the public in general."

Native Americans did not have the same clout as the immigrants who displaced them, but they protested just the same. A Nevada paper reported in 1911, "Taking his cue from other races, the American Indian has begun to protest against the caricatures of his race perpetrated by the cheap theaters [that are] misleading and libelous . . . Nearly every other race has filed protests, more or less vigorous against coarse and vicious caricaturing and lampooning. It is the one form of dramatic censorship that is effective and that deserves support."

Protest changed what was acceptable in vaudeville, drama, and comedy. Some comedians were forced to throw out racial material they had honed for years. In an era when comedians seldom wrote their own material and veteran comics rarely changed their act, coming up with an all-new routine seemed an insurmountable task.

"Should this disposition on the part of offended races that are for stage caricature continue, the poor vaudeville actor and imitator will be put out of business," reported the *Pittsburgh Post-Gazette* in 1915. "To object to the reproduction of the speech and supposed lineaments of Shylock, for instance, if done with intelligence should not be a ground for resentment."

The *Chicago Record-Herald* took the opposite view, encouraging comedians to adjust material to reflect the new era, "Let our humorists try fresh fields and new pastures. Let them exercise their ingenuity, their imagination, their power of observation . . . give us a sense of freshness and unexpectedness. Professional entertainers and comic writers must move with their age, as the rest of us do."

Humorist Montague Glass concluded that what had made America laugh in 1860 was no longer funny by modern standards. "Certainly our ideas of what is funny have changed," he wrote in April 1915. "Humor is an ephemeral thing. A generation ago we laughed at what today would merely make us ill."

Major theatrical agencies, usually bitter enemies, released a joint statement. A trade journal reported under the headline "Theatrical Men Taboo Offensive Racial Joke":

"There is to be no more offensive racial reference or caricature in the theaters of the United States. An understanding to that effect has been reached by A.L. Erlanger and Lee Shubert, the respective heads of the rival booking offices, which are now working in harmony by agreement. Offensive racial reference is any reference in story, dialogue, joke, gag, or song that would be held offensive by the members of the race it was aimed at. For instance, Jewish people object, and rightly enough, to tales about members of their race starting fires to collect insurance, Irish folk do not like to hear their countrymen depicted as living with pigs in their parlors."

Senator William E. Bauer of Ohio proposed legislation to make racial caricature illegal: "The bill forbids the impersonation of Irish, German, Jewish and negro characters on the stage, and any sketch or monologue with dialog which might arouse racial prejudice . . . The fine set for any offense is $200 to $1000."

"All that sort of 'offensive racial reference' from now on is out," concluded the *South Bend Tribune* in 1922. "No more of it to be allowed . . . if they can be in any way construed as offensive they will be deleted from [the] stage."

Vaudevillians who insisted on racist humor would have to contend with the potential blowback. "A near-riot was narrowly averted at the Alhambra,

New York, at midnight the other day," reported *Variety* in February 1927. "A young man came out during the show and started off saying: 'Well, folks, I am going to tell you a little [N-word] story, and I hope you coons will like it.' That was the touch-off. Upstairs the Negroes not only booed and hissed, but a bunch started walking down to get the chap. A panic or riot was sidetracked when another white entertainer, sensing the trouble, rushed on and kidded the audience until the other was forgotten."

Vaudeville comedians were in a constant panic as rules regarding what was permissible kept changing. Comedian Lew Kelly was best known for his popular drug-addled character Professor Dope, which made light of a slovenly narcotics junkie. Kelly had to throw the whole thing out when vaudeville announced a ban on portrayals of any "dope fiend, wherein the act of taking a hypodermic injection, the inhaling or eating of dope, or the use in any manner of dope."

All comedy concerning alcohol was banned in 1922. "All references to Prohibition, whether serious or humorous, have been ordered stricken from jokes, songs, and patter contained in the acts appearing on the Keith vaudeville circuit," reported the *Vancouver Sun*. "This ban includes the affiliated B.S. Moss and Proctor circuits and practically makes it impossible for actors to refer to Volsteadism [prohibition] on the majority of the stages of the United States."

President Warren Harding placed an unofficial taboo on political comedy. Will Rogers, the famous Cherokee comedian, made a joke suggesting the administration was on the take. The new attorney general, Harry Daugherty, was sent to the stage door of the Amsterdam Theater to deliver a message to Rogers: no more jokes about the president. Rogers dropped the joke and told his next audience, "I had a line here but the President doesn't like it. So I'll save it for the next President. I'm sure the Democrats will have a better sense of humor."

Xenophobia was on the rise again in the early 1920s. Anti-Semites in the farm belt objected to the dominance of Jewish comedians. The editorial staff of the *South Bend Tribune* proposed "a rule similar to the federal three per cent immigration quotas from foreign countries and in that way regulate the racial representation among the performers sent from New

York in road companies. From the standpoint of native-born Americans, there has been decidedly too much lower east side in the entertainment foisted upon the rest of the public."

A wave of bigotry swept through the United States, even as vaudeville suppressed racial depictions. A vaudeville comic named Alan Corelli was playing the Texas state fair when the Dallas police recruited him for a private gig. "While working this date, they booked me for a club date [a one-nighter] in the hills," said Corelli. "That was the craziest club date I ever had. I was picked up by a car filled with three big guys, all detectives from the Dallas Police Department. After about fifteen minutes we turned off into a dark path and there I was in the middle of a Ku Klux Klan gathering—white sheets, hoods, and everything. I did my act and got $1000."

The majority of vaudeville censorship focused on sexuality, immorality, and vulgarity. The *Moline Dispatch* wrote, "Wouldn't it be a blessing if something could be done to exterminate that loathsome pest, the vulgar comedian [who] is given opportunity to turn loose brothel jokes on an unsuspecting and suffering public?"

Clampdowns occurred throughout the country. Depictions of women smoking were banned in Kansas. References to pregnancy were forbidden in Pennsylvania. Detroit police banned "bare knees on the stage" and depictions of the "moral pervert or sex degenerate." Herbert Lloyd's *Vaudeville Trails*, a guidebook for traveling performers, featured an essay about vaudeville vulgarity:

"The trouble with profanity is not so much that it is wicked, but that it is just plain dirty. It is not so much that you shock religious people, as that you disgust decent people. Swearers are behind the times. They are hold-overs from a former century. A hundred years ago . . . ladies swore in the parlor. Husband and wife cursed each other across the breakfast table. The world has grown more decent since then . . . Americans, in former times, were so profane that the porters of the railway stations, in Europe, on seeing an American traveler alight from a train, would shout, 'Right this way, Mr. Goddam!' Nowadays anybody who swears is set down at once as being coarse and vulgar. Nobody wants a swearer in the office, nor in the theatre, nor on the train, nor in the hotel."

A clampdown on vaudeville profanity included a ban on the words "bloody," "damn," "floozy," "guts," "harlot," "hellcat," "hellion," "lousy," "punk," "screwy," "trollop," "wench," and "nuts." Vaudeville was in flux because America had changed. Several decades of complaint and protest had forced performers to evolve. Some felt it necessary, others considered it a giant step backward. Accused of racism, immorality, and vulgarity, the vaudeville theater struggled to adjust. And now it faced competition from an exciting and extremely profitable new medium: motion pictures.

2

DOWN WITH THE MOVIES

Soon after the movies were invented, they were subjected to criticism and censorship. A film short from 1897 called *The Dolorita Passion Dance* featured a bride preparing for her wedding night. A court order banned it as an "outrage to public decency." New York mayor Robert Van Wyck suggested outlawing nickelodeons "as immoral places of amusement."

Desperate for content, the new medium welcomed the very stereotypes that were being driven off the vaudeville stage. Some of the earliest nick-elodeons presented brief, sixty-second films featuring racist depictions of Native Americans, African Americans, and Chinese immigrants. Thomas Edison's film studio released a crude blackface loop titled *Watermelon Contest* in 1896. The Biograph company released [*N-word*] *in the Woodpile* in 1904. Essanay released *The Dancing* [*N-word*] in 1907. And an early Mack Sennett comedy, *Cohen at Coney Island*, was pulled from theaters in 1909 and reedited to remove potentially anti-Semitic content.

Silent comedian Fatty Arbuckle starred in *The Riot* in 1913. "In this film Arbuckle and his Jewish family run afoul of Irishman Charles Inslee and his brood, which has a ripple effect with others in the two ethnic neighborhoods," explains Brent Walker, an authority of silent comedy. "Far from the light Jewish/Irish humor that became popular . . . this film turns into an all-out race riot, with bombs thrown and many punches landed in one of the most extreme examples of an all-out Keystone [Cops] frenzy."

Race riots were not mere fiction during the silent-film era. A man named Thomas Dixon Jr. incited race riots nearly everywhere he went. A novelist, a playwright, and a Baptist preacher, Dixon Jr. was responsible for the most controversial novel of 1905, the most controversial play of 1906, and the most controversial motion picture of all time.

His father, Thomas Dixon Sr., had held thirty-two Black men enslaved on their farm in North Carolina. Dixon Sr. was one of the original Klansmen during the Reconstruction era.

Dixon Jr.'s first novel was *The Leopard's Spots*. Its racist theme claimed emancipation turned Black men "into a possible beast to be feared and guarded." His book was trashed in the Black press. Subjected to jeers and protest, Dixon was defensive, lamenting that Black people were going out of their way "to denounce me and declare my books caricatures and libels on their people. Their mistake is a natural one. My books are hard reading for a Negro."

Dixon's next book was *The Clansman*. In this book he called racial equality "an atrocity too monstrous for belief." The purpose of his novel, he said, was "to create a feeling of abhorrence in white people, especially white women, against colored men."

Dixon insisted *The Clansman* was based on historical fact. "During this period [Reconstruction] in South Carolina, 80,000 armed negro troops, answerable to no authority save the savage instincts of their officers, terrorized the state . . . with the intelligence of children and the instincts of savages, armed with modern rifles, paraded daily before their former masters. The children of the breed of Burns and Shakespeare, Drake and Raleigh, had been made subject to the spawn of the African jungle."

The Clansman was adapted for the stage in 1906 and banned throughout the country. "To claim that it is necessary for him to go girating [*sic*] about over the south," wrote an Atlanta paper, "stirring up such passions of hell, to keep the races apart . . . so vile . . . For God's sake, the negro's sake, and our sake, give the negro a rest from abuse and incendiarism!"

The play was deemed a threat to public safety in New Orleans. "We shall be agreeably surprised if innocent blood is not upon the head of the Reverend Thomas Dixon Junior, before he reaches New Orleans," said a civic official.

A Tennessee newspaper condemned the play: "It has been found necessary everywhere the 'Clansman' is presented to exclude negroes from the 'colored galleries' for fear of assaults and clashes . . . That very fact is enough to condemn it . . . and to recommend its withdrawal from the stage." A newspaper in Knoxville was mystified to learn Dixon was a Baptist preacher: "How the mind of a man who preaches love, and peace, and extols the principles embodied in the Golden Rule, could conceive of such a thing as 'The Clansman' is beyond ordinary comprehension."

When Dixon came to South Carolina he was taunted by an angry mob. "Some of the crowd," wrote Dixon's biographer, "registered their distaste by booing and hissing throughout the drama. When Dixon appeared on the stage, the diverse factions in the audience kept up a battle of 'boos' and 'bravos' for a full two minutes. Later that night, many prominent young men who had objected strongly to the play gathered at Dixon's hotel and taunted him to come down from his room."

In Philadelphia on October 20, 1906, a group of Black lawyers, doctors, and clergymen released a call to action:

"We, the Colored citizens of the City of Philadelphia, do unanimously and most positively protest against the exhibition of 'The Clansman' in this city . . . No agency has done more to arouse a spirit of antipathy against the Negro and to bring about a war of races than this play. Lynchings have been encouraged by the play . . . We, the citizens, have determined that it shall not play."

The Philadelphia performance went ahead. Black patrons sabotaged the performance. During a scene in which characters are shown *enjoying* slavery, a man hurled an egg at the stage and a police riot erupted.

"Two or three policemen was instantly upon him knocking him senseless with the first blow," reported a journalist with the *Broad Ax* newspaper. "And there upon the seat, helpless, these angels of hell vied with each other to see which could wield his club fastest and hardest . . . I am informed

[they] beat him as they were carrying him out. This display of brutality was no doubt intended as a determent to others who . . . resent the portrayal of himself as the brute, a rapist."

The lawyer T.J. Minton led a march to the home of Philadelphia's mayor, John Weaver. "We protest against this play because of the ill feeling it arouses in every community in which it is produced," said Minton. "The respect that we command is destroyed, we are slurred wherever we go; we are pointed out as brutes; our women are sneered at and our children on the streets and in the schools are subjected to indignities . . . we appeal to you on their behalf to suppress this vile and vicious play."

Mayor Weaver was persuaded. "From the evidence that has been brought to me," he said, "I am convinced that the intention of the play is to intensify the racial hatred . . . [and] we should do everything in our power to entirely remove it . . . I therefore forbid the play *The Clansman* to be continued . . . There shall be no further performance of the play in this city."

Thomas Dixon Jr. challenged the ban in court and lost. The judge ruled, "While the author may be entitled to his personal opinions concerning the Negro . . . the production of such a play in the city with a Negro population of more than 100,000 was a question of grave consequences. The mayor certainly had power to interfere with an injurious production and it was his duty to exercise that power."

Filmmaker D.W. Griffith optioned *The Clansman* for the big screen. Griffith would evenutally change the title from *The Clansman* to *The Birth of a Nation*. He saw nothing wrong with its content. Griffith had grown up in the Confederacy.

"They had a farm," recalled actress Lillian Gish, who starred in *The Birth of a Nation*. "It wasn't a big one, not enough to be a plantation. But they did have five slaves; and the father, D.W.'s father, was, as you know, a colonel in the Confederate Army."

Black protest mobilized in advance of *The Birth of a Nation* premiere on February 8, 1915. The *California Eagle*, the most influential Black newspaper on the West Coast, published editorials in opposition. Thirty thousand African Americans marched in opposition in Los Angeles. May Childs Nerney of the NAACP mailed "pamphlets by the thousands to the smallest of towns, compiling a list of pending state censor bills." She called *The Birth of a Nation* a "deliberate attempt to humiliate 10,000,000 American citizens and portray them as nothing but beasts."

The NAACP interviewed Thomas Dixon Jr. in 1915 and he stated a desire "to have all Negroes removed from the United States [and] to help in the accomplishment of that purpose by *The Birth of a Nation.*"

The film showed Black men committing voter fraud and, after being elected, scarfing down fried chicken and destroying government buildings. At one point, a white character commits suicide rather than having to contend with a Black man. The film ended with a climactic chase sequence in which the Ku Klux Klan drives the Black villains out of town.

Critics, scholars, and film fans overlooked the film's message to celebrate its technical achievements. The film created innovative and influential camera techniques, many of which became industry standard. But all of this was meaningless to African American viewers who could not ignore its racist intent.

"They would have none of the compelling beauty, rich narrative form, painterly composition," explained film historian Thomas Cripps. "For them it was a rough and cruel racist slander upon Afro-Americans during Reconstruction, and therefore they owed nothing to the tradition of opposing censorship."

Art house darling Sergei Eisenstein, like D.W. Griffith, was credited with many cinematic advances. He refuted the idea that the technical achievements overrode concern about content. Eisenstein called the film "disgraceful propaganda" that could not be "redeemed by purely cinematographic effects."

The Birth of a Nation was intentionally incendiary. Actors posing as Klansmen rode horseback through downtown Los Angeles to promote the film. At the Atlanta premiere, the real Ku Klux Klan rode through the streets. The *New Republic* condemned D.W. Griffith in their review: "He is yellow because he recklessly distorts negro crimes, gives them a disproportionate place in life, and colors them dishonestly to inflame the ignorant . . . His perversions are cunningly calculated to flatter the white man and provoke hatred and contempt for the negro. It degrades the censors that passed it and the white race that endures it."

The New York Board of Censors governed so-called immorality in the movies, but it had no problem praising Klan propaganda. Later renamed the National Board of Review, board member Rabbi Stephen Wise was the sole dissenter. "If it be true that the Mayor has no power to stop this indescribably foul and loathsome libel on a race of human beings," said Wise, "then it is true that Government has broken down. The Board of Censors which allowed this exhibition to go on is stupid or worse. I regret I am a member." The *New York Evening Post* and the American Bar Association were also opposed. During its second night at the New York Liberty Theatre, the screen was drenched with eggs.

The movie was banned in Illinois, Kansas, Ohio, and Pennsylvania. It was rejected in Newark, St. Louis, and Atlantic City. Screenings were delayed in Boston for eight weeks while protesters marched en masse.

"For eight long weeks they fought tooth and nail against the Birth of a Nation," reported *Motion Picture News*. "Peaceable meetings followed by protests to the mayor and governor; these by riots and arrests at the theatre; and the whole movement culminated in the passage of a law creating a censorship triumvirate." Forty policemen were assigned to protect each screening. Five hundred Black protesters occupied the lobby of the Tremont Theatre until police charged at them with nightsticks swinging. Street brawling went on long into the night.

Twenty-five thousand people marched to the Massachusetts State House, where Governor David Walsh denounced the film as racist propaganda that never should have been shown in his state.

While the Black press encouraged the protests, white newspapers condemned them. The *Macon Telegraph* said the protesters were "born of narrow-mindedness and ignorance." The *Houston Chronicle* asked whether "the people of Houston are to have their standards of thought or taste set or fixed or regulated by the negro citizenship." And the *New York Globe* suggested the act of protest was unconstitutional: "This is absolutely against public policy, against the spirit of the Constitution, against the very life and essence of what should be true American and democratic ideas."

A newspaper in Rhode Island warned that suppressing *The Birth of a Nation* would set a bad precedent, for "then there is no room on the stage for *The Merchant of Venice* or any other play that may be unwelcome to a relatively small element of the public in a given community."

D.W. Griffith said his right to free speech was being challenged and the controversy constituted "a fight for the whole institution of the screen." He published a pamphlet titled *The Rise and Fall of Free Speech in America.* "Today the censorship of moving pictures throughout the entire country is seriously hampering the growth of the art," he wrote. "So long as censorship holds the motion picture under its thumb, it is in every way enslaved."

★

Censorship was possibly at its height during World War One. President Wilson's Espionage Act and subsequent Sedition Act suspended civil liberties in 1917 and silenced critics of war. If anyone so much as questioned the morality of international bloodshed, they were subject to immediate arrest by Attorney General Mitchell Palmer. Simply for saying the country "could not afford the economic costs of sending an army to Europe," a deaf man from Atlanta was sent to the penitentiary.

Six thousand people were arrested, primarily in immigrant communities, during the "Palmer Raids." Palmer arrested those who "preached hate against America" and targeted suspects by identifying "sly and crafty eyes" of the "unmistakable criminal type."

The most powerful vaudeville chain, the Keith circuit, had zero tolerance for political commentary and a new law stopped draft-age vaudevillians from playing Canada. "The recent decision prohibiting men between 21 and 30 going into Canada is expected to badly cripple vaudeville acts and road shows playing Canadian territory," reported *Variety.*

Even after the war critics of foreign policy were imprisoned. Cartoonist Art Young was charged with conspiracy for an editorial cartoon in which he called the war a "satanic bloodbath embraced only by big-bellied profiteers."

American Legionnaires, unwilling to let go of anti-German sentiment, sabotaged a Los Angeles screening of *The Cabinet of Dr. Caligari.* The German expressionist film was playing downtown when the Legionnaires "broke through the crowd with a stepladder as a battering ram and, mounting it, waved for silence and announced that the film would be taken off immediately." The American Legion performed similar stunts around the country, leading *The Nation* to say it was "with the possible exception of the Ku Klux Klan . . . the most lawless and potentially the most dangerous organization in the country."

Seven years after *The Birth of a Nation*, D.W. Griffith released *One Exciting Night*. Again, it featured blackface, slavery nostalgia, and the N-word. One of Griffith's friends asked him, "Are you losing your sense of values . . . ? Do you stop to think that the [racist] foolishness appeals only to the empty-headed? And to the negro patron it gives only pain . . . ?"

★

Racism upset Black filmgoers, but white filmgoers focused on vulgarity. A minor scandal ensued when lip readers discovered that silent film actors, instead of mouthing dialogue, were mouthing profanity as a prank.

The New York State Censorship Board complained that Hollywood was corrupting America by depicting "idle women." "Too many women are screened reclining on a couch or otherwise reading a book and munching on chocolates," complained the board. "This showing of women idling is misrepresenting the American people for we are a working nation. Such scenes should be censored."

A call to clean up silent movies intensified when comedian Fatty Arbuckle was accused of rape. Arbuckle was a huge star and one of the most popular comedians in America. He was implicated in the death of thirty-year-old Virginia Rappe after she died underneath the weight of his body during a wild San Francisco party. The result was a media frenzy that deemed Arbuckle a sexual deviant and reckless killer. Arbuckle was held in a jail cell while hard-boiled novelist Dashiell Hammett lobbied for his release. Church groups used Arbuckle as an example of Hollywood's supposed degeneracy and hired representatives to impose strict censorship on the industry.

Guidelines were drafted by Catholic publisher Martin Quigley and Jesuit priest Daniel A. Lord. The protestant Will Hays was hired to oversee adherence to the new Motion Picture Production Code.

Jack Vizzard, a film censor with the MPPC recalled, "Hays had been Postmaster General in the cabinet of [President] Warren Harding, whom he had helped elect, and whom some would nominate as the worst we have ever had." Included in the Production Code was a total ban on "ridicule of public officials."

Fatty Arbuckle was acquitted of all charges, but film distributors were hesitant to associate with his name. Public opinion was torn. Arbuckle was guilty in the eyes of those who already distrusted Hollywood, even if Arbuckle was innocent of wrongdoing. An organization called Churches for Better Amusements mailed out postcards with the question, "Are We To Have Immoral Comedians as Heroes of American Youth?"

The Keith vaudeville chain forbade comedians from mentioning Arbuckle's name and temporarily banned any and all references to Hollywood. Even comedians doing impressions of famous movie stars were required to cease temporarily.

A new Arbuckle film had been completed prior to the trial, but film producer Adolph Zukor sat on it, nervous about how the public would react. Will Hays of the Production Code gave his blessing, encouraging Zucker to release the Arbuckle film "as we are confident the American public is eminently fair and realizes by this time that Arbuckle has been the victim of unfortunate circumstances."

An exhibitor in Buffalo presented a slate of Arbuckle films to celebrate his acquittal. "As long as the man has been acquitted of the charge against him and there has been sufficient doubt present as to the responsibility and honesty of the witnesses," he said, "it would not be fair to stand in his way to earn a living."

Others disagreed. Arbuckle films were banned in Waco, Texas, because "showing of Arbuckle pictures would be an outrage against morals and common decency." The State of Indiana said Arbuckle films would be "harmful to the children and youth of the state."

Will Hays retracted his approval. "I will state that at my request," said Hays, "they have cancelled all showings and all bookings of the Arbuckle films." Arbuckle was devastated.

"The decision is a complete surprise and a great shock," said Arbuckle. "I knew nothing of it until I read the decision in the newspapers. I don't understand it at all, for I thought I was well started on my come-back in the films."

He decided to appeal to his fans directly, venturing on a personal appearance tour in 1923. Many theaters refused to participate, but those that welcomed him found the house filled to capacity.

"Fatty Arbuckle is still popular among the movie fans of Milwaukee," reported *Moving Picture World*. "That was proved when, appearing in person at Saxe's Strand despite vigorous protests of the city motion picture commission, church organizations and women's clubs, the erstwhile comedian of the screen was greeted with wild demonstrations at every performance. On several nights prolonged applause at Arbuckle's appearance even was followed by whistling and stamping of feet."

From Milwaukee he traveled to Washington, DC, and Kansas City, Missouri. Some in the city council were opposed to the shows on moral grounds. Arbuckle met with Kansas City officials to explain, "I found God in the darkness of a prison cell. I am now leading a clean Christian life. All I want is the chance to live, to make a living, to pay my debt."

He was given a hero's welcome in San Francisco, the city where the scandal began. "He stepped into a two-minute ovation, timed by a stopwatch," reported *Variety*. "Before the day finished Arbuckle had broken the Pantages box office record for Sunday. Yesterday he repeated it with capacity even at the matinee, extraordinary for Monday. Last night the house management was figuring how and where to insert extra performances during the week."

Throughout the year he was welcomed in Detroit, New Orleans, Atlantic City, and Chicago. But he was canceled in Toronto, Boston, Fairbanks, and Tacoma. His career would never return to its previous heights, but the same could also be said of all silent comedians. Fatty Arbuckle would never again be a huge box office star, but then again, neither would Buster Keaton or Harold Lloyd. They suffered not from scandal, but from the evolution of public taste.

"The custard pie comedy is a thing of the past," reported the *Kansas City Kansan*, "in all parts of the state, and with all classes of society. Even the most primitive communities have grown tired of the comedies where physical violence and danger constitute the main theme of humor."

"The day of the slapstick is gone," explained Charlie Chaplin. "The public love for comedy is still great, but the taste in comedy has changed."

★

The war on Fatty Arbuckle was largely organized by religious lobbyists and church leaders. They had a great deal of experience attacking showbiz. In the lead up to World War One, Americans were warned about the menace of dancing. Preachers devoted Sunday sermons to the perils of physical movement, often invoking racist language to get their point across. Among the dances singled out were the tango, the shimmy, the turkey trot, and the waltz.

Reverend Barrett of St. Louis told his congregation, "In 1910 the first of the animal dances, known as the 'tango,' was introduced. This animal dance which is being practiced all over the country originated in the disreputable quarters of the South American republics . . . Never before has dancing been such a provocation to immorality."

Reverend William Brothers of New York warned, "Indulgence in the turkey trot, the tango, and other objectionable modern dances is as much a violation of the seventh commandment as adultery . . . These dances are a reversion to the grossest practices of savage man. They are based on the primitive motive of the orgies enjoyed by the aboriginal inhabitants of every uncivilized land."

According to a 1912 issue of *Harper's Bazaar,* when waltzing was introduced in Europe the "anti-waltzing party took alarm, cried it down, mothers forbade it, and every ballroom became a scene of feud and contention."

A booklet of dance instruction published in 1914 by the famous dance team Irene and Vernon Castle cautioned, "Do not wriggle the shoulders. Do not shake the hips. Do not twist the body."

New York City tried to outlaw the shimmy in 1919 because the "unladylike" dance contained "shameless evidence of debauchery." A court order shut down a dance club in Chicago where the shimmy was popular. The judge said the "evil genius of this place has artfully combined the grossness of primitive sensuality with . . . modern licentiousness." Police threatened to revoke the business license of any dance hall allowing "shoulder movements."

The music that usually accompanied the shimmy was jazz, which was considered a threat to all that was good and decent in America. The many condemnations of jazz music invoked language about wild savages and the primitive jungle.

"The so-called jazz music is an abomination and one of the most demoralizing influences in our social life today," wrote the *Greeley Daily Tribune* in 1920. "It should be banished."

"It is a sort of musical hysteria that incites to idleness, revelry, dissipation, discord and chaos," wrote a North Carolina paper in 1922. "It is musical chaos, to be sure, originating from the devastating volcanic spirit that has burst forth over the world in recent years. Half-savage voodooists are swayed by such music, somewhat as that are influenced by powerful intoxicants. Jazz music is an abomination."

The new medium of radio helped spread jazz throughout the country—upsetting the honky squares.

"Jazz bands are an abomination and should be absolutely eliminated," argued a magazine editorial in *Radio Broadcast*. "The scrambled mess of disjointed harmony that is jazz just cannot crowd into a telephone transmitter, with the result that all the public hears is a babel that bears no resemblance to music."

"Music should be censored," said Moissaye Boguslawski of the Chicago Symphony. "There is censorship for the film and for the stage, yet none for music, for which it is even more needed. I believe much recent criminal endeavor by youths has to a degree been influenced by jazz. Americans probably would not be so highly flattered if they knew they were paying tribute to the music of Africa."

Society matron Anne Faulkner Oberndorfer wrote an editorial for the *Houston Post* titled "Is Jungle Music Debasing Society?" and another for the *Ladies' Home Journal* asking "Does Jazz Put the Sin in Syncopation?"

"Jungle music, our American jazz, is setting the blood of our boys and girls on fire," said Oberndorfer. "It must be killed before it reduces us to savages, sadists, libertines and anarchists. Vicious primal instincts are awakened. The emotions triumph over the mind. Little wonder that we have more juvenile crime and immorality than ever before . . . When the negroes of the Mississippi Valley begin to sing out of tune, white women bolt their doors and lock their windows. And it is on the 'blues' of these Africans and their ancestors that jazz is founded . . . It is these principally who go wild from jazzmania . . . to commit atrocious and unbelievable crimes."

The anti-jazz crusade was anti-Black, but Henry Ford of the Ford Motor Company switched it up and made it anti-Semitic. One of the pamphlets he distributed through his Ford dealerships was titled "Jewish Jazz . . . the Moron Music of the Yiddish Popular Song." Ford wrote, "Many people have wondered whence come the waves upon waves of musical slush that invade decent homes and set the young people of this generation imitating the drivel of morons. Popular music is a Jewish monopoly. Jazz is a Jewish creation."

In the late 1920s, Rudy Vallée, Russ Columbo, and Bing Crosby embodied a new genre of singing known as crooning. It triggered another wave of hatred and hysteria. The Roman Catholic Church condemned it as "bleating and whining, with disgusting words, the meaning of which is a low-down source of sexual influence."

"I desire to speak earnestly about a degenerate form of singing which is called crooning," said an Ohio preacher. "No true American would practice this base art. I like to use my radio, when weary. But I cannot turn the dials without getting these whiners, crying vapid words to impossible tunes. If you will listen closely . . . you will discern the basest appeal to sex emotions in the young."

The National League for Decency in Radio emerged with the goal of ridding the airwaves of "sex delinquency and moral perversion." An NLDR spokesman said, "The only solution for the salvation of one of the greatest mediums for molding and forming public opinion rests in securing legislation which will insure the operation of radio in the best interests of all Americans."

Some of America's most famous songwriters were censored. Cole Porter's "Let's Do It," "Do It Again," and "You Do Something to Me" were all banned from radio playlists. An Irving Berlin lyric was changed from "perfume lingering on a pillow" to "seaplane rising from an ocean billow."

As the popularity of the tango and the shimmy waned, the doomsday prophets went after the latest dance craze, the jitterbug. It too was seen as a corrupter of youth, promoted by perverts, and a clear sign that America was on the road to ruin.

"Psychologists and doctors have truly said that the 'jitterbug craze' is a form of orgiastic sexual indulgence," wrote pamphleteer Dan Gilbert. "Jitterbuggery is an expression of perverted sexuality . . . What does it mean to have the emotional pattern of youth made to conform to the perversions of the sexually abnormal? What is to become of a generation under the influence of prostitute music and prostitute dancing? Those who have made a study of juvenile delinquency are convinced that the jitterbug, jive and hot music craze has led to a wide increase in drug addiction among youth . . . making a madhouse out of America and a generation of madmen, of jitterbug lunatics and jive loonies, out of American youth."

★

"Censorship *made* me," said Mae West.

An unlikely success story in a censorious time, vaudeville performer Mae West all but dared theater managers to fire her. Brash, cocky, and inspired by her free-spirited mother, West secured laughs with risqué numbers like "I Want a Cave Man" and "I'm a Night School Teacher." *Variety* said that while some of her material was certainly in bad taste, the young comic was "100% funny."

Mae West played vaudeville nonstop from 1910 through 1926. She had a cult following, but mainstream acceptance eluded her. She cowrote most of her own material, and when she and playwright Adeline Leitzbach put together a play called *Sex*, it made West the most talked about actor in America.

Sex was an action-comedy about a Montreal prostitute. It portrayed gangland slayings, corrupt policemen, seduction, and suicide. *Billboard* called it a "disgrace to all those connected with it." The *Daily Mirror* headline declared, "Monstrosity Plucked From Garbage Can—Destined to Sewer." And the *New York American* pleaded, "Wipe Out Those Evil Plays Now Menacing Future of Theatre."

A protagonist whore was too much for New York preachers and police. After forty-one consecutive weeks on the Broadway stage, the NYPD raided the production. The cast was arrested and charged with "giving an immoral performance and maintaining a public nuisance," stagehands were booked for "corrupting the morals of youth," and the stage manager faced three years in prison.

Sex went on trial in February 1927. Mae West's lawyer argued that the play had already been "widely viewed, with no apparent damage to civilization at large" and asked the jury to consider how much social mores had changed: "Standards of today permit open frank discussion of sex matters. Twenty years ago women appearing on the streets in knee-length skirts, in one-piece bathing suits on the beaches and smoking in public would have been considered immoral, but our wives do this same thing today and we think nothing of it."

The judge instructed the jury, "This show must be judged by the moral standards of today, rather than those of a century ago," but they didn't go for it. Mae West was found guilty on all counts.

The next night she was transferred to Welfare Island's women's workhouse and served ten days hard labor. Upon release she was offered one thousand dollars for a story about her jailhouse experience. She accepted and donated her payment to establish a prison library.

Between her arrest and conviction, the City of New York passed the Wales Padlock Act. It granted the NYPD increased powers "to jail, and release only under heavy bail, any actor who has participated in what any censor might consider 'obscene, indecent, immoral, impure scene, tableau, incident, part or portion of any drama, play exhibition, show, or entertainment."

Mae West closed the decade with a succession of plays designed to infuriate the censors and the prudes. *The Wicked Age*, *Pleasure Man*, and *The Drag* were all harassed by the police. She not only came to expect it, she exploited it. "I want to be filthy!" shouted the West character in *The Wicked Age*. "Low! Vile! Call it anything you please—but God—I want to live my own life!" *Billboard* said *The Wicked Age* would only entertain "tawdry morons to whom the theater is an intensified and expanded peep show."

Pleasure Man debuted in 1928. It featured homosexual characters. "No play of our time has had less excuse for such a sickening excess of filth," said the *New York Sun*. Mayor Jimmy Walker told the police to shut it down. Fifty actors were charged with "glorifying sex perversion" while Mae West was charged with "producing an alleged obscene play."

Drama critic George Jean Nathan supported the raid. "If the shutting down of the exhibition called *Pleasure Man* by the authorities constitutes censorship of the drama," wrote Nathan, "then I go on record as being head, foot and tail for censorship. I have seen a lot of degenerate stuff in my travels . . . but I have never seen perversion, inversion and such physiological idiosyncrasies so brazenly and shamelessly offered to the general public."

While awaiting trial, she produced *The Drag*, a murder mystery with an openly gay cast. Theater critic Jack Conway caught its out-of-town tryout: "It's the queerest show you've ever seen . . . The female impersonators, four strong, and some other Queens, all go in drag. Are you screaming?" It failed to make it to Broadway as the NYPD threatened every theater that tried to book it.

"It was about homosexuality," recalled West. "I showed forty men dressed up as women. It was about a love affair between two men. Can you imagine the shock it caused then? They banned it for New York!"

The trend of homosexual depictions in the theater created a backlash. The critic Hannen Swaffer complained in an editorial published in *Variety* in 1928, "They flaunt themselves upon the stage; they parade themselves in public . . . The male choruses have plenty of them . . . There were once so many male perverts in the company he [the manager] used to go into the dressing rooms and say, 'Good evening, ladies and gentlemen,' and there was never a murmur of protest. The truth is, of course, that nobody knows where it starts and where it ends. We are all equally guilty in the matter, because none of us dares to say a word."

The Constant Sinner was Mae West's final play before she entered the movies. The *Daily Mirror* called it "a three-ring circus of depravity and degeneracy," but not because of overt sexuality. The play featured a white protagonist in love with a Black man. The district attorney in Washington, DC, told the press he intended on shutting the whole thing down due to its "objectionable intermingling of color."

Preachers objected to sexuality while minorities objected to racial and ethnic stereotypes. The same battles waged against vaudeville recurred as the silent movies transitioned to sound.

The Callahans and the Murphys was a film released by MGM in 1927. It was a takeoff on the infamous Hatfields and McCoys, but instead of warring hillbillies, this family feud pitted one group of Irish stereotypes against another.

The Clan na Gael, triumphant against vaudeville stereotypes two decades earlier, returned to protest the film. They called on New York movie theaters to pull *The Callahans and the Murphys*. When a Forty-Second Street theater refused, the Clan na Gael burst through the doors, ran down the aisle with buckets of black paint, and destroyed the silver screen.

The following night, the Clan na Gael attacked a screening at Loew's Orpheum on East Eighty-Sixth Street. The Associated Press reported, "Electric light bulbs were broken against the screen and chemicals were poured on the floor."

When the 1927 film version of *Uncle Tom's Cabin* played in Atlanta, a Black organization demanded its immediate cancelation. After much protest, the mayor of Atlanta decided "the picture would be barred in Atlanta for fear racial prejudice might be stirred up."

★

Sensitivities increased in the 1930s as the Nazis took control of Germany. Parallels were drawn between the hatred in Europe and the Deep South at home. Film producer David Selznick announced his plan to turn a bestselling novel into a major motion picture, triggering a debate about the relation between Hollywood stereotypes and racial bigotry in real life.

Carlton Moss, a prominent Black theater director said, "Whereas *The Birth of a Nation* was a frontal attack on American history and the Negro people, *Gone with the Wind,* arriving twenty years later, is a rear attack on the same."

As soon as the novel was optioned in 1936, *Gone with the Wind* was compared to *The Birth of a Nation.* Margaret Mitchell, the novelist who authored the book, grew up on a plantation where her grandfather held thirty-five people enslaved. She was also a huge fan of *The Clansman.* Mitchell wrote Thomas Dixon Jr., "I was practically raised on your books and love them very much."

The book version of *Gone with the Wind* used the N-word liberally and featured a heroic Ku Klux Klan. The *Washington Post* and *New York Times* called it the best of all Civil War novels. *The Nation* and *New Republic* criticized it for being "none too sympathetic to blacks."

Margaret Mitchell felt critics did not speak for the majority: "The colored people I know here in Atlanta had nothing but nice things to say, especially the older ones. Shortly after the book came out the Radical and Communistic publications, both black and white, began to hammer, but all they could say was that the book was 'an insult to the Race.' For two years they could not think up any reason why."

The film critic for the *Daily Worker* wrote that it "glorifies the Ku Klux Klan and slavocracy, defends lynch law as a protective measure against the barbarous Blacks, hurls insults by the yard at Negro people and at the scandalous North for setting them free, and all in all gives as complete and deliberate a misreading of history as Thomas Dixon's 'The Klansman.' [*sic*] . . . The film must be stopped. The Klan must not ride again."

Selznick secured the film rights. Some of his contemporaries asked him not to go through with it. Screenwriter Ring Lardner Jr. told Selznick to avoid "glorification of slave owners and the Ku Klux Klan."

Concerns about Nazi bigotry increased between 1936 and 1939. Rabbi Barnett Brickner phoned Selznick and said, "Surely at this time, you would want to do nothing that might tend even in the slightest way to arouse anti-racial feelings."

Selznick released a statement to reassure all concerned: "These are no times in which to offend any race of people. I feel so keenly about what is happening to the Jews of the world that I cannot help but sympathize with the Negroes and their fears." He also sent a memo to Sidney Howard, the *Gone with the Wind* screenwriter who would be crushed to death by a tractor four months before the movie's premiere. "I personally feel quite strongly that we should cut out the Klan entirely," Selznick told Howard. "I do hope that you will agree with me on this omission of what might come out as an unintentional advertisement for intolerant societies in these fascist-ridden times."

On the recommendation of Margaret Mitchell, Selznick hired white journalist Susan Myrick as the technical adviser "on speech and customs, manners and costumes." Her first note to Selznick was about Hattie McDaniel, the Black actress who would play "Mammy."

"Hattie McDaniel is not the right Mammy," she told Selznick. "She lacks dignity, age, nobility and so on and she just hasn't the right face for it." Furthermore, the white consultant complained she was having a hard time "teaching Negro talk" to the Black actress.

The Black press was generally optimistic. Ruby Goodwin reported, "It is with decided relief that I can report from no higher authority than George Cukor, director for the opus, that the objectionable term 'n——' which was used a thousand times (to put it at a moderate figure) by Miss Mitchell, has been cut entirely from the script."

Margaret Mitchell was angry that the N-word was cut. "The Negro press has discovered the way in which they have been insulted," wrote Mitchell. "It is because I had various characters use the terms [N-word] and 'darkey.' Regardless of the fact that they call each other [N-word] today and regardless of the fact that nice people in ante bellum days called them 'darkies,' these papers are in a fine frenzy . . . I have had enough twisted and erroneous and insulting things written about me and 'Gone With the Wind' to make me sore on the whole Negro race if I were sensitive or a fool. But I do not intend to let any number of trouble-making Professional Negroes change my feelings."

The movie premiered to great fanfare and was an immediate box office smash, but the major Black papers, previously optimistic, were no longer charitable. The *Chicago Defender* called the film a "mockery of civil liberties" and the *New York Amsterdam News* said it was a "pus oozing from beneath the scab of a badly healed wound."

A union representative from the AFL-CIO said, "It's resurrecting all the racial inferiority theories which science has discarded and which Hitler and his fellow imperialists have picked up against the Jews and other minorities." The AFL-CIO joined the NAACP, the National Negro Congress, and the American Student Union in a protest march in front of the Chicago premiere. Among the protesters was Barney Rosset, the free speech champion who later published the banned books *Tropic of Cancer* and *Naked Lunch.*

Protests did not, however, diminish its tremendous success. *Gone with the Wind* was regarded as an instant classic, and it swept the Academy Awards. Accepting the first Oscar to ever go to an African American woman, Hattie McDaniel spoke with tears in her eyes: "I hope my winning the award will be inspiration for the youth of my race [and] encourage them to aim high and work hard and take the bitter with the sweet."

But showbiz columnist Jimmy Fielder was extremely cynical. "And where does this Negro artist go from here? Why, back to playing incidental comedy maids, of course. An actress comparable with the immortal [Oscar winner] Marie Dressler has flashed across the screen—and now must disappear because Hollywood can't give her adequate parts."

3

RADIO, PROTEST, AND SCANDAL

Racial stereotypes became largely taboo in vaudeville and were subject to protest in film, but they flourished in the growing medium of radio. It was a pattern repeated each time a new form of media emerged. Vaudeville suppressed stereotypes, radio resurrected them. The film industry phased them out, television brought them back.

Sam 'n' Henry was a comedy hit in Chicago in 1926. Created by Charles Correll and Freeman Gosden, the program went national in 1928 under the name *Amos 'n' Andy*. Fifteen minutes a day, five days a week, each episode of *Amos 'n' Andy* ended with a cliffhanger. The to-be-continued structure conditioned people to keep listening, and as a result the program became the most popular radio show in America.

Gosden and Correll were both white, but their characters were Black. They delivered each line with the minstrel dialect they learned as blackface performers.

Charles Correll's father fought for the Confederacy during the Civil War. His grandfather was a judge who dispensed Southern justice after Reconstruction. Correll started out in show business performing a blackface parody of *Uncle Tom's Cabin*.

Freeman Gosden's father was a Confederate veteran, and the Gosden family attended Confederate statue ceremonies. When he was a teenager, Gosden left home to join a blackface troupe.

Gosden and Correll performed at American Legion fundraisers around Chicago. They became roommates in 1924, formed a team, and played local vaudeville, where they witnessed the Black comedy team Miller and Lyles.

From 1903 to 1934 Miller and Lyles were considered "the biggest and best" of the Black comics. They authored a dexterous bit of verbal word play called the "Multiplication Routine," which Abbott and Costello later claimed as their own. Miller and Lyles released comedy routines on shellac discs under the names Sam 'n' Steve four years before Correll and Gosden entered radio as Sam 'n' Henry.

"We recall having seen the two white radio comics on Keith [vaudeville] years ago on the same bill with Miller and Lyles," reported the *Pittsburgh Courier* in 1930. "And we remember going back stage . . . there stood Amos 'n' Andy in the wings watching Miller-Lyles . . . The two white fellows have since then begun to score and collect on what they learned from our boys."

It didn't matter if you had done it in vaudeville for a decade. If someone stole your material and did it on national radio, it would be identified with them from then on. Radio reached millions of people at the same time, whereas the biggest vaudeville show reached maybe four thousand. Radio didn't employ Black comedians at the time. It was easy for white comics to steal from them without anybody knowing.

Miller and Lyles pursued legal action in May 1930. Their lawyer asked for an injunction to stop "the white comedians from using the material unless they pay a large sum to the owners of the copyrighted material." The case was thrown out of court.

The white press praised *Amos 'n' Andy* as a "Mark Twain of the air," but some Black listeners were less charitable. The NAACP pointed out that *Amos 'n' Andy* was using Joseph Breil's "The Perfect Song" as its theme music, a number that was originally composed for *The Birth of a Nation*.

An early condemnation came in 1929 from a preacher at Chicago's Methodist Episcopal Zion Church. He called the program "moronic" and "dangerous." Gosden and Correll insisted *Amos 'n' Andy* was presented without malice. To demonstrate their goodwill, they traveled to Black neighborhoods to sign autographs—in blackface.

According to historian Mel Watkins, the name "Amos," like "Sam" and "Sambo," was associated with "post slavery tales and jokes" long before *Amos 'n' Andy* came along. As the show increased in popularity, the names Amos and Andy became a demeaning way to address Black men, much like "boy." A letter to the *Pittsburgh Courier* said, "Yes, I have been called Andy. It happened at a drug store. A soda clerk gave me the moniker in offering to serve me. I like laughter programs but there is absolutely nothing funny in *A 'n' A*."

"They are a shame and a disgrace to our race," wrote a Black listener. "I think the same of them as I do of the KKK."

"Amos 'n' Andy must go," wrote Raymond Foust to the *Pittsburgh Courier*. "We, the colored race, just will not stand for these two to continue cashing in at our expense any longer."

The *Pittsburgh Courier* called the program "dirty propaganda." They announced a campaign with a front-page statement that readers could clip and sign: "A Nation-wide Protest Against 'Amos 'n' Andy.' . . . We, the undersigned, do most solemnly join the protest of the *Pittsburgh Courier* and ask that the comedians so exploiting our group be driven from the air as a menace to our self-respect, our professional, fraternal and economic progress."

"I think that all the members of our race throughout the country should help wipe out this broadcast," wrote a *Courier* reader in October 1931. "The white people of today are using every scheme they possibly can to make it appear that the Negroes are still living in ways *Amos 'n' Andy* portray. It is up to the members of our race to get them off the air. We must crush them now!"

The white journalist H. L. Mencken told the program's detractors to lighten up. "It seems to me that in objecting to such things," said Mencken, "the Negro shows a dreadful lack of humor."

Some listeners did indeed wonder what the big deal was. After all, it was just a comedy show. The *Pittsburgh Courier* answered in an editorial: "What is the damage done? It is almost everywhere to be met where white people encounter Negroes . . . On the streets, in the banks, in the business places . . . Negro help is often referred to as Amos or Andy. Negroes are being put down."

The Elks Club, the Knights Club, the National Association of Colored Waiters, the Hotel Employees Union, and the National Baptist Convention all called for the program's cancelation.

One hundred thousand letters of objection were mailed during the first month of the *Pittsburgh Courier* campaign. Three months later, five hundred thousand. By November 1931, there were seven hundred forty thousand signatures on the petition to remove *Amos 'n' Andy* from the air. The NAACP presented copies to the program's sponsors, NBC, and the Federal Radio Commission, later known as the FCC.

"There is little doubt," wrote the *Pittsburgh Courier*, "that the Radio Commission will rule that Amos and Andy propaganda is harmful to a portion of the citizenry of the United States."

They never received a response.

★

Amos 'n' Andy continued, but its popularity diminished as more sitcoms entered the field. Meanwhile, the NAACP and the Black community pressured network radio to eliminate Black stereotypes wherever they occurred.

Eight songs were removed from radio in 1935, including "Carry Me Back to Old Virginny," "My Old Kentucky Home," "Swanee River," and "That's Why Darkies Were Born." *Variety* reported, "Any program carrying one of the above songs or words is sure to get howls if caught. For instance, the *Kraft Music Hall*, Thursday-evening NBC show with Paul Whiteman, got severe censuring for offering 'Darkies are Born' and Helen Hayes got a rap on Sanka Coffee commercial week before for uttering the word 'pickaninny' which appeared in the script . . ."

Those suffering the most censorship were comedians. The popular comics were constantly dealing with sponsor interference. Unfunny businessmen checked every joke to ensure nothing subversive or offensive made it through. Milton Berle complained, "The guys that run radio are even worse than the assholes who run vaudeville."

Even innocuous political comedy was out of the question. CBS radio comedian Phil Baker rattled off the ages of the Supreme Court Justices, "62, 68, 72, 75," and then yelled, "Bingo!" The censors scolded him, "You can't make passes at dignity over the radio."

An NBC executive complained in an internal memo, "We are getting many protests about Bob Hope from both Democrats and Republicans. Each time he refers to things political, and that's been pretty consistent for some weeks, we've had protests. Can't we do something about it?"

"This country is in a state of fear," concluded Morris Ernst of the ACLU. "That is why we have censorship . . . It wouldn't surprise me if in the next year the President took over control of all the radio stations."

In the years since her Broadway arrest, Mae West had ascended to mainstream stardom as one of Hollywood's great movie stars. When she appeared on Edgar Bergen's radio comedy in December 1937, it resulted in one of radio's most notorious moments.

The Chase and Sanborn Hour was named for its sponsor and starred comedian Edgar Bergen and his ventriloquist dummy Charlie McCarthy. Mae West joined them for a sketch that took place in the Garden of Eden. The routine seemed innocent on the page, but delivered in West's sultry voice, the effect was pornographic.

Bergen recalled, "She said to Charlie, 'Why don't you come up and see me sometime?' And Charlie said, 'What do?' And she said, 'Oh, I'll let you play around in my woodpile.' Well, that's kind of cute—until *she* said it."

The *Christian Science Monitor* called it "a quality of humor only acceptable in the lowest types of burlesque theaters." The FCC said it was "offensive to the great mass of right-thinking, clean-minded American citizens." Senator Clyde Herring proposed a new government censorship agency "to prevent the recurrence of such broadcasts."

Church organizations prepared a boycott of Chase and Sanborn products and thousands of angry letters poured in. "After listening to radio from 1920 until the present time," wrote one man, "I have the Sunday night sponsors to thank for the smuttiest, filthiest, most degenerate, sacrilegious program I have ever heard."

Despite the tremendous controversy, NBC sensed it was part of an orchestrated campaign and not an indication of listener consensus. Too many of the letters they received were written with identical language for it to be a coincidence. "It was like a great wave of witless drivel that broke upon our shore, rolled foaming up the beach and flowed out again," said one NBC executive. "What coincidence, or as yet undiscoverable force, activated these variant minds and set them thinking along identical channels . . ."

Regardless, Chase and Sanborn did not want to be identified with any controversy and they convinced NBC to ban Mae West from the network for twelve years.

"We got into all kinds of trouble," recalled Edgar Bergen. "The network apologized, Chase and Sanborn apologized, and I went and hid for a week. And the net result was our rating went up two points—so we weren't really too sorry."

After the hysteria died down, a survey determined that 59 percent of listeners approved of Mae West's performance. Another 60 percent said that they would like to hear "more sexually suggestive programming over the radio than currently existed."

They wouldn't get it. Instead, sponsors and network censors became far stricter. Radio censors forced comedian Fred Allen to delete the word "saffron" because it "had sexual connotations." And he was required to remove a reference to "nuptials" because "marriage ceremony is not a suitable topic for comedy."

NBC vice president Clarence Menser reminded radio comedians that any jokes about him or the network were also "strictly taboo." He would censor comedians "who think they have the right to say what they want." Menser met with the Young & Rubicam advertising agency to devise "a way to silence" comedians who used "libel, derogatory reference, [or] vulgarity" to get laughs.

4

NAZIS, RACISTS, AND WORLD WAR TWO

The Nazi politicians of Germany hated many of the same things being demonized in the United States. Crooning, jitterbugging, and jazz music were among the first things banned by the Nazis. German Vice Chancellor Franz von Papen called the genres a "corroding poison [that] threatens to destroy the moral code" and categorized them as "Cultural Bolshevism."

A comedian named Werner Finck was performing in a Berlin nightclub in 1935 when it was raided by police. Reuters reported, "Werner Finck, one of the best-known vaudeville stars in Germany, has been put in a concentration camp for 'pulling the leg' of Nazi leaders . . . He has been detained since in a secret police prison in Berlin. His 70-year-old mother has been unable to obtain any information regarding his whereabouts."

Actress Käthe Dorsch learned Finck was incarcerated at the Esterwegen concentration camp. She met directly with Nazi minister Hermann Göring to secure his release, and the comedian was freed in 1936.

"You know, it's funny," said Finck. "I walked around the camp and saw the walls, guards with their guns, and the heavy gates. Everybody told me how hard it was to get in—but all I did was speak one sentence."

Nazi propaganda minister Joseph Goebbels called Berlin comedians "society rabble and intellectual snobs." Goebbels said, "There is plenty of humor in Germany, more than enough. But we do not permit ourselves to be ridiculed . . . Such jokes make us wretch."

Five more comedians were banned "for publicly ridiculing Nazi party and state functionaries [and making] Nazi leaders the butts of their jokes."

"Comedians have no right to be jocular about such things as the Nazi four-year economic plan or Adolf Hitler's demand for colonies because they are too important and require too much careful thinking on the part of big minds," said Goebbels. The Nazis banned nearly all comedy—with the exception of anti-Semitic jokes and racist humor.

Warner Bros. pulled their films from Germany after Philip Kaufman, their point man in Berlin, was brutally beaten by Nazis. The other film studios, however, were keen to retain the German market. Joe Kennedy, the former Hollywood studio head and father of John F. Kennedy, said, "Americans should accept Adolf Hitler as a fact of life."

Films starring Jewish comedians were banned wherever fascism reigned. The Marx Brothers movie *Duck Soup* was banned in fascist Italy and fascist Spain. It was also banned in Portugal for fear that the surname Marx would trigger sympathy for communism.

American radio preachers spread anti-Semitism during their weekly radio sermons. Reverend Edwin Moll of Wisconsin called comedian Eddie Cantor a "cheap Hebrew wit" because he advocated on behalf of Jewish refugees. Moll received letters of praise from domestic Nazis: "I congratulate you that you have taken up the challenge—too long unanswered—of these cheap, immoral radio comedians among which the Jew Eddie Cantor is the most shining as well as the most harmful example."

Father Charles Coughlin of Michigan was the most famous of the radio preachers. Initially a supporter of President [Franklin D.] Roosevelt's social safety net, he turned against him when the president refused to hire him as an advisor. Coughlin began quoting from *The Protocols of the Elders of Zion*, the anti-Semitic conspiracy theory pushed by the Nazis.

Father Coughlin's rise to prominence was underwritten by millionaire George Richards, the anti-Semitic owner of the Detroit Lions. Richards owned major radio stations including WGAR in Cleveland, KMPC in Los Angeles, and WJR in Detroit. He referred to President Roosevelt as "a Jew-lover who was out to communize the nation" and directed his news bureaus to report negative stories about "that Communist bastard." He told his station managers, "We have got to get these kike actors out of Hollywood." Without the support of Richards, there's no way Father Coughlin could have stayed on the air.

Father Coughlin's program aired on station WMCA in the New York area, but his anti-Semitic commentary became too much, and his program was pulled. Two thousand Coughlin supporters marched in front of WMCA, claiming the station had declared war on the First Amendment. Many held anti-Semitic signs.

An editorial in the *Reading Times* noted, "Freedom such as we Americans enjoy is a broad thing with no sharply-defined limits. Perhaps the simplest way to define it is to say that it gives every man the right to speak or act absolutely as he pleases, provided that in doing he does not infringe on the rights of others. That means that freedom is not quite unlimited. Freedom of the press, for instance, does not give an editor the right to commit libel . . . Political freedom does not give any citizen the right to get down on the floor of Congress and disrupt business by yelling his head off . . . And so it is with freedom of speech. You may have the right to say what you please; but if you elect to stir up race hatred . . . you have no business trying to hide behind the freedom of speech clause."

Comedian Eddie Cantor called Father Coughlin a phony opportunist. "Father Coughlin is a great orator but I doubt he has a sincere atom in his entire system," said Cantor. "We Jews have nothing to fear from good Christians. We are their brothers and sisters. But I am afraid of people who *pretend* to be good Christians."

The Eddie Cantor Show was sponsored by Texaco Oil from 1935 through 1938. The comedian used his platform to speak out against the Nazi threat. At the end of one episode, he pleaded with listeners to support Jewish refugees fleeing Germany. "If you believe in the things that I do, believe in America, love your country," said Cantor, "then join in the fight for civilization and humanity." For his statement, Texaco threatened to cancel his program while American Nazis threatened his life.

Cantor's wife picked up the phone and heard an anonymous voice on the other end: "Tell Cantor to get out of Los Angeles before he is carried out in a pine box." He hired bodyguards to protect his family. "My home, my wife and my children have been threatened," said Cantor. "I don't care if they do get me now. This, the help of fellow Jews, is my life work. If I am gotten, someone else will carry on."

Broadcasting from Columbia Square, an art deco megaplex at 6121 Sunset Boulevard, Cantor was heckled by fascists. The *Los Angeles Times* reported, "Jokes about Adolf Hitler told by Eddie Cantor, Jewish radio and film comedian, in an after-program talk in the Columbia Broadcast Studio . . . led to a fight between members of the audience and two men."

"We were sitting near the rear of the theater," said audience member Charles Gollob. "And as this final address started I suggested to my wife that we leave, because we didn't want to hear any propaganda. As we neared the door, a woman asked us if we didn't like the program. We explained that we liked it but didn't want to hear any propaganda against Hitler." When comedian Bert Gordon overheard the comment, he sucker punched the man, and a shoving match spilled into the street.

Texaco Oil considered Eddie Cantor a problem. After the comic emceed several rallies for the Hollywood Anti-Nazi League, Texaco pulled their sponsorship, and the program was canceled. Six months later, Texaco chairman Torkild Rieber resigned after he was exposed for secretly supplying oil to Hitler and providing classified information about American shipping routes to the Nazis.

Not everyone agreed about the extent of the Nazi threat—or cared. Many in the corporate sector considered fascism the lesser of two evils. After all, if Hitler hated communists as American capitalists did—and criminalized their philosophy, as some American capitalists desired—how bad could he be?

NBC and CBS presented a joint broadcast of a Nuremburg rally on September 12, 1938, and *Variety* gave it a glowing review: "One of the most momentous speeches in modern history was given America first-hand via shortwave from Nuremburg Monday when both the NBC and CBS nets [networks] broadcast Adolf Hitler's closing address to the annual Nazi congress . . . A dynamic, spellbinding speaker, the broadcast was most impressive when he worked up the thousands of Nazis in attendance to frenzied cheers, 'Heil Hitlers' and 'Sieg Heils.'"

NBC and CBS had no problem broadcasting a Nuremberg rally, but references to Hitler were forbidden in "song parodies, comedy skits [or] dramatic productions." The novelty song "Even Hitler Had a Mother" was banned in England because British censors had a firm rule: "No head of state should be ridiculed."

Criticism of Hitler was cut from *March of Time* newsreels in Ohio so as not to anger local Germans. Charlie Chaplin's anti-fascist satire *The Great Dictator* was banned by Franco in Spain, Mussolini in Italy, and the police in Chicago. Chicago's Police Censor Board approved the pro-Hitler film *Campaign in Poland*, but banned newsreels that mentioned Nazi atrocities. They called the anti-Hitler films *Goose Step*, *Professor Mamlock*, and *Pastor Hall* "purely Jewish and Communist propaganda against Germany."

Texas congressman Martin Dies, a precursor to Joseph McCarthy, chaired the House Committee on Un-American Activities in 1938. He condemned the Hollywood Anti-Nazi League and declared, "Racial equality forms a vital part of communistic teachings and practices."

Dies was one of the first politicians to demonize Hollywood for political gain. He was detested by the major stars of the day. "I do not believe in the so-called revelations made by the Dies Investigating Committee," said Oscar-winning actress Luise Rainer. "I believe their purpose is purely destructive, aimed at discrediting worthwhile peace and anti-fascist organizations, which are so much needed in these worried times."

"May I express my whole-hearted desire to cooperate to the utmost of my ability with the Hollywood Anti-Nazi League," said conservative filmmaker John Ford. "If this be Communism, count me in."

Congressman Dies belonged to a political dynasty. His father was elected to Congress in 1909, railing against "the dangers of foreign immigration" and opposing the woman's right to vote on the grounds it would "thrust the ballot into the hands of millions of ignorant negro women of the South."

As his anti-Hollywood campaign accelerated, Dies received a congratulatory telegram: "Every true American, and that includes every Klansman, is behind you and your committee in its effort to turn the country back to the honest, freedom-loving, God-fearing American to whom it belongs."

His committee inspired several pamphleteers to join the fight. A leaflet titled *Behind the Scenes in Hollywood* railed, "Hollywood has a Russian background. Hollywood has Communistic leanings. This alien influence which the movies have enthroned over America has perverted the character of our people; it has dried up the sources of spiritual strength; it has plagued us with the pagan spirit of materialism and sexuality."

★

The United States entered the war in December 1941 and anti-fascism was suddenly a noble cause rather than a Commie plot. And as fascism ran over Europe, racist humor was objected to in the United States.

Irving Caesar, a songwriter who wrote hit songs for Al Jolson, said, "I am unalterably opposed [to] dialect humor at this particular time. Today, with all too many bigoted, moronic, intolerant, and well-organized forces loose in the world, the similarity of all Americans should be emphasized, not their ethnological differences."

Many of the best comedians were deployed overseas, either as servicemen or as entertainers. It left a domestic vacuum that was filled by mediocre, lackluster talents. Broadway producer Billy Rose noted an ironic trend of racist comedians filling the vacant spots. "Before the war, most of them didn't work two weeks in fifty," said Rose. "During the war, these brassy, not-so-classy comics got their chance."

Alan Carney of the movie comedy team Brown and Carney was one of them. "I saw comedian Alan Carney's performance on the Paramount stage last Thursday," complained an anti-fascist. "Although it was done in jest, it contained some of the same arguments used seriously by the enemies of democracy. It poked fun at some of our basic freedoms . . . He caricatured the various national minorities in this country . . . Carney's anti-Jewish caricature got the biggest laugh. There was even a note of hysteria in the laughter. It could easily have been turned into a Christian Front meeting at that point."

Fibber McGee and Molly was a popular radio comedy that used Greek,

Irish, Black, and Asian stereotypes. When the program was pressured to eliminate them, head writer Don Quinn was angered. He called the campaign "snoopery, meddling, finger pointing and thin-skinned cry-babyism." Quinn felt Americans had gone soft: "We've got an epidemic of war-born touchiness; a mass yearning to regulate and restrict . . . Everybody wants to be a censor [or] maybe it's just that a few people are getting louder."

Armed Forces Radio broadcasted several pleas for racial tolerance and they featured Black performers speaking in their own voice, without adopting dialect. On the AFR program *A New World A-Comin'*, white journalist Lillian Smith criticized racist comedy:

"We are now in the midst of a total World War and changes are already taking place, changes for the better, changes which concern all of us deeply . . . The next time you hear someone start to tell what he considers to be a great joke, using certain distasteful words concerning colored people . . . you might urge the individual to stop using those words and, even better, to stop telling that kind of joke. These days, jokes like that are not very funny except to the Germans. It's a little thing, yes, but the little things do as much as the big things to wear out the nerves of decent, self-respecting Negroes in our community."

March of Time released an anti-racist newsreel in 1944 called *Americans All.* "Deep seated in the American citizen," opened the narration, "is born of the concept that all men are free and equal. But at a time when unity is desperately needed, American is being set against American, systematically and purposefully, by singling out one minority or another as a target for old and reasonless hatred." Warner Bros. ordered several copies of the film for its chain of theaters, but the message was undercut by the Warner Bros. cartoon that played with it, *Angel Puss,* based on the slowpoke stereotypes of actor Stepin Fetchit. *Angel Puss* was heckled in the Black neighborhoods where it played.

Members of the Screen Cartoonists Guild objected when they were asked to animate racist drawings, but they were overruled by superiors. The SCG insisted they held "distinct dissatisfaction with the type of racial caricature material used in the making of animated film cartoons."

The American Guild of Variety Artists, a union that represented nightclub performers, drafted a resolution in July 1944 that forbade "all clichés and racial caricatures for comedy purposes."

"Feeling has long been manifest in some quarters that racial disunity is being engendered by frequent cracks in niteries at the expense of minority groups," reported *Variety*. "More often than not contempt . . . is implied via makeup and costume, to the embarrassment of many in the audience." *Variety* addressed the issue in a July 1945 editorial: "Comedians persist in being among the worst offenders against racial minorities. This is not because comedians are biased, but because so many are thoughtless of consequences. Anything for a giggle. Moreover, a comedian's habit of thinking exclusively in terms of gags . . . often makes him unwilling to admit—when challenged—that much of what used to be innocent fun is now vicious political propaganda . . . They do not acknowledge the offense, protest good intention, or indicate a disposition to watch more carefully in the future. Instead they counter-attack."

★

Attacks on African Americans increased after the war as bigots targeted Black veterans. Vigilante beatings, police brutality, and lynch murders sought to "make an example" of Black men in uniform. The situation was inflamed by Mississippi governor Theodore Bilbo, who said Black soldiers "had shown a lack of intelligence and initiative and had been a disgrace to the uniform."

Historian Philip Dray explains, "Even before the soldiers had walked down the gangplanks of the returning troopships, Southern demagogues were warning of the dangers of having allowed 750,000 blacks to engage in a great war for democracy. Senator James O. Eastland of Mississippi claimed, ludicrously, that black soldiers in the Occupation Forces in Germany were routinely raping white women." And when the vocal white supremacist Eugene Talmadge was re-elected governor of Georgia in 1946, the "Grass-Roots Fuhrer" was blamed for the new "outbreak of racist violence" sweeping across the state.

Black celebrities were not immune to racist attack. Bandleader Lionel

Hampton invited jazz legend Cab Calloway to be his guest at the Pla-Mor Ballroom in Kansas City. But when Calloway tried to walk through the stage door, a white police officer intervened and struck him "several times over the head with a .45 automatic pistol." Calloway was charged with "interfering with a police officer" and sent to a hospital, where he received eight stitches. Hampton was informed of the fracas during intermission and refused to return to the bandstand. The Pla-Mor issued fifteen hundred refunds.

Journalist Eugene Gordon concluded, "It is obviously not only a frameup but, more seriously, according to accumulating masses of evidence, it is a part of the same general pattern, a studied effort by fascist-minded Americans to shove black fellow Americans back to their prewar status."

★

"We're Hitler's boys! We're going to get Robeson! Lynch Robeson!"

White supremacists chanted in the fairgrounds above Peekskill, New York, while a cross burned on the hill.

Paul Robeson was a well-known African American actor, baritone, Communist sympathizer, and Soviet apologist. He played Othello on the stage in London, starred in *Show Boat* on Broadway, and sang in a Royal Command Performance at Buckingham Palace.

Hired by a labor union to sing in Peekskill in August 1949, a consortium of American Legionnaires, Nazi sympathizers, and Klan associates conspired with police to run Robeson out of town. Concertgoers who arrived to enjoy a night of music were swarmed by "thousands of local vigilantes" who pelted them with rocks and beat them as they fled.

The *Pittsburgh Courier* reported, "For five hate-filled hours Sunday, wild-eyed 'defenders of law and order,' with teeth bared and wearing the uniforms of New York State Troopers and special deputies, joined the vicious mob of hoodlums disguised as 'World War II veterans' in putting on one of the . . . most shameful spectacles in American history."

Twelve hundred police officers were sent to restore order but, according to the *Courier*, "their flying nightsticks wrought as much mayhem in the rioting they helped carry out as did the stones, clubs and bottles hurled by the 'veterans' who tried—unsuccessfully—to keep Robeson from singing. The officers openly and brazenly broke the very laws they had sworn to uphold . . . Everybody who seemed to be a Negro was automatically taken . . . and received the full weight of the joint attack of the police."

★

While bigoted politicians encouraged vigilantes, the Vatican influenced lay Catholics to endorse Spanish fascism, which was considered preferable to the communist alternative. Stand-up comedian Frank Fay, a devout Catholic, followed the pope's lead.

Fay belonged to Actors' Equity, a union representing Broadway performers. When the union criticized the Spanish Catholic Church for endorsing the execution of anti-fascists, Fay considered it a slur on his religion. Fay broke with his union and criticized their stance in the press. As a result, he was censured by Actors' Equity, and his cause was taken up by fascist sympathizers.

Five months after World War Two, thousands of fascist sympathizers gathered in Madison Square Garden to deliver speeches in support of Franco. A banner hanging from the podium said: "The Friends of Frank Fay." Showbiz columnist Maurice Zolotow wrote, "Several personalities connected with the Fascist lunatic fringe were the organizers and speakers. Naturally, a terrific controversy was aroused by Fay's association with these persons." Speakers included the Klan ally Joseph Scott; an anti-Semitic author named John Geis; and Joseph P. Kamp, a man who used the Klan's mailing list to distribute anti-Semitic conspiracy theories about FDR.

★

Debates about ethnic characterizations intensified in the late 1940s. Mister Kitzel, a hot dog vendor with a Yiddish accent played by Artie Auerbach on *The Jack Benny Program*, and the malaprop-prone Mrs. Nussbaum played by Minerva Pious on *The Fred Allen Show*, had been popular for years. But now, in the postwar atmosphere, their purpose was questioned.

"I'm not suggesting Fred Allen get rid of Mrs. Nussbaum or Jack Benny dispense with Rochester and Kitzel," said Broadway producer Billy Rose. "I am suggesting these two highly talented gentlemen make sure those yocks aren't knocks. The race crack is the crutch of the stumble bum who is too scared, too stupid or too stingy to lay it on the line for good material."

The Jack Benny Program had another Jewish character named Schlepperman, played by comic actor Sam Hearn. Most listeners considered it harmless fun—until it was embraced by anti-Semites.

"I was vacationing in the country with my family when we came across a clambake held in the woods by a group from town known to be anti-Semites," recalled Jewish humorist Sam Levenson. "We were in a rowboat at the time. I pulled up close to shore just to take a peek and found the group laughing like crazy, listening to a loud-speaker that was playing 'Schlepperman' records." Levenson felt it was time for showbiz to evolve.

"The classic vaudeville dialecticians did not tell the truth about my father's generation," said Levenson. "If they had presented the whole picture, then perhaps there would have been room for some dialectical kidding, but when every Jew is presented as a pawnbroker or his next of kin, I say good riddance . . . It is dated at best."

Billy Rose agreed. "Let me start with the flat statement that, without exception, the fellows peddling race ridicule are inferior comedians and midget talents," he said. "These jokes not only make me mad—they make me sleepy. I laughed at them 20 years ago. I yawned at them 10 years ago. I winced at them five years ago. Today they nauseate me."

The Jack Benny Program also featured Eddie Anderson, the country's highest-paid African American comedian. He was beloved for the role of Rochester, a sarcastic manservant who ridiculed the vanity of his white boss. In real life Anderson owned racehorses, designed his own sports car, and purchased a Los Angeles city block, which he renamed Rochester Circle. Enjoying his fame and wealth, he denied the existence of discrimination.

"I believe those who have shown that they had something to offer have been given an equal opportunity," said Anderson. "I haven't seen anything objectionable. I don't see why certain characters are called stereotypes."

Lillian Randolph was a radio contemporary of Anderson's. She was well-known for playing maids on radio sitcoms like *The Great Gildersleeve*, and she was the only Black woman in attendance at the American Federation of Radio Artists convention in 1947. At the convention, her union proposed a resolution condemning stereotypical roles. Although it was offered in the spirit of civil rights, Randolph objected, feeling that the resolution specifically targeted her livelihood.

The resolution read:

"Whereas, radio is one of the most potent mediums of education, information and entertainment, and should not portray minorities, in general terms, at their worst, but should rather treat all people as individuals, each with his own failings and shortcomings; and should not show members of minorities as stereotypes . . . Whereas, it is common for AFRA members to be compelled by economic pressures, to perform such stereotyped characters, against their own better judgement, and thus give what amounts to tacit, approval of a bad practice . . . copies of this resolution [will] be forwarded to Radio Writers' Guild, Radio Directors' Guild, and all agencies, stations, networks and producers."

The membership applauded, but Randolph stood up in protest. She defended herself among the sea of white do-gooders. "I am very proud that I can portray a stereotyped role," she said. "When you take that away from me, you take away my birthright. We are not doing anything to disgrace anybody. Such things as that should be left alone. There are certain traditions we can't get rid of. [I will] fight the above resolution to eliminate the stereotyping of Negroes on the radio."

Randolph was criticized in the Black press. The *Pittsburgh Courier* wrote, "Negro delegates spoke of portraying . . . stereotype as their birthright—I am embarrassed as a human being and as a Negro. They might well look to other of their birthrights for which such men as Frederick Douglass fought rather than those for which Uncle Tom sang and danced."

5

TV: IMMORAL AND FILTHY
AND POSSIBLY RACIST

In 1946, there were only ten thousand households with a television set. By 1949, there were one million. By 1955, thirty-three million televisions were in use. During the same period, bookstores suffered a massive slump in sales and movie theater attendance dropped 40 percent.

The corporate interests that dominated radio quickly seized control of TV. Censorship decisions were made solely in the name of protecting sponsor profit. Programming was sanitized to the point of blandness so as not to offend the consumer. America seemed ready for greater maturity, but sponsors, television networks, and the government imposed even heavier censorship.

The Texaco Star Theater with Milton Berle was an early television hit and it frequently featured the comedian in drag. Wearing a wig and crooked makeup, the laughs came from Berle's homely appearance, but critics accused him of perversion.

"Abnormalities are currently regarded by some of the most famous comedians as top subjects for good clean fun for mommer, popper and the kiddies," complained the *Rochester Democrat and Chronicle*. "During the past few nights the video fans saw two highly exploited comics, sponsored by great industries, behave as if there was nothing so funny in the American home as the female impersonator, the freak of nature, the male-hands-on-hips character and the pathetic biological problem case."

"Berle started to do what was then called, 'swish,' or 'nance' comedy," recalled his writer, Irving Brecher. "Here he was, swishing around the living room telling jokes."

TV Guide published numerous complaints. "Milton Berle's show has too many two-sided jokes," wrote a woman from Waynesville, Ohio. "People wonder where their children pick up all this trash. Could it be due to TV shows such as this?"

"I think Milton Berle ought to be banned," wrote Mr. Bosko of Illinois. "We had some out-of-town guests at the house who had never seen TV. When they saw Miltie they said, 'Why do they allow it?'"

Another viewer was enraged that Berle, a Jewish comedian, presented a Christmas episode: "Why station WNBC or the sponsor, Phillip Morris Cigarettes, should permit this interloper to ridicule a sacred occasion many cannot fathom. It was thoroughly anti-Christian."

NBC censors complained about the "swishy manner" of comedy team Olsen and Johnson, banned all references to transgendered woman Christine Jorgensen, outlawed any mention of the Kinsey Report, and scolded comedian Jack Carter for making a live appearance "in too-tight long johns causing the home audience to clearly see the contours of his penis."

On an episode of *The Jack Benny Program*, the comedian bragged about the brutal toughness of his new bodyguard, Killer Hogan. The studio audience exploded in laughter when the bodyguard delivered his first line in a sing-song lisp. NBC told Benny to immediately delete all "effeminate gentlemen or sex-perverted characters."

Senator William J. Keenan of Massachusetts called for government action. In a speech delivered in January 1951, he said, "It is about time for us to see that we get decent shows that do not make parents blush in explaining double meaning gags to their children." He proposed "a year's imprisonment" for any television comedian "deemed immoral or tending to corrupt morals."

One of the great debates of early television concerned how women dressed. "It is shocking, I say, the way some women dress on TV," wrote a reader of the *Cincinnati Enquirer*. "I am ashamed and disgusted for my sex at times. The modest woman gets the man to the altar."

A woman from Dayton, Ohio, complained about a television appearance by Judy Garland: "I don't like the way Judy Garland is always running around with her legs showing from here to there. I remember Judy as such a sweet young thing. I like to see her in clothes like the ones she wore in *Wizard of Oz* . . . Now she is running around in short, short pants with jazz musicians."

Cleavage, or the suggestion of it, was another furious debate. "Television, popular magazines, and theater advertising have led us to believe that the majority of women have adopted this style," said a letter published in the *Dayton Daily News*. "It is not the majority but a degenerate minority . . . These women cannot escape responsibility for provoking immoral thoughts . . . Few women stop to think when they read of the mangling of a little girl's body that they may have been responsible for the initial impulse."

Minnesota congressman John Chenoweth wanted television cleavage regulated. "In boxing, if you hit below the belt, it's a foul," said Chenoweth. "Just where should the neckline be—where should we draw the line?"

"I am glad to see someone in government interested in TV censorship," wrote a TV viewer from Barkley, Michigan. "The number of . . . raw jokes as well as scanty low cut dresses is disgusting."

Senator E. C. Gathings of Arkansas chaired a 1952 congressional hearing about "immoral material in radio and television." The hearings lasted several days and received wide media coverage. "Recently a program put on by a peanut butter firm [had] one particular act [that] was most obscene and lewd," said Gathings. "It had a grass-skirted lady and a thinly clad gentleman dancing the hootchy-kootchy to a lively tune and they both shook the shimmy. Then the attractive lady shook down backward all the way to the floor with the young man standing close by. I tried to turn it off but the children wouldn't let me."

George Q. Lewis, a joke book writer who taught comedy workshops, testified before the committee. "Barnyard and bathroom humor has no place in the American living room," he said. "And the people aren't seeking dirty or smutty entertainment—they're looking for laughs not smutty jokes and limp-wristed female impersonators." Lewis told the committee they needed "to outlaw suggestivity, the innuendo, flagrant use of male effeminacy. These immoral uses reflect a contempt of the entertainment industry for the public."

Lloyd Halvorson, a spokesman for the farming lobby National Grange, testified, "Television is the greatest menace to clean-minded farmers since the traveling salesman."

Senator C. Eugene Farnam of Massachusetts expressed his concern about immoral commercials: "It's terrible to flick on a TV set at home and have women's undergarments flaunted in your face and hear talk about curvier cups and smoother separation. [They are] undermining the moral foundations of society."

"We have waited for TV to show some signs that it is growing up to its responsibilities," said Congressman Thomas Lane. "Instead it seems to be plunging down to the primitive state of nudism and the manure pile."

A Chicago archdiocese told the committee they should hire "bedridden veterans" as watchdogs. From the purgatory of a VA hospital, they could participate in marathon viewing sessions and flag "any moral infractions."

After the initial testimony about sexuality, Senator Gathings moved on to the topic of politics. He proposed federal censorship for television programs that depicted politicians in a negative light. He took his cue from the many letters to the editor that complained about mockery of American institutions and historical figures.

"I was disappointed in Sergeant Bilko making a burlesque of George Washington's crossing of the Delaware," said a letter to the *Cincinnati Enquirer*. "Some things are sacred and this is one of them. It is not gratifying to see a low comedian make fun of our beautiful history. This can lead to Milton Berle making a stooge of Abraham Lincoln or Martha Raye making fun of Eisenhower."

References to religion were another sticking point, and largely informed by the growing religious fervor at the White House. President Dwight Eisenhower said America was "getting too secular" and signed a bill that added "under God" to the Pledge of Allegiance. He invited celebrity preachers Billy Graham and Norman Vincent Peale to lead "prayer breakfasts" at the White House and he added the phrase "In God We Trust" to US currency.

The Eisenhower administration promoted religion as a way to differentiate itself from the "Godless Communism" of the Soviet Union.

A sitcom viewer from St. Clair, Ohio, complained about the gentle sitcom *December Bride*, which she accused of tearing "down the home, one of the finest and most Christian institutions there is . . . I suppose these obnoxious people who delight . . . in seeing marriage and the home knocked would like to replace marriage with free love and the home with taverns and cocktail lounges."

The general contempt for anything even remotely related to sex led New York state censors to ban Walt Disney's *The Vanishing Prairie* because it had a "two-minute sequence showing the birth of a buffalo."

Lassie, the popular family program about an intelligent border collie, raised the ire of a viewer because it showed a litter of puppies. "If I wanted my kids to watch sex shows," he said, "I would take them to burlesque."

I Love Lucy was the most popular television comedy in America. When its star, Lucille Ball, was expecting a baby in real life, a storyline was proposed about Lucy Ricardo being in a family way. Desi Arnaz, who produced the show and played the Cuban bandleader-husband, received immediate resistance from the sponsor, Philip Morris. "There's no way you can do that," they told him. "You cannot show a pregnant woman on television."

"She's pregnant," Arnaz insisted. "There is no way we can hide that fact from the audience. We have already signed the contracts. This is the number-one show on the air. There is only one way to do it—Lucy Ricardo will have a baby."

Getting nowhere, Arnaz wrote a letter directly to Alfred Lyon, the UK-based chairman of Philip Morris. He reminded him that *I Love Lucy* had made huge profits for the tobacco company, and now his American underlings were putting that at risk. Lyon sent a directive to his American representatives, "To Whom It May Concern: Don't fuck around with the Cuban."

Arnaz hired priests and rabbis to supervise the process, but despite precautions, complaints poured in. "We are not the only ones disgusted with Lucy having a baby," said a letter published in a February 1953 issue of *TV Forecast*. "I don't think we will ever watch the program again." Another wrote, "I did not find them [the pregnancy episodes] funny, but considered them in very bad taste. The three ministers who supervised must have been taking a nap." A viewer from Crown Point, Indiana, said, "If we want to know about having babies and all that junk we don't have to watch it on TV."

Viewer complaints affected comedy content. Sid Caesar abandoned the oversize glasses worn by his jazz musician character on *Caesar's Hour* after a complaint from the Maryland School for the Blind. *The Garry Moore Show* dropped its Happy Mailman character after a complaint from the postal service. *Variety* reported that a pharmaceutical company threatened to sue comedian Louis Nye for cracking a joke about one of their products.

"You crack a joke about lawyers, there's a letter the next day from a legal group," complained Groucho Marx. "You make funny about doctors, the AMA writes in. You have an audience of thirty million and your sponsor receives eight letters saying his comedian is a jerk, and he's terrified. This is what has cramped humor."

"The few comedians who continue to function despite the trend," said *Tonight Show* host Steve Allen, "are subject to increasingly heavy attacks from critics, audiences, rating services, and from the vaguely defined spirit of the times."

Television became one of the most common household appliances, and with hundreds of thousands of new TV viewers, there were nearly as many complaints about its content.

"In television everything known to man is sacred," complained satirist Henry Morgan. "Absolutely nothing can be made fun of lest it offend someone . . . This has led to the formation of a sleazy group of cowards whose business it is to guess ahead of time what joke will offend whom. They are the termites of television."

The hearings chaired by Senator Gathings did not lead to much, and the press generally concluded that it had been an exercise in self-aggrandizement. Still, members of the industry felt threatened by talk of legislation and decided to impose a degree of self-censorship.

The National Association of Broadcasters unveiled their Television Code in 1952. It required television stations to conform to certain standards in exchange for a Seal of Good Practice, assuring viewers of inoffensive content. NAB's Television Code covered several subjects:

"Religion. The subject of religion should invariably be treated with respect. Reverence should mark any mention of the name of God. His attributes or powers . . . baptism, marriage, burial and other sacraments— should be portrayed with accuracy. A priest or minister, when portrayed in his calling, should be vested with the dignity of his office.

"Marriage and the Home. Respect for the sanctity of marriage and the home should be maintained. Marriage or extra-marital relations should not be made a vehicle for suggestive or offensive lines. Adultery and other infractions of moral law should not be presented . . .

"Divorce should not be casually treated or advanced as the normal solution to marital problems. No material tending to break down juvenile respect for parents, the home or moral conduct should be broadcast.

"Programs for children and young people should be designed to meet the following: They should convey the commonly accepted moral, social and ethical ideals characteristic of American life . . . No dramatization of political issues should be permitted . . .

"Profanity and Obscenity. Sacrilegious, blasphemous, profane, salacious, obscene, vulgar or indecent material should not be broadcast . . . Sex abnormalities are not desirable subjects for broadcast."

As the NAB deliberated about what the Television Code and its Seal of Good Practice should include, they were pressured by civil rights groups to include restrictions on racial stereotypes. The NAB board voted unanimously to reject any such condition.

The Gathings commission equated "immorality" with sexuality. Some politicians went further and equated immorality with so-called race mixing. Georgia governor Herman Talmadge was appalled when a Christmas episode of *The Ken Murray Show* presented an integrated children's choir singing Christmas carols. "Good taste alone should prevent such a situation," said Talmadge. "But if the television executives and producers do not have this good taste then the great millions of people in the Southern states can turn their own resentment, individually, toward the products which sponsor the shows."

Corporate sponsors were far more likely to placate bigots than Black viewers. Southern racists possessed greater purchasing power than the average African American, and as such, their considerations were more important to advertisers.

★

Amos 'n' Andy was still on the radio in the 1950s. After the major protests of the early 1930s, its stereotypes were diluted. The lead characters were still performed by two white guys, but the cast had been expanded to include several Black and Asian actors. While it remained on radio, it had fallen out of the Top 20, and the controversy had long since cooled. The program was neither loved nor hated so much as ignored.

Many radio sitcoms made the transition to early television—*The Goldbergs*, *The Burns and Allen Show*, *The Jack Benny Program*—and succeeded. But with blackface out of favor in the postwar era, it seemed unlikely that *The Amos 'n' Andy Show* could do the same.

With its popularity on the wane, the stars and creators of the show, Freeman Gosden and Charles Correll, came up with a gimmick to generate excitement. *The Amos 'n' Andy Show* would come to television in 1951 with an all-Black cast.

The Kingfish was the boastful, larger-than-life character who provided the TV program with its biggest laughs. The Kingfish was played by Tim Moore, one of the great Black comedians of the 1910s. In his early days, Moore did a one-man version of *Uncle Tom's Cabin* in which he painted one half his face white and applied blackface to the other. Eventually, he teamed with his wife, and the Moores became one of the most critically acclaimed acts in comedy.

By the time he was cast in the television version of *The Amos 'n' Andy Show*, Moore was a showbiz veteran of forty-seven years. Those who worked with him said he was one of the funniest men on the planet. "The words on paper were just words," said *Amos 'n' Andy* director Robert Justman. "He could take these things and turn them into something so funny that you could barely stand it." Comedian Jack Carter concurred, "He was the funniest man that ever lived, the funniest person I ever knew." Comedian Nipsey Russell said every Black comic owed him a debt: "Of all the comedians from what we call the 'old school,' Tim Moore, who became Kingfish in the *Amos 'n' Andy* series, was possibly the most imitated and the most emulated . . . those intonations were copied by everyone."

The Amos 'n' Andy Show hired comedians Johnny Lee, Nick Stewart, Spencer Williams, and Alvin Childress and respected Black actors Ruby Dandridge, Amanda Randolph, and Lillian Randolph. It was a historic moment for Black performers even though the content was controlled by the program's white creators. Cast member Johnny Lee said Freeman Gosden would take the actors aside and coach them to "talk as white people believed Negroes talked."

The program's writing staff included former Bob Hope scribe Dave Schwartz, future Bob Hope writer Hal Kanter, *Green Acres* creator Jay Sommers, *Leave It to Beaver* creator Bob Mosher, and Joe Connelly, future head writer of *The Munsters*.

The Amos 'n' Andy Show premiered on CBS Television on June 28, 1951. The old radio theme song, originally composed for *The Birth of a Nation*, was scrapped. Flournoy Miller, formerly of the Miller and Lyles comedy team that once sued Gosden for plagiarism, was hired as the "consultant on racial matters."

A columnist from the *California Eagle* wondered why this "slow and steady poison" was being resurrected: "To my way of thinking, the *Amos 'n' Andy* show is not controversial. It just doesn't belong on TV or anywhere else."

The television program was not attacked for its content so much as the stigma it carried from the early days of radio. Despite the Black talent involved, the title automatically conjured up memories of stereotypes.

The Committee for the Negro in the Arts held a press conference at the Hotel Theresa in Harlem and called for Black control of Black stories: "What is needed is a representative presentation of Negro life, written by Negro writers preferably, many of whom have such material available, and fuller use of Negroes in all aspects of radio and TV on a dignified level of merit and equality. All democratic-minded citizens should make known their objections to this program and urge its withdrawal."

Schenley Distilleries sponsored the show. The makers of Blatz beer, they received a letter from the NAACP announcing a boycott of their products.

The Coordinating Council for Negro Performers, an offshoot of the Negro Actors Guild, was organized by the program stars to oppose the boycott. The NAACP "does not speak for the majority of Negroes," they said, and the boycott "actually threatened the greatest opportunity given Negro actors in recent years."

A joint statement from Tim Moore, Lillian Randolph, and other cast members said *The Amos 'n' Andy Show* "at last gives us the Negro actors and actresses of America, some understanding spokesman who can protect and extend the gains we have made in recent years." They said their careers were being "threatened by ill-informed people of our own race who have irresponsibly threatened a boycott of our sponsor (Blatz Beer) and have unfairly characterized the show, its producers and ourselves."

James Edwards, a Black actor who played a soldier in the critically acclaimed film *Home of the Brave*, said the stars of *The Amos 'n' Andy Show* were selfish. "For the sake of the 142 jobs which Negroes hold down with the 'Amos 'n' Andy' show, 15 million more Negroes are being pushed back 25 years by perpetuating this stereotype on television. The money involved (and there's a great deal) can't hope to undo the harm that the continuation of 'Amos 'n' Andy' will effect."

There was certainly a great deal of money involved; the actors were paid well. Nick Stewart used his salary to start the Ebony Showcase Theater in South Los Angeles. His theater was a training ground that provided work for Ossie Davis and Sidney Poitier before they were famous.

"In the daytime I played Lightnin', but at night I was presenting Blacks in the best of Broadway shows," he explained. "And [the producers of *The Amos 'n' Andy Show*] called me in the office and told me I was diverting my attention in too many directions. 'Either give [your energy] to the theater or the program.' I said, 'You keep your program.' They said, 'Well, we'll call you.' I said, 'Don't call me no more 'cause I won't come."

The Amos 'n' Andy Show lasted sixty-five episodes. The network, the sponsor, and the producers blamed NAACP pressure for its demise, but CBS was happy to be free of the controversy. Television executives were reluctant to admit it, but programming decisions were made with the Southern bigot in mind, not the concerns of African Americans.

"It's all part of the segregation issue and the resistance from the south," said *Variety*. Television affiliates in the South were "growing more and more fearful of boycott repercussions from potential white customers if Negroes are showcased. At one major agency the word has gone out: 'No Negro performers allowed.'"

The Amos 'n' Andy Show left the air and the all-Black cast struggled to find new jobs. "Gosden and Correll are millionaires," complained Nick Stewart. "But *us*? We have nothing to show for it."

★

The Amos 'n' Andy Show was canceled in 1954, the same year that the Supreme Court ruled for school desegregation in *Brown v. Board of Education*. Racists widely considered the ruling as the first step toward tyranny.

"In Virginia, outraged state officials responded with legislation to force the closure of any school that planned to comply," wrote political historian Nancy MacLean. "Some extremists called for ending public education entirely."

Phil L. Ryan, an obscure B-movie director, sought to cash in on the racist backlash. He announced his intention to remake *The Birth of a Nation*. There were immediate objections from civil rights groups, but Ryan rejected their concerns: "Until they know the subject material which will be presented, how can they question without knowing the grounds? Our production of *The Birth of a Nation* will be the greatest denunciation of totalitarianism ever to appear on the screen."

Thirty-three years after D.W. Griffith unveiled *The Birth of a Nation*, the veteran filmmaker was living alone at the Hollywood Knickerbocker Hotel, where he drank himself into a daily stupor. Freelance writer Ezra Goodman showed up at the Knickerbocker unannounced, hoping to interview the old man.

"Griffith had been holed up in his hotel room drinking for days and refusing to answer telephone calls," wrote Goodman. "His mailbox was crammed with three weeks' letters. Occasionally he would have food and liquor left at his door and, after making sure that there was no one around, would whisk it inside."

Goodman came with a fellow journalist and used a woman friend as a decoy. He slipped a note under Griffith's door saying he wanted to introduce him to a female fan.

"Griffith opened the door warily, saw the young lady and grabbed her by the arm, pulling her into the room and quickly trying to slam the door shut," said Goodman. "But we moved quickly, too, elbowing our way in after the girl. Griffith was tremendously displeased. He asked us to get the hell out. We stayed put. Griffith finally plunked himself down in the easy chair and continued drinking, from time to time lunging at the girl . . . Griffith started talking about the movies . . . It was partly incoherent, but partly it was eloquent, compounded of gin, wisdom, and long years."

"The best pictures I did were not popular," Griffith told him. "The lousy ones, like *The Birth of a Nation*, only a cheap melodrama, were popular." Recalling the protests Griffith said, "According to the Constitution, you are allowed to say anything you please, but you are responsible for your speech and conversation by law and may be so punished. No one is really allowed to say what he pleases."

★

A few months later, D.W. Griffith suffered a cerebral hemorrhage in the lobby. The old director passed away, but the controversies that surrounded his most famous film lived on. Throughout the 1950s, *Little Black Sambo* was pulled from library shelves. Tributes to the minstrel era were condemned. Songs containing the slur "darkie" were purged from the airwaves. When singer Kate Smith held up a blackface mammy doll on her television show in 1954, a viewer wrote, "We fail to see how such things can promote good relations among groups of people. The mammy days are gone forever."

The songs of Stephen Foster, classified as "Americana," were censored. Foster's slavery-era compositions were a source of Southern pride, but his songbooks were removed from schools and purged from radio and television.

"My Old Kentucky Home," "Swanee River," "Shortnin' Bread," and "Waiting for the Robert E. Lee" were rerecorded with slurs removed. The song "When It's Sleepytime Down South" was rewritten so the phrase "darkies" was replaced with "people" and the line "when old mammy falls upon her knees" changed to "sweet magnolias in the trees." Frank R. Crosswaith, the only Black member of New York's Housing Commission, demanded a social housing development called Stephen Foster House be renamed. Meanwhile, Southern politicians resisted the affront to their "heritage."

"There is a mounting resentment throughout America against the shocking censorship by the major networks of the songs of Stephen C. Foster," said Congressman William Jennings Bryan Dorn of South Carolina. "Our people will be further shocked and alarmed when they learn that many music books taught in the public schools have already been censored . . . When the news of this unwarranted action of publishing houses and broadcasters gets through to the American people in every one of our states, they will be resented."

Elizabeth Fossey, a voice teacher in Jackson, Tennessee, complained, "They have no more right to change Stephen Foster's lyrics than I have to enter a museum and paint a red necktie on Whistler's mother. It's stupid to stir up trouble over something that is part of our common heritage."

Congressman Frank Chelf of Kentucky concurred, "The American people as a whole agree with my theory that it is wrong whenever any group of people in this nation, or any other nation, for that matter, take it on themselves to set up rules and regulations by and through which they can arbitrarily control what songs shall or shall not be heard and get away with it—then they can censor speech, censor religion, censor or even control the press."

The Florida Association of Broadcasters refused to conform with the trend. Their president promised Floridians would "still hear 'Old Black Joe' the way Stephen Foster wrote it." Former president Harry Truman said he was firmly opposed to the "misguided people" who altered material "on the grounds of racial descriptions considered . . . offensive to Negroes."

Southern politicians wanted a new law to make suppression of racial stereotypes illegal. "Action is a direct result of the 'censorship' of several

Stephen Foster songs by the radio and tv networks," reported *Variety.* "A bill to prevent 'unwarranted' censorship of songs without permission of the author or of the FCC, has been introduced by several members of the House."

Some liberal politicians proposed exactly the opposite. New York State Assemblyman Felipe N. Torres introduced a "racial libel bill" that would outlaw "malicious publication which exposes any group of persons of a particular race, color, creed or national origin, to hatred or ridicule."

NBC executive Harry Ward supervised the deletion of "racial clichés in hundreds of old movies purchased for television broadcast" and "redacted dozens of comedies, cartoons, and silent films showing sycophantic black cooks, maids, and chauffeurs." It became official NBC policy in May 1956 that "best interests would be served if all minstrel or blackface presentations were deleted." "We deleted any material which we consider derogatory to any minority group—that's on a common sense and public relations basis," explained executive Bob Wood. "Our outlook on society is supposed to enlighten the rest of the world, and NBC wants to present that intelligently. We don't want to say slavery never existed, but we don't want to play it up."

The ongoing controversy led to a resurrection of Confederate symbols. The flying of Confederate flags from automobile antennas became a craze—and led to conflict when people drove beyond the South.

"A motorist was about to park in Capitol Plaza today when a Capitol policeman stepped up and asked him to take down the Confederate battle flag that flew from the radio antenna of his car," reported the *New York Times.* "The motorist, somewhat taken aback, grinned and then complied. This is a scene that has occurred many times in the past, and with the increasing vogue for display of the Confederate flag, it is likely to occur many times in the future . . . The current fad for the Confederate flag . . . has kept the Capitol police busy."

Comedians, authors, and newspapers obsessed over the changes. Columnist Erskine Johnson complained that there were too many "taboos under which all comedians now work . . . No dialect jokes, no working in blackface, no this and that."

"Slowly but surely the wellsprings of humor are drying up," wrote the *Saturday Evening Post*. "Personal caricature is libel, parody is illegal . . . The minstrel show is a thing of the past, and blackface comics like Al Jolson or Eddie Cantor would be barred from the stage."

"Americans are losing their sense of humor," said former burlesque comic Jack Albertson. "Minority groups carry chips on their shoulders . . . Blackface comedy, a traditional American form of humor, is unfashionable now."

Retired vaudeville performer Patrick H. Ginty defended the minstrel legacy: "As an old-time amateur player, I have played many minstrel shows in blackface, with never a thought in my mind but to entertain. Certainly great professional blackface performers like Eddie Cantor and Al Jolson never ridiculed the black man. In fact, they endeared him to all."

Paul Gallico, who later wrote the novel *The Poseidon Adventure*, longed for the days when comedy was "full of racial jokes with caricatures . . . blackface comedians, Irish comedians, Jewish comedians, and Italian comedians; the Germans, the French, the Dutch, the Mexicans [who] were merrily and mercilessly lampooned and nobody got into a sweat about it."

Black people should not be upset with stereotypes, went the argument, because Italians, Irish, and Jewish people never complained. But all of the aforementioned groups had indeed complained, picketed, and protested, sometimes violently, decades earlier.

In an article published in September 1958, the *Saturday Evening Post* concluded things had gone too far: "Dialect jokes are taboo, a political gag may brand you un-American, and racial jokes bring a deluge of enraged mail from sensitive 'minority groups!' In fact, most of the material that immortalized our old-school comics is strictly out of bounds today!"

"Now you can't kid anyone anymore," complained broadcaster Arthur Godfrey. "Negro and Italian jokes are out. It's sad."

"We're losing our sense of humor," warned author Corey Ford. "One by one we've herded all our sacred cows behind a high barbed-wire fence of patriotic or social or racial sensitivity. If a comedian trespasses inside, he is promptly punished. They're seeking to censor."

Popular comedian Danny Thomas said he was sick of "over-sensitive groups and individuals" who were "too thin-skinned" to appreciate comedy. "From now on I'm going to use as much dialect material as possible in my guest appearances," said Thomas. "I'll do Yiddish, Greek, Arabic, Negro, Italian and Irish vernaculars, and to heck with the squawks."

"The area of life in which ridicule is permissible is steadily shrinking," wrote Malcolm Muggeridge in the April 1958 issue of *Esquire*. "Never since American television began has the viewer's comedy ration been smaller than it is today . . . This decay of humor . . . haunts the lives of so many today."

Comedian George Gobel lamented that the comedians of the 1950s needed "a seismograph to know where the next rumble of public wrath is coming from."

"Is American Humor Dying?" asked an editorial in the *Lake Charles American Press*. "Taboos have killed off most sources of American humor. Only Jews can tell jokes about Jews. Only Catholics can tell jokes about Catholics. Only Negroes can tell jokes about Negroes . . . It is no wonder that comedians can no longer survive on television."

★

Racial stereotypes were censored by the television networks, but so was anti-racism. "I'd like to do a definitive study of segregation from the Negro's point of view," said *Twilight Zone* creator Rod Serling. But any such attempt was sure to be thwarted by corporate sponsors.

Serling wrote a thinly veiled teleplay about the murder of Emmett Till for the *US Steel Hour* in 1956. US Steel was threatened with a boycott by the White Citizens' Council.

The White Citizens' Councils were a collection of racist civic organizations formed shortly after *Brown v. Board of Education*. Commonly referred to as "the uptown Klan," the White Citizens' Council dressed in suits rather than robes and preferred professional organizing to cross burnings. "The Citizens' Council is the South's answer to the mongrelizers," explained one of their spokespeople. "We will not be integrated! We are proud of our white blood and our white heritage . . . If we are bigoted, prejudiced, un-American etc., so were George Washington, Thomas Jefferson, Abraham Lincoln, and other illustrious forebears, who believed in segregation."

The White Citizens' Councils applied pressure to US Steel. The *Alabama Tribune* reported, "The doctoring, trimming and emasculation [of Rod Serling's script] were done on orders of U.S. Steel upon the demands of the White Citizens Council elements of the South. U.S. Steel was hit by nearly 3,000 letters from pro-segregation elements in Mississippi, Alabama and several other Southern states. Serling's script was cut, revised and twisted because of U.S. Steel's fear of economic pressure. "

Rod Serling recalled, "Till was changed to suggest an unnamed foreigner. Then the locale was moved from the South to New England . . . It became a lukewarm, eviscerated, emasculated kind of show." The word "lynch" was deleted, and the character of a murdering racist changed to "a nice guy who committed the crime accidentally."

The White Citizens' Council coordinated a violent assault on Nat King Cole when the popular singer played a concert in Birmingham, Alabama. Cole was not political and kept his distance from the burgeoning Civil Rights Movement, but that didn't matter to racists. Prior to his concert, the White Citizens' Council circulated pamphlets titled *Cole and His White Women* and *Cole and Your Daughter*.

He was in the middle of a song when six bigots overpowered security guards, rushed the stage, and pulled Cole from the piano. Thrown to the ground, he was kicked repeatedly until his face and ribs were broken.

"I can't understand it," said Cole from a hospital bed. "I have not taken part in any protests. Nor have I joined an organization fighting segregation. Why should they attack me?" He placed blame not on his assailants, but on the political leaders who emboldened them with racist incitement. "It's not the people in the south who create racial problems," said Cole. "It's the people who are governing the people in the south."

Other major celebrities contended with similar situations. Racist terrorists detonated explosives "a couple of hundred yards away" from the stage in Knoxville, Tennessee, while Louis Armstrong & His All Stars were performing. The trumpet legend tried to calm the crowd. "That's all right, folks, it's just the phone," he joked.

Lena Horne was not so diplomatic. At the Luau in Beverly Hills, an intoxicated patron shouted the N-word in her direction. "I jumped up," recalled Horne. "I started throwing things. The lamp, glasses, an ashtray . . . and I hit the man with something. He got a cut over his eye and he was bleeding." The man, nursing a bloody forehead, demanded an apology. Horne told the press, "My anger is directed at something that was wrong, not at something I have to apologize for."

While not as well-remembered as Lena Horne, Louis Armstrong, or Nat King Cole, comedian Timmie Rogers was an important Black performer. He did stand-up comedy in a nicely tailored suit, using his own voice rather than dialect, and addressed white crowds directly. Until he came along, this was unheard of for a Black comedian. Rogers started out as a dancer working in several failed dance teams. When legendary comedian Tim Moore saw him perform, he suggested Rogers go solo.

"The Kingfish told me I ought to be a comedian because I had a funny looking face," recalled Rogers. "Besides, if I ever broke a leg I'd be out of the business."

It was understood that Black comedians were not to address white crowds directly. "He can't talk directly to that white audience like that," warned theatrical agent Nat Nazarro. "That's too aggressive. That's too impudent."

"See, the white boys like Bob Hope and Milton Berle, they were all using smart material and dressing very fine," said Rogers. "They had freedom of speech, could say whatever they wanted to say, and they could wear what they wanted to wear on the stage. I couldn't speak directly to the audience . . . They didn't allow that."

Booked at the Beverly Hills Country Club in Covington, Kentucky, a venue run by white mobsters, Rogers was lectured by the manager: "Boy, you trying to do a white man's act [with] that tuxedo on? You get back in your funny clothes like the rest of the colored comedians or else you're fired."

But the novelty of a Black comic being himself onstage would be the key to his success. "The sight of a Black man dressed in formal clothes was a sensation around New York," recalled Rogers. "The older colored comics were the most astounded. Most of them were doing Uncle Tom stuff and some of them were even blackening their faces."

Rogers played a triumphant week with Duke Ellington and Sarah Vaughan at the Paramount in New York in 1950. The Black press said the gig would "go down in theatrical history as the day Timmie Rogers arrived on the theatrical firmament as a full-fledged star, becoming one of the few comics to crash that cloistered circle heretofore reserved to the Milton Berles, Eddie Cantors, and Bob Hopes."

Among those in the audience was comedian Jackie Gleason, who hired him for *The Jackie Gleason Show*. He was a regular on the program for over a decade, and Rogers called Gleason the "first guy to give a Black comedian a chance."

Popular on television and beloved as a comic, Timmie Rogers was hired to do a two-month tour of US military bases in 1958. He arrived at the Officer's Club in Baumholder, Germany, shortly after midnight on a warm August evening. Strolling through the door fifteen minutes before showtime, he encountered a drunken sergeant shouting, "Where is that fucking emcee?"

Rogers turned to identify himself, but was interrupted by the screaming soldier, "You're late, you Black bastard! I'll teach you to be late!" Rogers was struck in the mouth and knocked to the ground. Rising to his feet, Rogers was punched again and then dragged to a foyer, where he was kicked repeatedly until his ribs were broken.

The *Pittsburgh Courier* reported that the "severe beating" left him "with three broken ribs, black eyes and several bruises." Rogers reeled from contusions and internal bleeding, but the sergeant denied any responsibility: "I'm in a blouse uniform and I'm going to beat up some [N-word] in the back yard? That would be ridiculous. I never laid a hand on him. I know better than that. I've been in the army sixteen years."

But the Officer's Club pianist positively identified the assailant. He was court marshalled for "inflicting grievous bodily harm, felonious assault, and conduct unbecoming an officer and a gentlemen." He faced five years in prison and a dishonorable discharge.

After much press coverage, speculation, and anticipation of a harsh sentence, the seven white army officers presiding over the case decided to acquit the soldier and reinstate his post. Meanwhile, Timmie Rogers was bedridden for months, unable to do stand-up—because he was unable to stand up.

"Man, the jury was Little Rock," said Rogers. "And the judge was Governor Faubus."

6

THE CIVIL RIGHTS MOVEMENT AND THE JOHN BIRCH SOCIETY

Governor Orval Faubus summoned the Arkansas National Guard to prevent Black students from entering Little Rock Central High School in 1958. Faubus was a hero to bigots, but a punchline to everyone else. On an episode of the *Tonight Show*, comedian Henny Youngman joked, "Alaska is coming into the Union as the forty-ninth state. You know, we could avoid changing the flag if we just get rid of Arkansas."

In the mid-twentieth century, mobilizations for Black equality were frequently characterized as a Communist plot. By the late 1950s, accusations of Commie conspiracy had touched nearly every facet of American life. Robert LeFevre, a mentor to economist Milton Friedman, accused the Girl Scouts of being a Communist front. Jack Benny was called un-American for cracking a joke about Joseph McCarthy. And the book *Robin Hood* was flagged by an Indiana school district as Communist propaganda. Support for the hysteria came from some of America's most powerful corporations. The president of Quaker Oats praised "the net overall job" of McCarthyism. The CEO of Sears complimented McCarthyism for pushing "traitors and spies out of our government." Campbell's Soup, Eversharp, Hewlett-Packard, Kraft, and Paper Mate invested millions of dollars in Red Scare campaigns. Richfield Oil and Sun Oil funded Fred C. Schwarz's Christian Anti-Communist Crusade, a lecture series of Red Scare prophecy. "At the present rate of progress, Communism will conquer the United States by 1973," said Schwarz. "People will be animals, to be disposed of . . . The hour of their final conquest draws near."

The extent of the Red Scare went beyond any concern for those living in a country that the Soviets invaded. Domestically, the anti-Communist movement attacked those who favored racial equality and labor unions seeking better working conditions. Characterizing someone as a "dirty commie" was the perfect way for a corporate boss to marginalize anyone who criticized their way of doing business.

The most powerful corporations gave birth to the "think tanks," sophisticated propaganda outfits that worked to further corporate interests through elaborate disinformation campaigns. Think tanks planted articles in magazines, editorials in newspapers, and placed their representatives on radio and television. Each spokesperson gave an illusion of scholarship—without disclosing the corporations that paid them. According to economic historian Kim Phillips-Fein, the think tanks used "nightmarish fears inspired by anti-communism and turned them against the entire liberal state, as though the minimum wage and labor unions were about to usher in a new era of political enslavement."

Think tanks were influenced by the methods of the advertising industry. Advertising agencies like Batten, Barton, Durstine & Osborn combed television scripts on their clients' behalf. BBD&O crossed out terms like "peace" and "brotherhood" to prevent television from presenting anything that might be "Communistic."

One sponsor ripped into NBC for presenting a dramatization of *A Christmas Carol*: "There is not one in a thousand employers who even faintly resembles Scrooge, any more than there is one Jew in a thousand who resembles Shylock . . . Nothing which can be said of continuing to play *A Christmas Carol* because of its classic nature that cannot also be said of *The Merchant of Venice*. Let us now ban the other because of the injustice it does the employer."

The American Gas Company deleted all references to Nazi gas chambers in Rod Serling's teleplay for *Judgement at Nuremberg*. "It mattered little to these guys that the gas involved in concentration camps was cyanide, which bore no resemblance physical or otherwise to the gas used in stoves," said Serling. "[It was] an example of sponsor interference which is so beyond logic and so beyond taste."

Corporate money sustained an organization called the John Birch Society. The John Birch Society focused on harassing people, censoring things, and spreading wild conspiracy theories, but their stated purpose was to "save our 'Christian-style' civilization from destruction." They attacked musicians, comedians, reporters, professors, and the Civil Rights Movement.

The head of the organization was Robert Welch, the confectioner responsible for Junior Mints. His parents had been slaveholders before the Civil War and his older brother was a North Carolina politician who pledged to eliminate African American voting rights in 1898. But for Welch, it was *The Decline of the West* by Oswald Spengler, an anti-immigrant book first published in 1918, that motivated him politically.

In the late 1940s, Welch was head of the National Association of Manufacturers. NAM's purpose was to diminish the influence of labor unions and combat government regulations. Welch claimed to be a foe of bureaucracy, but he wanted to expand military spending and establish new laws to restrict immigration, suppress civil rights, and increase censorship.

Welch founded the John Birch Society in 1958 with oil tycoon Fred Koch. The wealthiest man in Kansas and father of the infamous Koch brothers, Fred Koch said the Civil Rights Movement was "a massive Communist conspiracy that is seizing control of every phase of American life."

It was the John Birch Society's main talking point: the Civil Rights Movement was a Commie conspiracy that would lead to a tyrannical dictatorship. A John Birch Society pamphlet concluded, "Civil Rights is a perfect example of Communist strategy to fasten the tiny but almost infinite chains of a central Communist tyranny around their bodies and their lives."

Fred Koch published *A Business Man Looks at Communism* in 1961, in which he described socialism as a "disease of the mind." Ironically, he owed his initial fortune to the Soviet Union.

"In 1930, his company, then called Winkler-Koch Engineering, began training Russian engineers and helping Stalin's regime set up fifteen modern oil refineries," explained investigative journalist Jane Mayer. Koch's employee William Rhodes Davis secured a contract for Winkler-Koch to build "the third-largest refinery in the Third Reich" in 1935. Koch defended fascist countries in 1938: "I am of the opinion that the only sound countries in the world are Germany, Italy, and Japan, simply because they are all working and working hard."

Another founding member of the John Birch Society was a Holocaust denier named Revilo P. Oliver. He edited the John Birch Society newsletter *American Opinion* and gave lectures on the "conspiracy of the Jews," whom he referred to as "degenerates, scum, dregs, savages, debased squealing enemies, dear little cockroaches, howling mobs, parasites and lazy illegitimates." Oliver's anti-Semitism eventually became a liability, and he was removed from the *American Opinion* and replaced with a Libertarian economist named Ludwig von Mises.

The John Birch Society received support from corporations including DuPont, Schick, Campbell's Soup, and Paper Mate. Some of the largest donations came from Allen-Bradley, manufacturers of internal resistors for television sets. Allen-Bradley became a major company through military contracts, and they used those government handouts not only to fund existing organizations, but to establish the Bradley Foundation, an influential think tank that sought to abolish public services.

The John Birch Society began actively recruiting members, eventually nicknamed "Birchers." An early Bircher was the accomplished Hollywood screenwriter Morrie Ryskind. His credits included many great comedies of classic Hollywood: *My Man Godfrey, Stage Door, Penny Serenade,* and the Marx Brothers films *The Cocoanuts, Animal Crackers,* and *A Night at the Opera.* Ryskind grew disgusted with fellow screenwriters Dalton Trumbo and Ring Lardner Jr., whose affinity for the Communist Party moved him to the right. A member of the John Birch Society for two years, Ryskind resigned when Robert Welch accused President Eisenhower of being a Communist stooge.

The John Birch Society was mocked on radio by actors Rita Moreno and Robert Ryan. They performed a sarcastic reading of Robert Welch's most outlandish essays. Two weeks later, while Robert Ryan was filming a movie in France, his wife received a phone call telling her their "home would be bombed" if he didn't stop.

"We had round-the-clock police protection," recalled Robert Ryan's daughter, Lisa. "I was maybe nine years old, and I didn't quite understand what was going on, and they really didn't want to tell me what was going on."

Threats became increasingly common as the John Birch Society turned fanatical. The disarmament group Committee for a Sane Nuclear Policy (SANE) included Hollywood luminaries Steve Allen, Harry Belafonte, Ossie Davis, Henry Fonda, Marilyn Monroe, and Marlon Brando. Birchers accused it of being a Communist front and devoted ample space to it in the *American Opinion* newsletter. Soon a letter arrived at Marlon Brando's office:

"You . . . have a queasy smell of left-wingism and Communist treason and treachery . . . You think you're beguiling and deceiving with your phony, pseudo-tactics with S.A.N.E., as well as all of your other Communist activities, such as supporting [Adlai] Stevenson for President . . . Where do Communist bastards and pigs like you and Steve Allen get the sauciness and the effrontery to tell 180 million Americans that Russia should overthrow this nation?"

Steve Allen was one of SANE's most visible members, endorsing its work on his comedy-variety program *The Steve Allen Show*. After he was named in a John Birch Society newsletter, the popular comedian received death threats for the next year and a half. The first letter said:

"I have nothing to lose taking my revolver, going down to your home, or better yet, to your office in Sherman Oaks, and, on the whim, firing two or three bullets into the head of the biggest liar, cheat, humbug and communist in this country."

Initially the former *Tonight Show* host did not take it seriously. "I was not a Communist, rather I was quite an active anti-Communist," said Allen. "So, when I began to get mail, 'You dirty Communist bastard,' at first I laughed."

A second letter arrived a few days later:

"I'm not quite certain just who you actually feel you [are] tricking by your dirty Communist Front . . . You're the biggest and most rotten traitor to America . . . You hand out your anti-American views, committing a vicious and outright treason . . . You know darn well that you're a hypocritical, beguiling, treacherous Red liar . . . Here's hoping that you, a no good Communist traitor, are in the worst of health—Unsincerely (You Communist pig)."

Twenty-four hours later, another one: "You have committed treason against the United States and you belong behind bars on a ball and chain with the rest of the filthy Communist bastards."

Allen began to dread opening his Sherman Oaks mailbox. The next letter was dated October 1960 and said: "There could be only one ending for such pieces of communist shit like yourself—a horrible death, murder if possible."

The *Los Angeles Daily Mirror* received a hostile letter after running a profile of the television comedian:

"Dear Editor, I just got finished reading an article in your newspaper on the tv comic, Steve Allen, and I must say that I'm very disappointed that your writer went to such disgusting extremes to glamorize a man who is working viciously for the violent overthrow of this country . . . Steve Allen is a liar and a traitor . . . a vicious, evil, wicked, lying, sanctimonious bastard . . ."

The letters came frequently and grew more intense.

November 4, 1960: "Here's sincere[ly] hoping that you either die of a heart attack, or some fatal disease, or that you get killed in a car crash or meet with some tragedy."

November 14, 1960: "In the name of God, my dear STEVE, I'm going to do something to stop your filthy treason . . . I have a highly regarded gun collection . . . If you should die suddenly, it would be the biggest loss that the American commies have suffered . . . I am going to fight for my country. I am going to kill the biggest communist, the biggest fraud, liar, cheat, monger, hoax, and filth in this country . . ."

Soon the hostility greeted Allen in person. Booked for a lecture about nuclear disarmament at the Queens Arms Restaurant in Encino, California, in January 1961, he was confronted by twenty-four members of the John Birch Society in the parking lot. A woman holding a "Dead Before Red" sign told the press, "We just wanted to make sure he knows there are some who care about the United States." Other protesters held signs that said, "Steve Wants to Crawl on His Knees to the Kremlin" and "Is Steve Allen a Fascist Pig?"

As the hostility turned to death threats, Steve Allen contacted the FBI. Eighteen months after the first letter arrived in Sherman Oaks, the FBI interrogated a former playwright named Myron C. Fagan. Fagan had a grudge against show people ever since his Red Scare play *A Red Rainbow* was trashed by drama critics in 1950. Theater critic Brooks Atkinson wrote, "Mr. Fagan believes that he is helping to save America. That leaves us with an unworthy thought: Who is going to save America from Mr. Fagan?"

Fagan wrote Richard Nixon a series of fan letters in the early 1950s, praising his anti-Communist record, but in a private memo Nixon warned that Fagan was "a Fascist and will pop up again six years from now."

Fagan believed newsmen Edward R. Murrow and Chet Huntley were the "chief supporters of Communist propaganda in America" and that the purpose of the Civil Rights Movement was "martial law under control of the United Nations." He spent most of his time publishing pamphlets with titles like *How Hollywood Is Brainwashing the People*; *How Greatest White Nations Were Mongrelized, Then Negroized*; and *Civil Rights, Most Sinister Tool of the Great Conspiracy*. In his pamphlet *Red Stars Over Hollywood,* he accused Gregory Peck, Katharine Hepburn, Edward G. Robinson, Myrna Loy, and Eddie Cantor of taking orders from the Soviet Union.

The FBI was unable to find enough evidence to prosecute Fagan, but after his interrogation, Allen no longer received death threats.

The pamphlets of Myron C. Fagan were carried by John Birch Society bookstores, franchised under the name the American Opinion Library. Robert Welch supplied each American Opinion Library with newsletters, film strips, books, biographies, and 16mm propaganda films. The American Opinion Library in Wichita, Kansas, was run by the son of Fred Koch—and heir to his oil fortune—Charles Koch.

Koch opened the store in July 1965, during the height of the John Birch Society's anti–civil rights crusade. The pamphlets that surrounded him informed his political point of view and he operated the store for at least three years, until he inherited his father's wealth.

Among the available titles were *The Politician*, a book in which Robert Welch claimed President Eisenhower was a Communist; *Brainwashing in the High Schools*, which attacked the theory of evolution; and *The Invasion of Mississippi*, which wrote of Dr. Martin Luther King Jr., "Behind his façade of religiosity [he] is a trouble-maker who gambles the lives and fortunes of his fellow Negroes, for self-glorification and the fulfillment of what has the earmarks of a deep hatred for his white brethren."

Republican senator Thomas Kuchel criticized the John Birch Society for manipulating "thousands of Americans with hoaxes and lies." Kuchel was disturbed "to find many educated people falling hysterically and emotionally, without reservation, for the unaltered venom spewed by out and out crackpots for paranoia and profit . . . So many Americans have been so cruelly swindled, and have allowed themselves to be so cruelly duped."

Fred Hall, president of the California Republican Assembly, said that based on the "evidence of anti-Semitic and segregationist attitudes on the part of society members" the Birchers were the "closest thing to a totalitarian party in this country." He considered them a serious threat: "Their chief aim now is to get control of the Republican party and get into legislative processes. I believe this group is conspiring to capture control of the Republican party, and their philosophy is a totalitarian-type philosophy. I do not believe the Republican party can survive this kind of thing."

Robert Welch said it was not the John Birch Society that was a threat, but the Civil Rights Movement. Welch described civil rights marchers as "a horde of termites from all over the country, led by half-crazed ministers and professors . . . in [a] typical demonstration of Communist activism."

The John Birch Society purchased a full-page newspaper ad in Bedford, Indiana, and designed it to look like actual news. Arranged in a series of newspaper columns, the paid advertisement said, "The average American Negro is no more the blame for what is happening under the banner of 'civil rights,' than was the average Chinese peasant for Mao Tse-tung's agrarian reform . . . There is almost nothing being written, preached, or done under the 'civil rights' slogan today, which is not in accordance with the planning and instruction laid down [by the Communists] nearly forty years ago." Beneath a photo of Dr. King, the caption said, "Blood lust was in the air [with] the obvious fact that the whole racial agitation was designed and directed by the International Communist Conspiracy . . ."

George Carlin was a brand-new comedian when he appeared on a black-and-white episode of *The Merv Griffin Show* and mocked the John Birch Society. Carlin delivered his monologue in character:

"Thanks very much, the name is Lyle Higgly. I'm the head of the local chapter of the John Birch Society . . . That's the New York chapter that takes in New York, New Jersey—and parts of Idaho . . . At this time I was going to have a guest speaker for us tonight. I had invited the head of the Ku Klux Klan, the Grand Imperial, Almighty, Omnipotent, Invincible Stomper. However, his wife won't let him out of the house tonight. In his place we have the supply officer in charge of sheets and robes . . . He's just been acquitted of murder for the sixth time."

Carlin's performance went over well. He walked to the panel and Merv Griffin said, "Geez, George. You don't usually do little things with a *sting*." Carlin agreed, "No, usually it's nonsense stuff, but I just thought it was topical and . . . why not give it a little try?"

While many in the John Birch Society resented being compared to Klansmen and Nazis, the associations dogged the organization throughout its existence. George Lincoln Rockwell, the leader of the American Nazi Party, said of the John Birch Society, "At times our purposes bring us together. [They] would like to be Nazis but don't have the guts."

The father of the Nazi leader was an old vaudeville comedian with the stage name Doc Rockwell. "He was one of the funniest men in the world," according to showbiz columnist Jack O'Brien. "He used a banana stalk and on it hung coat hangers and he used that for a biology lesson . . . It was funny and rather naughty."

George Lincoln Rockwell dressed in a full Nazi uniform and toured the United States in a "hate bus." From the sides of the bus hung banners that said, "We Hate Jewish Communists" and "We Hate Race-Mixing." In 1961, Rockwell and his fellow Nazis protested screenings of Otto Preminger's *Exodus* and they blocked the doors of an NAACP office, shouting, "Racial strife is Communist inspired!"

A man named Speros Lagoulis operated the Joe McCarthy Book Store in Boston, where he positioned American Nazi Party pamphlets next to those of the John Birch Society. And he let Rockwell use his name to book hotels so that the hate bus wouldn't be turned away.

Rockwell was mentioned in Bob Dylan's latest composition, a satirical song called "Talkin' John Birch Paranoid Blues." Dylan was booked on *The Ed Sullivan Show*, but CBS got nervous when they learned he was going to perform the song. "Dylan went through it," recalls *The Ed Sullivan Show* director John Moffitt. "Ed said, 'That's fine by me.' And CBS said no. Usually they left Ed alone because he censored the show himself and was very strict. It was the only time they ever overruled him."

It became a showbiz trend to make fun of the John Birch Society. The Chad Mitchell Trio, a popular folk group which later featured John Denver, sang a song that called the Birchers "tools and cranks." During their gig in Camellia, Illinois, those lyrics placed them in peril.

"The hazards of doing political material in a time of heightened tensions caught up with the Chad Mitchell Trio during a performance of a song on the John Birch Society," reported *Variety*. "A fist fight ensued, and both parties filed assault charges at a nearby police station. According to one report the brawl occurred when a member of the trio picked up the pennies tossed at him by a heckler and brought them over to the customer's table and was slugged. Mitchell went out and called the cops, and when he returned the fight started over again."

The John Birch Society attacked comedians who parodied American history. Two of them, Bob Newhart and Stan Freberg, were bestsellers in the genre of vinyl comedy records.

"Those satires on American history Bob Newhart indulges in on his weekly NBC-TV series have drawn the ire and fire of letter-writers described by an NBC-TV source as 'extreme right-wingers,'" explained *Variety*. "The writers take issue with Newhart's irreverent fun in the satires and charge that he is 'un-American' and 'must be Communist-tinged,' the net executive said."

Stan Freberg was arguably the most censored comedian of his era. His comedy single "John and Marsha," a parody of insipid soap operas with a couple passionately repeating each other's names over and over, was deemed too lurid for radio. Freberg tried negotiating with the censors when he was booked on *The Ed Sullivan Show*, *The Dinah Shore Chevy Show*, and *The Dick Clark Show*—and lost each time. Hearing of Freberg's frustration, a Canadian television producer named Ross MacLean invited Freberg to perform all the censored material on CBC in Toronto.

"Freberg was given the freedom of the Canadian airwaves," reported *Variety.* "Freberg did 75% censored writings by the American networks, including his Southern States jibe which American TV networks had banned." The program featured sketches about Arkansas Governor Orval Faubus, the hydrogen bomb, and censorship itself.

The most controversial project of Stan Freberg's career was a comedy record satirizing the clichés of American history. *Stan Freberg Presents the United States of America* parodied Christopher Columbus, Abraham Lincoln, and the Boston Tea Party. It starred eleven reputable voice actors and a full studio orchestra. Freberg claimed it was the most expensive comedy record ever made, boasting, "I've become the Stanley Kubrick of the record world."

But thanks to the agitation of the John Birch Society, radio stations were "deluged with anti-Freberg phone calls and letters." *Stan Freberg Presents the United States of America* was banned in Dallas, Phoenix, Tucson, and San Diego. Most of the anger was directed at the album's showcase number: "Take an Indian to Lunch."

"Take an Indian to Lunch" featured white politicians determining that "for the first time that a minority group—Indians for example" can be utilized as a political pawn. The suggestion that historical figures were dishonest was seldom expressed in the mainstream and as a result, many people objected to the album.

"Take an Indian to Lunch" caused an uproar. NBC and CBS would not play it or accept advertising for it, claiming it was "not up to programming standards." Seven independent radio stations banned the album in New York. On the West Coast, two record stores refused to restock it despite customer demand, and Capitol Records scaled back their promotion. The Daughters of the American Revolution wanted a full-scale ban. One of its members phoned Capitol Records and told them she would fight Freberg's album "to the death."

"What they're trying to say," concluded Freberg, "is that we mustn't toy around with American history."

Booked on *The Tonight Show Starring Jack Paar*, Freberg was granted permission to sing "Take an Indian to Lunch," as long as it occurred after midnight. Freberg performed the song and then joined Jack Paar on the panel. The host asked him, "Are you a hypocrite? How often do you yourself take Indians to lunch?" Freberg replied, "All right, listen, I invite any American Indians within the sound of my voice to come to my hotel at noon tomorrow, and I'll take you to lunch." Twenty-eight Indigenous New Yorkers, including the Pima jazz trombonist Russell Moore, crammed the hotel lobby the following day. "Call all the papers," Freberg told his publicist. "Have them send a photographer over to the Algonquin immediately."

Despite attempts to suppress it, *Stan Freberg Presents the United States of America* became a bestseller. It received two Grammy nominations and the endorsement of the National Congress of American Indians. Helen Peterson, executive director of the NCAI, said, "We commend the use of political satire to help tell the Indian story and to promote respect and appreciation for all men's values and aspirations."

The intention of Freberg's album was not overtly political, but his detractors in the John Birch Society made it that way. It was not the first time, nor the last time, that instigators in the Culture War would pressure radio stations to pull a record from the air.

7

ROCK 'N' ROLL AND
JUVENILE DELINQUENCY

In the 1950s, radio was unable to compete with the popularity of television. Most scripted programming was canceled or transferred to TV. Radio censors stopped combing scripts for offensive jokes and instead focused on song lyrics.

Irving Berlin's "Love for Sale," Cole Porter's "Let's Do It," Nat King Cole's "Can I Come in for a Second," "The Persian Kitten" by Phil Harris, "An Occasional Man" by Jeri Southern, and "Drunk With Love" by Joyce Bryant were all considered too obscene for radio. Rosemary Clooney's "Come On-A My House" was censored for "suggestive implication," Leroy Van Dyke's "Walk on By" was banned for "plain vulgar suggestiveness," and the Kitty Wells song "It Wasn't God Who Made Honky Tonk Angels" was censored for fear it would offend Christian fundamentalists.

Corporate sponsors diverted their advertising dollars to television, and radio could no longer afford the big-name stars. Into the vacuum, for the very first time, came numerous Black personalities. African American deejays like Lavada Durst and Nat D. Williams entered radio and turned it into a medium for rock 'n' roll.

Young people loved it. Old racists did not. Early R&B stations like WSOK in Nashville, WDIA in Memphis, WERD in Atlanta, and WEDR and WENN in Birmingham were subjected to constant acts of violence from the Ku Klux Klan. Black disc jockey Daddy Sears was on WGST in Atlanta when the Klan burned a cross in front of the station. Radio deejay Peggy Mitchell, known for popularizing the music of B.B. King, had her home destroyed in a drive-by shooting. The radio station fired her to stop "any further trouble with the Klan."

The language once used to condemn jazz music was back. References to savagery and the jungle were recycled for rock 'n' roll.

Church leaders were especially upset about the new musical genre. A preacher named James DeForest Murch railed, "Through Dixieland jazz it has spiraled down through swing and bebop to the wild, sex-crazed, sometimes crime-instigating, voodooistic rock and roll. It has the same qualities which are resident in the music of all pagan religions . . . which causes youths to mutter dirges in low monotones, females to moan nasal notes interpreted with seductive gestures . . ."

A minister in Dayton, Ohio, asked, "Are we experiencing a satanic assault? Is the lawless one at work? There are certainly evil forces behind it . . . pandering to the lowest urges of a morally loose generation."

Letters to the editor were filled with rock music haters. "Rock 'n' roll music is the most barbaric form of nonsense ever heard by human ears," said a letter in the *New York Daily News*. "Its attraction stems from barbaric beats that would not even appeal to a smart caveman . . . The solution to this problem is to send these savage rock n' roll punks to Mau Mau country and everybody will be happy except the Mau Maus."

The so-called loose morals were a frequent complaint. "The rhythm in blues called rock and roll is really suggestive," said a letter to the editor published in 1955. "'I want to hug you' or 'I want to dance with you,' with the suggestive manner of saying 'hug' and 'dance,' is really offensive."

Representatives of 1940s pop music expressed their objections to the sounds of a new decade. "The people of this country do not have any conception of the evil being done by rock n' roll," said Meredith Willson, composer of *The Music Man*. "It is a plague as far-reaching as any plague we have ever had and now it [has] become international in scope."

"Rock n' roll is lewd," complained Frank Sinatra. "It fosters almost totally negative and destructive reactions in young people. It smells phony and false. It is sung, played and written for the most part by cretinous goons and by means of its almost imbecilic reiterations and sly, lewd—in plain fact dirty—lyrics, and as I said before, it manages to be the martial music of every sideburned delinquent on the face of the earth. This rancid smelling aphrodisiac I deplore."

Jerry Lee Lewis, the Everly Brothers, Bo Diddley, and Chuck Berry all received plenty of hatred, but nobody stirred more anger among the letters to the editor than a young singer from Tupelo, Mississippi.

"I find Elvis Presley appalling," a woman wrote to the *Cincinnati Enquirer* in June 1956. "That long, greasy hair, that surly expression, that stupid howl, that savage dance he does as he wails. Are we returning to the jungle?" "Elvis Presley's body contortions are obscene and I am no prudish old maid," wrote another hater. Even the mainstream press piled on. "Mr. Presley has no discernible singing ability," wrote the *New York Times* in 1956. "His specialty is rhythm songs which he renders in an undistinguished whine . . . For the ear he is an unutterable bore . . . Watching Mr. Presley it is wholly evident that his skill lies in another direction. He is a rock-and-roll variation on one of the most standard acts in show business: the virtuosos of the hootchy-kootchy."

A letter to the editor in the *Cincinnati Enquirer* from July 1957 warned of a hex placed on those who dared badmouth Elvis: "Creep!!! Goon!!! We have warned you before of the horrible, dire consequences if you kept talking against the great Elvis Presley. Now you have done it again, oh, foolish one! Beware, oh, stupidest of men! We hold the midnight teenagers black mass over everything you write against the great Elvis! Smeared with the famous Hound Dog Orange, it is consumed in sulphurous flame as the litany of destruction is chanted!"

Several radio stations rebelled against rock 'n' roll and tried to boost ratings with publicity stunts. Radio KWK in St. Louis staged Record Breaking Week. Disc jockeys played one last rock song before breaking it into pieces, live on the air, so listeners could hear the audible smash.

Acts of staged violence led to real-life aggression. A man poured gasoline on six hundred rock 'n' roll LPs on the steps of a Nashville courthouse and lit them on fire. At a March of Dimes fundraiser in Uvalde, Texas, in 1957, a collection of brand-new Elvis Presley records were auctioned off for charity. The winning bid went to an anti-rock music organization that threw the records "into a bonfire and howled with glee as the waxworks melted."

A rock-hating maniac attempted to murder a Tucson deejay in 1958. "A disc jockey was stabbed yesterday by a listener who screamed that he hated rock n' roll music," reported United Press International. "Deejay Ron Irvin was sent to the intensive care unit with the knife stuck in his back."

Teenage rock fans issued their own threats of violence. Wisconsin radio station WSPT banned Elvis as part of publicity stunt and received a threatening phone call, "You play Elvis Presley, or else." A week later someone threw a rock through the window with a note attached: "I am a teenager—you play Elvis Presley or else we tear up this town."

Dick Clark's *American Bandstand* was the most popular rock 'n' roll program on television. Any rhythm and blues it showcased was heavily sanitized, but it was still repugnant to the elders. A letter to the editor asked, "When are they going to stop all that suggestive Rock and Roll dancing on *American Bandstand*? I think today's teenagers are terrible young brats who haven't grown up yet." A letter to the editor in the *St. Louis Dispatch* said, "I don't think that the decadent gyrations of the young people participating in this program should be telecast, nor that the type of musical entertainment praised and recommended on this show should be encouraged or even allowed." A viewer from Minnesota sent his letter directly to Dick Clark: "You better get off television soon or else I will kill you. I have a rifle and I will use it."

When Dick Clark brought his rock music tour, Caravan of Stars, to Kansas City, Missouri, eight policemen were hospitalized after being pummeled by hostile teenagers. "Two weeks later, five teenage girls were hospitalized in another such show," reported *Variety*. "It was necessary to send five police squads . . . when a gang of youths amassed an attack on 12 off-duty policemen."

Rock music was labeled garbage, accused of encouraging violence, and banned around the world. Colombian dictator Gustavo Rojas Pinilla "banned all public exhibitions of rock n' roll dancing" in his country on the grounds it was "Communistic." Rock 'n' roll was against the law in

Indonesia because it was "crazy and immoral." The Batista regime in Cuba outlawed rock because it was "immoral and profane and offensive to public morals and good customs." Rock concerts were against the law in various American cities including Boston, Miami, New Haven, and Newark. The district attorney of Suffolk County, New York, warned, "The rock n' roll record hops only give young hoodlums an excuse to get together."

"Black Denim Trousers" and "Chicken," two songs written by Jerry Leiber and Mike Stoller for the Cheers, were accused of promoting juvenile delinquency and banned by radio stations throughout California. Bobby Darin's "Mack the Knife," hardly a rock song, was banned in New York because its lyrics were "too close to Gotham's juvenile delinquency problem. Mack and his blade might further inspire teen-age hoodlums in the big city."

A wave of juvenile violence—dramatized in popular movies like *The Wild One, Rebel Without a Cause*, and *Blackboard Jungle*—filled adults with fear. The movies themselves were banned for a variety reasons. Some feared they would trigger gang violence in movie theaters while others worried what the Russians would think.

Blackboard Jungle starred Glenn Ford as a schoolteacher grappling with hostile students. Its soundtrack featured Bill Haley & His Comets and popularized their hit song "Rock Around the Clock." Clare Boothe Luce, America's ambassador to Italy, used her political clout to remove the movie from the Venice Film Festival. "There is little doubt but that the picture would give foreigners a distorted picture of the United States and the Reds an added fillip to their propaganda," concluded one film critic. The American Legion labeled *Blackboard Jungle* the film "that hurt America the most in foreign countries in 1955."

A police chief in Santa Cruz, California, banned rock concerts claiming they triggered "juvenile delinquency and degeneracy." He canceled a scheduled Fats Domino appearance because the show might attract "a certain type of crowd that would not be compatible to this particular community." When kids of all races poured from the grandstand to dance together at a Fats Domino concert in Houston, police intervened and announced over the loudspeaker that only white kids were allowed to dance. Fats Domino said fuck that noise: "Man, I could not go for those happenings as my people *made* me—and to play for a jim-crow dance would hurt me all over the country."

At another Fats Domino concert in Newport, Rhode Island, fifteen sailors ended up in the hospital and another seven landed in jail. According to the Associated Press, "Beer bottles, beer cans and pitchers were hurled through the air and out the windows of the club as the battle reached its peak."

The Towne Casino in Cleveland, Ohio, was targeted by terrorists for presenting integrated rock shows. "Planted upstairs early morning when only a night watchman was on the scene, the three sticks of dynamite ripped a big hole in the club's ceiling," reported *Variety*. "It also tore up floors, walls and broke 200 windows in the neighborhood, which has been rocking with bitter controversies ever since the Towne Casino installed Harlem entertainment for a mixed clientele . . . Racial prejudice by unknown parties was blamed . . . All the bombings came at various times when the current management was bringing in new name colored bands."

Blame was deflected from racists and placed on the shoulders of youth and their favorite musical genre. "From puritanical Boston to julep-loving Georgia, the new revolt is being waged against a musical tyranny," reported the *New York Daily News*. "Its hazards, morally and musically, have been stressed by church groups, youth organizations and public officials."

When they arrived in Birmingham, Alabama, Bill Haley & His Comets were picketed by the White Citizens' Council. Racists marched through town holding signs that said, "Why Negro Music?," "Be-Bop Promotes Communism," and "Jungle Music Leads to Integration."

The protest was coordinated by Asa Carter, an aspiring writer who later wrote speeches for Alabama governor George Wallace—including the famous line, "Segregation today, segregation tomorrow, segregation forever." Carter said of rock 'n' roll, "The NAACP uses this type of music as a means of pulling the white man down to the level of the Negro."

The rock 'n' roll controversy evolved into a clampdown on dancing. "The Twist" by Hank Ballard & the Midnighters was released on Federal Records in early 1959. The song instructed listeners how to perform a brand-new dance. It seemed simple and innocuous, perhaps even dull. You merely planted one foot on the ground, rotated your midsection, and moved up and down. But in nearly every city in America—and nearly every country in the world—the twist was banned.

The City of Tampa outlawed the twist because it was "unwholesome for children and teenagers." The Texas Liquor Control Board banned it because it was "vulgar" and "lewd." A civic official in Huntington, West Virginia, said he forbade the twist because "the youngsters put a little *too much* twist into it." The manager of the Roseland Dance Hall in Times Square disallowed the twist because it was "lacking in true grace." He predicted the fad would quickly fade "because a girl likes to be held while dancing."

The twist was banned in Mexico, the Isle of Formosa (Taiwan), Egypt, and Iran. Syria outlawed it for being "sexually provocative," and riot squads arrested dozens of Lebanese twisters in downtown Beirut. The London Dance Institute forbade twist instructions. "The Twist is far too uninhibited, abandoned and frankly sexy to be performed in Britain," said one of the teachers. "It belongs to the African bush."

By now it was a hackneyed refrain. The jungle. The savage. The bush. It was a constant reminder that concern for children was but a cover for bigotry. A twist club in Madeira Beach, Florida, was stormed by eleven racists who attacked a bartender, the waitstaff, and the manager. Police said the chaos "stemmed from a desegregation policy."

Chubby Checker covered "The Twist" in 1960. It turned him into one of America's most popular stars. He was flown overseas to perform "The Twist" for US troops stationed in Yokohama in March 1963. The performance did not go as planned.

"Chubby Checker, given some not too subtle hints he was not being appreciated during a tour of Japan, abruptly ended the junket last week by storming off the stage during a performance at the Golden Dragon Yokohama Officers Club," reported music journalist Doug Hall. "The Negro twist originator reportedly was disturbed by ringside patrons in blackface, decorations of Confederate flags, and the prominent display in the club of [hecklers shouting] an unfavorable review."

Soldiers in the audience yelled the N-word, and a woman stormed the stage. "The straw that broke the twister's back," said Hall, "was when

Checker was upstaged by a blackfaced woman patron who joined him on the stage to do her own version of the twist."

One of the first big hits recorded by the Beatles was a cover of "Twist and Shout." It was the swan song of the twist craze. As the popularity of the dance bottomed out, the dance craze was supplanted by Beatlemania. And the hostility previously directed at rock music and the twist now focused on John, Paul, George, and Ringo.

Burt McMurtrie, a radio commentator, attended a Beatles concert in August 1964. He concluded, "It was not only trash, it was lewd, disgusting, revolting and an insult to the money charged . . . That entire evening seemed designed to arouse every animal and sex instinct in the audience up to [an] uncontrollable pitch . . . The sort of emotional lack of control, out-of-control, found in a savage jungle."

The Beatles were blamed for leading American youth down the road to "decadence" and they were condemned for their style. Schools around the country banned "Beatle haircuts." A high school in Kenosha, Wisconsin, suspended seventy-five students for "failure to trim their ugly long hair." A thirteen-year-old boy in Virginia shot himself "because his father forced him to have his Beatle-style hair trimmed."

But the hostility did nothing to stem the tremendous influence of Beatlemania. The majority of older people despised them, but a majority of young people helped make them the biggest rock band in the world.

The John Birch Society spread a rumor that the Beatles had been devised by the Soviets to destabilize America. Baptist preacher Billy James Hargis claimed, "Communist scientists have discovered that music with a broken meter in the treble, played over in an insistently regular beat which increases to the point of frenzy can produce hysterical effects to young people."

A Bircher wrote to the *Fort Myers News Press*, "These Beatle lovers should secure the facts and see how the Beatles have been pushed on America and the world. The groundwork was accomplished by three Communist Russian scientists, Ivan P. Pavlov, A.R. Luria and K.I. Platonov. These Beatles and their music records are a Communist plan through their scientists, educators and entertainers contrived by elaborate, calculating and scientific technique directed at rendering a generation of American youth useless through nerve jamming, mental deterioration and retardation."

The conspiracy theorists felt vindicated when John Lennon told a reporter, "Christianity will go. It will vanish and shrink." The statement triggered an anti-Beatles campaign. Their music was pulled from dozens of radio stations and detractors organized a nationwide boycott.

"I'm glad to see the boycott," said Robert Shelton, Imperial Wizard of the KKK. "We brought it out in the past about the atheistic views of a few of them."

The Beatles were banned in Israel, Indonesia, and South Africa. Four Pennsylvania senators introduced a law to ban them from every radio station, television channel, and jukebox in the state. The St. Catherine of Siena Church in Indianapolis organized a "Beatle bonfire" that spiraled out of control. Flames jumped from a pile of *Help!* soundtrack albums to neighboring homes. When the fire department arrived to extinguish the flames, churchgoers pelted them with rocks.

British television host David Frost was shocked by the reaction. "Should not on principle," asked Frost, "a civilized society be beyond the point where one paragraph by anyone about anything can produce this sort of hysteria?"

The John Birch Society sponsored a series of lectures by Reverend David A. Noebel. "The Beatles, judged by Christian culture, symbolize Western degeneracy," said Noebel. "They are . . . rude, profane, vulgar, irreverent, pornographic, uncouth, smutty, anti-Christ, anti-Christian . . . they are also immoral."

Noebel published *Communism, Hypnotism, and the Beatles*, a booklet distributed by John Birch Society bookstores.

"Teenage mental breakdown is at an all-time high and juvenile delinquency is nearly destroying our society," wrote Noebel. "Both are caused in part by emotional instability which in turn is caused in part by destructive music such as rock and roll and certain kinds of jazz. But no matter what one might think about the Beatles . . . the results are the same—a generation of young people with sick minds, loose morals, and little desire or ability to defend themselves from those who would bury them. In conclusion, it seems rather evident to this writer that Communists have a master music plan for all age brackets of American youth."

Noebel encouraged people to destroy their record collections. "Throw your Beatle and rock and roll records in the city dump," he pleaded. "We have been unashamed of being labeled a Christian nation; let's make sure four mop-headed anti-Christ beatniks don't destroy our children's emotional and mental stability and ultimately destroy our nation."

8

WE SHALL OVERCOME (BLACKFACE)

In 1963, the NAACP unveiled a plan to integrate television. They asked for greater African American representation onscreen and behind the scenes. They chose the family sitcom *Hazel* as their test case. Like most sitcoms of the era, *Hazel* had an all-white cast. It was something of an ironic target. The title character in *Hazel* was a maid.

The NAACP told the production company, Screen Gems, that if they did not start hiring African Americans onscreen and off, they would register an official complaint under California's Fair Employment Practices Act.

"Any other teleseries or features that go into production after the start of *Hazel* must also have integrated crews," reported *Variety*. "If integration is not effected by *Hazel*'s fall production start, the NAACP is prepared to hit Ford, who sponsors the program, with a nationwide consumers boycott."

Godfrey Cambridge, the popular Black comedian, suggested federal action. "Not only the FCC, but the Interstate Commerce Commission, should intervene," he said. "The government should enforce anti-discriminatory statutes in the Communication Act."

"The average Negro actor is starving to death," said veteran Black comedian Nick Stewart. "Dogs have shows! Monkeys have shows! *Lassie! Mister Ed!*"

Luther James, a Black production assistant on the NBC drama *Dr. Kildare*, said civil rights legislation was being "thwarted by the picture we have on TV, which is that of a segregated nation. When there are Southern stations that won't carry a show because Negroes are on it, or they involve racial issues, it is the function of the government to prevent segregation in programming . . . Their licenses should be revoked until they can show they serve the interests of the people."

Screen Gems hired several Black actors to play incidental parts and an African American assistant to work with *Hazel* producer James Fonda. Production companies in Hollywood seemed willing to proceed with affirmative action, but they were often stopped by advertisers.

The Farmer's Daughter, an ABC sitcom starring Swedish American actress Inger Stevens, was another Screen Gems presentation. It was threatened with cancelation when its sponsor, Phillip Morris, learned Stevens had a Black husband in real life. Gossip columnist Rona Barrett was ready to run a series of articles on the controversy when Screen Gems paid her to squash the story.

The costar of *Hogan's Heroes,* Werner Klemperer, was instructed not to embrace singer Leslie Uggams on a CBS variety program because she was Black. "I must reiterate what was related to me in our last pre-production meeting," Klemperer told *Variety.* "It was that one should avoid this situation because . . . the sponsor or somebody would be upset."

General Motors tried to kill an episode of the popular western *Bonanza* because it dealt with discrimination. The episode, titled "Enter Thomas Bowers," concerned a famous Black opera singer, played by William Marshall, falsely accused of being a fugitive slave. Denied accommodation at a local hotel, he's hosted by the one Black family in town. When the family is targeted by racist vigilantes, it's up to Hoss and the Cartwright family to fight back.

"General Motors last week was applying all the pressure it could muster in an attempt to force NBC-TV to shelve a 'Bonanza' episode," reported *Variety.* "General Motors raised its objections on the premise of not wanting to whip up national anxieties during the current integration crisis."

General Motors withdrew its advertising. Roy Wilkins of the NAACP scoffed, "This is no time for a major American corporation to line up in open support of exclusion based upon race. It is a time for men and corporations to take affirmative action in behalf of human rights for all." The episode aired without General Motors commercials—and without further incident. It went down as one of the best episodes in *Bonanza* history.

The stars of *Bonanza*—Dan Blocker, Lorne Greene, and Michael Landon—did regular publicity tours throughout the United States. When they were booked at the Mississippi Commerce and Industry Exposition in Jackson in January 1964, Landon announced they would only appear if the venue was desegregated. "If I get a guarantee with the proper language—not Mickey Mouse style—that there won't be segregation, we will appear," he said. "If they will put all seats on sale for anybody, we will keep our date."

The fair organizers complained that the *Bonanza* stars would be in violation of their contract if they refused to appear. Furthermore, they said that even if they wanted to integrate the audience, to do so would be against Mississippi law.

Dan Blocker, who played the character Hoss, responded with a telegram: "I have long since been in sympathy with the Negro struggle for total citizenship, therefore I would find an appearance of any sort before a segregated house completely incompatible with my moral concepts—indeed repugnant."

Jackson mayor Allen Thompson was livid. He called Blocker's telegram "the greatest insult to the intelligence and activities of the people of Jackson" and called on all Mississippians to "help destroy" *Bonanza.*

A letter in the Jackson's *Clarion-Ledger* accused the actors themselves of bigotry: "Since Dan Blocker, Lorne Greene, and Michael Landon refused to perform before a group holding views opposing theirs, I find it 'repugnant' to watch a performance by any one so extremely prejudiced."

It was a common argument. Anti-racists were the actual bigots because they were prejudiced against prejudice.

"We White Southerners are accused incessantly of using foul and unfair methods of intimidation against our Negro neighbors, while in fact it has been the club most frequently and effectively wielded by CORE, NAACP and other Negro pressure groups," said a letter to the editor published in the *Clarion-Ledger*. "I should like to see WLBT, which carries the program 'Bonanza,' replace it with one whose stars find our company and traditions less 'repugnant.'"

The organizers decided to violate the contract themselves and canceled the appearance. "Nobody would come to watch them after this," said one fair organizer. "There is no possibility of them drawing a crowd now." With the loss of Hoss, they booked Donna Douglas from *The Beverly Hillbillies* instead.

Pernell Roberts, another *Bonanza* cast member, joined a civil rights protest in Torrance, California. Sponsored by the Congress of Racial Equality (CORE), protestors objected to a discriminatory housing complex euphemistically advertised as a "selective community."

An image of Roberts holding a sign that said "Fair Housing For All" was published in *TV Guide*. The *Bonanza* star said it was time "to stop hating, start loving." Roberts was hounded by a counter protester with a sign that said, "Down with CORE." The letter *C* was shaped like a hammer and sickle.

Marlon Brando and Rita Moreno also participated. Moreno, best known for her starring role in *West Side Story*, explained her presence to the *Los Angeles Times*, "I think recent events have shown that demonstrations do work. Apparently they're the only way to make people realize the problem. I can't see how anyone with a conscience could possibly not want to contribute what he could to the cause for equal rights."

When they arrived in Torrance, the actors were confronted by a hostile mob. A man shouted at Brando, "Communist! Communist!" A small boy in a Klan outfit carried a sign that said, "Down with CORE." An adult Klansman held a sign that said, "Brando is a stooge for Communist race mixture!" And a maniac wearing a full Nazi uniform held a placard that said, "Marlon Brando is a [N-word]-Loving Creep."

Thirty members of the Torrance Police Department and seventy reserve officers were assigned to protect the housing complex. Twenty-four civil rights marchers were arrested and charged with trespassing. The City of Torrance filed an injunction against Roberts, Moreno, and Brando. LAPD chief William Parker insisted the civil rights demonstration had no support in the Black community.

★

"When God has drawn a line of distinction, we should not attempt to cross that line," said a young Baptist preacher named Jerry Falwell. "Integration would destroy the white race."

Twenty eight years old at the time, Jerry Falwell rejected the idea that Dr. Martin Luther King Jr. was following the teachings of Christ. "Jesus was not a pacifist," insisted Falwell. "He was not a sissy."

In the name of balanced reporting, anti-MLK viewpoints received mainstream coverage. The *Saturday Evening Post*, one of the most widely circulated magazines in America, ran an editorial in April 1965 by Baptist minister Clayton Sullivan in an attempt to present both sides of the civil rights issue:

"I wonder if it ever has dawned upon critics of the South that one of the reasons Southerners find the idea of integration so abhorrent is because of the rural Negro's physical uncleanliness . . . White Southerners do not relish the idea of instantaneous integration with people who live under such primitive conditions."

In reaction to the Civil Rights Movement, the defunct genre of black-face minstrelsy had a resurgence in the mid-1960s. In a run-down Atlanta strip club, a comedian named Cotton Watts applied burnt cork and sang minstrel songs. He used shocking blackface imagery in his advertisements, and he inserted Dr. King's name into old, racist street jokes.

A folk trio from South Carolina called the Mavericks toured the night-club circuit singing pro-segregation folk songs. Its members—Ronnie Gammon, Arnie Gammon, and Freda Burrell—delivered their repertoire in blackface.

Performing at the Top Hat Supper Club in Windsor, Ontario, in January 1965, the Mavericks told a local journalist "only Communists from up North" complained about their act and were "consistently pounding on the fact that Negroes were being made fun of by these jokes."

"The average Negro never took offense until he was told he should," said Arnie Gammon. They claimed their biggest fans were the Black janitors and dishwashers in the nightclubs where they appeared: "They love it."

Philadelphia's annual Mummers Parade featured blackface for a century, but conceding that times had changed, festival organizers announced a new no-blackface policy in 1964. A newspaper editorial in Salt Lake City said it was evidence that the Civil Rights Movement had gone too far:

"And what, we ask, does the presence of blackface clowns in a parade have to do with civil rights? It would be bad enough if CORE were merely thin-skinned . . . they cannot evade responsibility for building up a potential for riot. The episode will hang like an albatross around the neck of the civil rights movement."

As ratification of the Voting Rights Act of 1965 neared, a man in blackface stormed the US Capitol Building. UPI reported, "Clad in black from head to foot and wearing blackface minstrel makeup, he pranced and grimaced before the stunned House members, shouting, 'I'se de Mississippi delegation.' He waved a large, unlit cigar and wore a jaunty, slightly crushed top hat. A fur loincloth hung from his waist. Capitol policemen, caught unaware by the bizarre invasion, surged onto the floor . . . He later was charged with two counts of disorderly conduct and released after forfeiting a $20 bond . . . Chairman Emanuel Celler, D-N.Y., of the House Judiciary Committee said he was irked at the relative lightness of [the] fine. He said he would have 'thrown the book' at the intruder . . . It seemed incredible that a man so dressed could have obtained entrance into the Capitol at all."

The Lions Club in Camarillo, California, announced plans for a blackface show in April 1965. A debate over its merits played out in the letters to the editor section of the local paper. A reader from Ventura wrote, "The black-face minstrel show . . . was retired some time ago and why the shortsighted members of the Camarillo Lion's Club should choose to revive it at this sensitive time is beyond comprehension."

The Lions Club insisted there was "nothing derogatory to the Negro race in the use of blackface" and suggested those objecting to it should acquire a sense of humor. The NAACP called the Lions Club plan "a cruel and unjust hoax" and "an outright insult to all Negroes." The ACLU, usually quick to defend all forms of speech, turned down a request to defend the Lion's Club. An ACLU spokesperson explained, "It was felt that a form of comedy belittling to the Negro people should not be included in any entertainment."

Dr. Ted Greathouse of Oxnard, California, wrote, "At the risk of being branded 'racially prejudiced,' I would like to suggest that the [protesters are] being somewhat ridiculous and highly over-sensitive . . . If in the Negro's quest for dignity, equality and social maturity he loses his sense of humor or ability to laugh at himself, then his cause is a forlorn one . . . This attitude, presently popular among some Negroes, of 'either do as we say or we'll fix you' is the method used by Al Capone, the KKK, Hitler and the playground bully."

A reader from Ojai responded, "I would like to ask Dr. Greathouse whether he thinks I was over-sensitive when I objected to a so-called comedian, in a Ventura night club recently, who told anti-Semitic, anti-Mexican and anti-Negro jokes and ended with, 'I don't have anything against [N-word]s.' I wonder if I am over-sensitive because I say that the terrible things that have been done to human beings in the past is no excuse for these things being condoned in the year 1965."

★

"I don't have anything against [N-word]s, I'm just sick and tired of making excuses for being white." It was a line from the act of a famous stand-up comedian whose persona was that of a ne'er-do-well, straight-talking, chain-smoking preacher.

Brother Dave Gardner sold millions of comedy records in the early 1960s. After a successful appearance on *The Tonight Show Starring Jack Paar*, he was signed to RCA, released several comedy albums, and was placed under contract to NBC. For five years, 1958 through 1964, he was one of the top comedians in the country. But by the end of the decade, he had all but disappeared from the scene.

Fans wondered what became of the comic. Intent on solving the mystery, *Harper's* magazine commissioned journalist Larry L. King to write a piece titled "Whatever happened to Brother Dave?"

Gardner was initially a musician in the "dingy bottle clubs" of the "Bible and boll-weevil belt." He recorded a calypso number, "Fat Charlie," and was part of the house band on Wink Martindale's Nashville-based show.

Music gave way to stand-up. Gardner paid his comedy dues in rough roadhouses throughout the Deep South. With an affected preacher cadence and a cigarette between his fingers, he punctuated his routines with the phrase "belove-ed."

His first national television appearance was on *The Garry Moore Show*, the variety series that had made Carol Burnett famous. But it was his first time on Jack Paar's *Tonight Show* that led to the three-year contract and "sixty-odd appearances on the Paar show alone."

"Brother Dave rattled off a monologue presenting Brutus in the execution of Caesar," wrote King. "Paar received a thousand letters and telegrams begging more. He appeared in a Broadway play, banked up to thirty thousand dollars per week for campus one-nighters, and made connections with Las Vegas gambling emporiums."

With his new wealth, Gardner purchased a yacht, several Cadillacs, a thirty-two-room mansion in the Hollywood Hills, and a fancy new home in Biloxi. And he started hanging out with other wealthy Southerners, including the billionaire oil tycoon, and financier of the John Birch Society, H. L. Hunt.

"I got interested in Mr. Hunt's patriotic work about six years ago," said Gardner. "So I checked him out and he checked me out and we got our heads together. We've become real good friends."

Long before the emergence of the Koch brothers, H. L. Hunt used his tremendous oil wealth to manipulate American politics in his favor. He was the ultimate reactionary oilman, often ridiculed in the pages of *MAD* magazine. Hunt felt anyone who collected welfare should be denied the right to vote, and he called Dr. Martin Luther King Jr. a fraud. "I cannot detect that King has any regard for the truth, religion, sincerity, peace, morality," said Hunt. His former assistant recalled, "Mr. Hunt believed that Jews controlled Wall Street, banks, press, radio, and TV." And most famously, he ran a syndicated radio program called *Life Line*. On the morning of November 22, 1963, *Life Line* broadcasted "a dire warning" about President John F. Kennedy's "leftist plot . . . to deprive the people of their right to bear arms."

Larry L. King drove to the Pecan Grove Club in rural North Carolina to see Gardner perform. On his way to the gig, King passed a billboard that said, "Welcome to Klan Country." When he arrived, the comedian was missing and the manager was issuing refunds.

King phoned Gardner's house to find out what happened. His wife answered and said, "We were detained by some Indians. I've called in the FBI. I'm not sure I trust the telephone."

Brother Dave picked up the other receiver and shouted, "Aw, man, don't you know what's happening? Who attacked a meeting of the Klan here in North Carolina two or three years ago, when the Klan cats wasn't doing nothing but burning crosses and singing hymns?"

"The Cherokees?" asked King.

"Damn right," said Gardner. "They're part of this thing!"

Brother Dave Gardner showed up at the Pecan Grove Club the following night, but the crowd was sparse. Among the few attendees was an African American family. The manager walked over and told them, "I don't think this is your type of show."

Brother Dave took to the stage and opened, "James Baldwin is a low-life, bug-eyed, queer [N-word]." He gestured to one of the Black patrons and said, "Here's one of them bastards."

The heckling started immediately. Gardner powered through the jeers. "We gonna get our country back someday," he said. "I'd love to join a patriotic outfit like the Klan, only I ain't got enough morals." He went into a spiel about the Middle East that was full of racial slurs and then did the same with Vietnam: "I think we ought to go in there and blow them damn slopeheads off the damn map." He complained there were too many words you couldn't say anymore: "This here's a thought for you—cause this here's about this little boy and he's with his mammy. I don't know whether you can say 'mammy' anymore. I don't care. I tell ya, listen, I just go so far with them civil rights."

King saw a table of "good old boys" roaring with laughter, but most of the audience walked out. "Ask him to leave that offensive material out," a patron told the manager. "People want to hear the old routines that made him famous, not this crap."

"I'm losing my ass," the club owner confessed. "I'm paying this guy a thousand bucks a night. And look at the [empty] house . . . I had him here about three years ago and made good money. He was doing more straight comedy then—not so much of this political nonsense. A year later he was deeper into the political thing and I just broke even. This time he's knocking everything—religion, the colored, even the dead Kennedys. It's a disaster. People are calling up to complain."

Asked about his drastic shift in personality, Gardner said, "Well, everything grows and events change too. For ten years there I was paralleling the Civil Rights Movement. I'm a Southerner, so I'm not gonna change that accent to appease ignorance. You dig it? I never had a demonstration against me anywhere. We got off the colleges because we saw this thing building."

King joined Gardner at his home for a lengthy interview. As the tape recorder rolled, Brother Dave dismissed Bob Hope and John Wayne as too left-wing. He said he was grateful for the break provided by Garry Moore "even though he's a Jew." And he started quoting *The Protocols of the Elders of Zion* and speaking of a Jewish plot: "Hell, man, the Rothschilds put FDR in. The House of Morgan. And they started us toward one-world government. And now, belove-ed, we can't even control our kids. We can't even be white without having to make excuses for it, and I'm sick and tired of making excuses for being white."

Gardner's young son ran into the room and interrupted. "Dad, quick, J. Robert Jones is out here." J. Robert Jones was the grand dragon of North Carolina. He had released a vinyl record titled *Why the United Klan Burns the Rugged Cross*. Jones was there to personally thank Brother Dave for performing at his birthday party. Gardner excused himself and left his son alone in the room with King. Breaking the awkward silence, Gardner's son told the journalist, "The Klan watches over Dad everywhere he goes."

★

Dr. Martin Luther King Jr. was an inspiration to millions of Americans, but he was also relentlessly criticized, condemned, and defamed during his many campaigns. He was not revered in life as he would be in death.

On April 4, 1968, Dr. Martin Luther King Jr. was assassinated. Two months later, on June 6, 1968, presidential candidate Robert Kennedy died the same way. Conservatives blamed violent TV shows. Liberals blamed the National Rifle Association. Extremists blamed Dr. King.

Variety said post-assassination outrage "focused chiefly on two issues, violence in the popular arts . . . and the fact that America, with an estimated 100,000,000 firearms in private possession, has no Fed statutes on registration of guns nor curbs as to who may acquire same. As has often been remarked in recent days, the U.S. is the only civilized western nation without such controls. Efforts to legislate gun clubs have repeatedly been stymied by the tax-exempt National Rifle Assn."

The John Birch Society resisted gun control proposals. "The real purpose of such enforced registration would be to make ultimate seizure of such firearms by the government both easier and more complete," said Birch leader Robert Welch. "As the Communists get nearer to taking us over . . . the pressure for this firearm legislation grows stronger."

Showbiz was hypersensitive during the mourning period. The Academy Awards were delayed several days while violent clips from the Oscar-nominated *Bonnie and Clyde* were deleted. An episode of the sitcom *The Second Hundred Years* was shelved because it took place in a funeral parlor. The secret agent sitcom *Get Smart* was rewritten so that Don Adams and Barbara Feldon would no longer carry guns. ABC pulled an episode of *The Flying Nun* that featured a political assassination, and Ed Sullivan briefly removed all comedians and rock acts.

Newspapers paid tribute to Dr. Martin Luther King Jr., but letters to the editor were full of vitriol. "I come into contact with a lot of people every day of my life and I have yet to find one who is prostrate with grief over King's demise," said a letter published in the *Livingston County Daily Press.* "He preached nonviolence yet . . . violence followed him wherever he went . . . I fail to find any place for any great sorrow in my heart for his death."

Racist politicians had only negative eulogies to deliver. Republican senator Strom Thurmond said King only "pretended to be non-violent."

Democrat senator Robert Byrd said, "He usually spoke of non-violence [but] violence all too often attended his action." Georgia governor Lester Maddox said King "carried out the policies and programs of Communists in this country [which] led to the burning of Washington, Watts [riots] and murders during civil rights disturbances." Maddox called for a congressional investigation into public television station WETV for airing *A Tribute to Martin Luther King*. "We're just inquiring why it's being shown," he said.

Carol Burnett appeared on *The Merv Griffin Show* and made a plea for world peace in memory of Dr. King. Holding a wristband up for the camera, she explained, "These are the bands that we have been wearing in support of a non-party organization. In other words, if you are for peace—we all are—to kind of even show it—and say *yes* you are . . . in hopes that some good might come . . . It couldn't hurt!"

The audience applauded.

CBS cut it out.

"Griffin Show Edits Out Pleas for World Peace," said the AP headline. "Two appeals to send mail for world peace to Mrs. Martin Luther King Jr. were edited out of two Merv Griffin Shows in accordance with what the Columbia Broadcasting System said is its official policy."

Variety believed CBS was afraid of being punished after Vice President Spiro Agnew accused the media of bias: "Apparently hypersensitive to anything which might upset the White House, CBS-TV censors jump-cut text out of peace appeals made by Carol Burnett."

"I felt like an absolute jerk," said Burnett. "It made me look like I said something dirty, or off-color—or maybe un-American."

Vice President Spiro Agnew delivered a speech in Des Moines, Iowa, in November 1969, written by White House staffer Pat Buchanan. The speech characterized the news media as a collection of pompous snobs, "a small and unelected elite," who slanted news in favor of "violent protesters and demonstrators." Agnew accused the media of promoting "campus unrest, antiwar marches, lawlessness on picket lines, police brutality, and the apparent bankruptcy of the American system."

The speech was widely debated, praised, and condemned—and it became the defining moment of Agnew's political career. Bob Hope joked, "Spiro has a new show coming out—*Beat the Press*."

In the weeks that followed, large volumes of hate mail were addressed to journalists, newscasters, and reporters. *New York* magazine said Agnew's speech "elicited record numbers of letters with words like 'kike,' 'homo,' 'Jew bastard,' '[N-word] lover,' and 'Commie.'"

Merv Griffin said that after the Agnew speech, network pressure to balance opinions was intense and irrational. Griffin said CBS "used to keep track of the hawks and the doves and any references to the Vietnam War. By that time there was nothing but doves . . . Trying to even that up was impossible."

While many showbiz luminaries like Carol Burnett and Merv Griffin were concerned about the ramifications of political assassination, Oscar-winning actor Walter Brennan was "not sorry about it." Revered for his iconic performance in John Huston's *The Treasure of the Sierra Madre*, Brennan had great success starring in the long-running sitcom *The Real McCoys*. But offscreen he was a difficult man.

"He feels strongly that there is a plot," said a *TV Guide* profile, "not just a plan, but a *plot*—to take over the country. This operation is run by the Communists, of course."

Brennan was devastated when he found out that Kathleen Nolan and Richard Crenna, his costars on *The Real McCoys,* voted for John F. Kennedy. "How can I do this?" asked Brennan. "How can I work with these Commies?"

Brennan endorsed American Party candidate John G. Schmitz for president after concluding that Richard Nixon and George Wallace were too far to the left. Schmitz had been ejected from the John Birch Society for being too extreme. According to the American Party's platform, "women's liberation is an insidious socialistic plan to destroy the home, make women slaves of the government and their children wards of the state" and the United Nations was "an organization controlled by communists, run by communists and contrived by communists."

Irving Pincus, creator and executive producer of *The Real McCoys*, said Brennan was the "world's biggest anti-Semite [and] very verbal about his feelings."

"Walter showed me his bunker," said production assistant John G. Stephens. "He was positive the Russians were going to invade the United States. He had firearms and a two-year supply of food."

Brennan even recorded a spoken-word album on which he railed against the tyranny of "zip codes, area codes, and interstate highway signs." Reflecting on the Watts riots, he said, "They could have stopped that thing in Watts with a machine gun. I'd have *made* them observe the laws."

And while Brennan's viewpoint was extreme, it wasn't totally uncommon. A survey published in a Tampa newspaper in July 1968 asked television viewers whether they were "offended by jokes against church, government, charities etc." Of those polled, 53.9 percent replied that they were indeed offended by such humor, 74 percent of senior citizens were disgusted, 53 percent of middle-aged viewers were appalled, 35 percent of those under the age of twenty-five felt comedy had gone too far, and 44.9 percent of all those surveyed felt there were "too many Negroes on TV."

★

The Equal Employment Opportunity Commission conducted an investigation into the film and television industry in 1969. They wanted to determine if the studios were upholding their end of the Civil Rights Act or if they were engaged in a "practice of discrimination." Executives from Disney, Warner Bros., Universal, and 20th Century Fox were summoned for an all-day hearing. Network executive Perry Lafferty was asked if CBS had any Mexican American producers, technicians, or news reporters. Lafferty said no, but it would be unfair to characterize that as racist.

Latino actor Ray Martel came to the opposite conclusion during his testimony. Martel had appeared on *Mission: Impossible, I Spy,* and *The Girl from U.N.C.L.E.* He told the commission that "the entire industry" practiced "overt racism" and that the studios were run by "bigoted and racist dogs." Martel said he intended to destroy bias in the television industry "even if we have to tear these studios down."

Lack of diversity was seldom noted in the press, but frustration was evident. *The Dean Martin Show* featured a chorus of beautiful women each week and a letter published in *TV Guide* noted, "The bevy of girls surrounding Dean all conform to the white, Anglo-Saxon version of beauty. Not one is black, Oriental, or even Latin."

A number of programs were created to diversify the industry. The Writers Guild started its Open Door Workshop for aspiring Asian, Black, Latino, and Indigenous screenwriters in June 1969 and CBS promised to cover the cost.

Budd Schulberg, the screenwriter responsible for classic films like *On the Waterfront* and *A Face in the Crowd*, started a similar program. After the Watts riots, Schulberg wanted to use his position to help in some way. He met with Jack Valenti of the Motion Picture Association of America to discuss the "problem of whiteness."

"Lots and lots of buildings were in rubble," said Schulberg. "I saw this building called the Westminster Neighborhood Association. I parked, went in, and said, 'I'm only one person, but as a writer maybe I can start a writing class.' So I did. I simply put up a notice saying: Creative Writing Class—Every Wednesday—3 O'clock.' I came back a week later. People had written suggestions as to what I could do with my workshop and where I could put it."

Nineteen-year-old Charles Eric Johnson attended one of the first classes. "Nate Monaster and Stanley Shapiro were there," recalled Johnson. "They were the writing team that did all the Rock Hudson–Doris Day films like *Pillow Talk* and *That Touch of Mink*. We talked about film and they invited me out to Universal. They took me under their wing. I ended up following them around the lot, smoking their Garcia y Vega cigars, and I started wearing an ascot just like them. They taught me screenwriting. They had an office above a tailor shop on Santa Monica Boulevard. They gave me a key and said if I wanted to go in there and write, I could use it . . . They introduced me to Walter Newman, who won the Academy Award for writing *Cat Ballou*. Walter told me, 'You have to *feel* and *care*. It can't just be for the money. You have to have a vision and speak to something . . . and *never* dehumanize people.' With that, he gave me my foundation for writing." Johnson became the go-to screenwriter for Black action films in the early 1970s like *Hammer*, *That Man Bolt*, and *Slaughter's Big Rip-Off*.

Schulberg named his project the Watts Writers Workshop. "It was amazing," he said. "Just amazing. It was like all of Watts could write. An awful lot of people in Watts had a lot to say."

Harry Dolan graduated from the Watts Writers Workshop and sold a script to *The Partridge Family*. In his episode, the Partridge Family's multicolored bus breaks down in a Black neighborhood. They're confronted by an unwelcoming pair of Black Panthers, portrayed by Lou Gosset Jr. and Richard Pryor, but the family wins them over. By the end of the episode, a young Danny Bonaduce is gifted a black beret and made an honorary Panther.

The Watts Writers Workshop acquired a solid reputation and evolved into a full-fledged theater. Sammy Davis Jr. donated a piano, Quincy Jones taught music classes, and Sidney Poitier taught acting. But as a prominent new center for Black culture, the FBI considered it a threat.

The FBI assigned an informant, Darthard Perry, to infiltrate the workshop. He scored a job as an audio-visual assistant and used his position to wire the venue, just in time to spy on a speech by Black Panther leader Bobby Seale.

"First I planted two mics in the workshop office," recalled Perry, "slipped their wires up through the ceiling and down onto the stage where I hooked them into a big Ampex recorder. When Seale showed up I took him into the office and got him talking privately about all sorts of Panther activities. During his talk I photographed the entire audience with a wide-angle 35mm camera. And when he was finished I videotaped a nice long interview for the workshop. When I brought all this material back to FBI headquarters, my superiors were barely able to contain themselves."

The FBI's next step was to destroy the venue—literally. "The Bureau had it burnt down," confessed Perry. "I did the arson. At the time . . . it looked like there was a possibility of a grant [but] if there was no theater, there would be no grant. Two cans of kerosene, Purex bottle, gasoline, and a flare."

9

DIRTY MOVIES AND DRUG MUSIC

Perhaps the only thing the FBI despised more than Black Power was the growing antiwar movement. Influential opponents of the Vietnam War were widespread in the field of music.

"Eve of Destruction" was a hit song performed by Barry McGuire. Its lyrics intimated that war and racism were leading the United States to "the eve of destruction." Some considered it troublesome when it made it to number one on the charts. Los Angeles disc jockey Bob Eubanks asked, "How do you think the enemy will feel with a tune like that number one in America?"

David A. Noebel, author of *Communism, Hypnotism and the Beatles,* said the song was "obviously aimed at instilling fear in our teenagers as well as a sense of hopelessness . . . to induce the American public to surrender to atheistic international communism."

Radio tycoon Gordon McLendon blamed rock bands from England. He proposed an "updated version of the Boston Tea Party" to dump records by the Animals, the Dave Clark Five, and the Rolling Stones into the water. "I suppose we might call it the Wax Party, one in which we purge all the distasteful English records that deal with sex, sin, and drugs. At the same time, I think it is past the time that we made an attempt to stop whatever few irresponsible elements of the British music and record industry there are in existence from influencing our children with their double entendres and, in some instances, single entendres of unmistakable meaning."

Detroit preacher Jack Van Impe joined the campaign. "If you love Jesus Christ, go home and smash those crummy records," he sermonized. "Get rid of the Beatles and the Herman's Hermits and the rest of that crowd . . . the rottenest music that has ever come out of the pit of hell is rock n' roll."

McLendon Broadcasting operated powerful stations in Chicago, Dallas, Detroit, El Paso, Louisville, Oakland, San Antonio, and Shreveport. They announced their new policy in May 1967: "The McLendon radio stations will not air records that offend public morals, dignity or taste either innocently or intentionally. We've had all we can stand of the record industry's glorifying marijuana, LSD, and sexual activity." McLendon placed an open letter to the record industry in *Billboard* imploring producers to partner with them in enforcing the boundaries of "good taste." "Please, let's work together. Clean things up before some unnecessary regulatory action is taken or before the broadcasters' listening audience indignantly tunes out."

Among the rejected songs were "Let's Spend the Night Together" by the Rolling Stones, "Try It" by the Standells, "Sock It to Me, Baby" by Mitch Ryder and the Detroit Wheels, "Penny Lane" by the Beatles, and "I Think We're Alone Now" by Tommy James and the Shondells. McLendon said any radio station that played them was "as guilty as those who do the pushing of drugs."

Major hits like "Mellow Yellow" by Donovan, "Eight Miles High" by the Byrds, "Rainy Day Women #12 & 35" by Bob Dylan, and "Lucy in the Sky with Diamonds" by the Beatles were accused of having "a permissive attitude to drug taking." Radio KNEL in Brady, Texas, banned Aretha Franklin's "Respect" because the refrain "sock it to me, sock it to me, sock it to me" was supposedly a reference to sexual penetration.

McLendon stations demanded each record label provide lyric sheets in advance. "Record manufacturers," reported *Billboard*, "while acknowledging the right of McLendon to screen material which he airs on his own station, are, nevertheless, not about to bend over backwards to accommodate him." An executive with McClendon said, "The compliance has not been very good. We've only received three lyric sheets, but we're sticking to our demands."

★

The antiwar movement turned public opinion against the Vietnam War. Two pieces of popular culture tried to circumvent the trend: "The Ballad of the Green Berets," a hit song performed by Sgt. Barry Sadler in January 1966, and *The Green Berets*, a pro-war action movie starring John Wayne in June 1968.

The Green Berets was a formulaic war movie set in Vietnam. At its premiere in New York, it was picketed by Veterans Against the War in Vietnam and the GI paper the *Bond*. They carried signs that said, "Green Berets— Saga of Fascist Terror" and "Drop Acid, Not Bombs." The NYPD trailed thirteen of them back to the subway, where some were beaten until their legs were broken.

John Wayne wished violence upon the antiwar movement. "I think they oughta shoot 'em if they're carrying the Vietcong flag," he said. "A lot of our boys are getting shot lookin' at that flag. As far as I am concerned, it wouldn't bother me one bit to pull the trigger on one of them myself."

Violence followed screenings of *The Green Berets* in England, Italy, France, and Germany. The premiere in Frankfurt "was marred by eggs, tomatoes and rioters" and a screening in Copenhagen devolved "into rioting that police called the most violent ever to hit the Danish capital."

The film benefited from the popularity of Sgt. Barry Sadler's unlikely one-hit wonder, "The Ballad of the Green Berets." The square-jawed veteran with no previous music experience said his five-minute, undanceable pro-war record about "fearless men who jump and die" was "written in a whorehouse in Nuevo Laredo, Mexico, while I was on leave." It went to number one on the Billboard charts and made him a mascot for the pro-war movement.

Sadler enlisted at the behest of an army recruiter. "This guy came up to me in a f*ggoty-looking hat," recalled Sadler. "'You look like a big strong boy. Do you want to be in the Green Berets?'"

Sadler was praised as a true American. "Who knows, the words and the music may inspire some of the pickets and street demonstrators to put on a uniform and try to win the coveted green beret," wrote the *Sikeston Daily Standard*. "Now that the American people know what can be done with a good musical score and words that are not a jumble of chatter but make sense, they may be willing to forsake rock and roll for all time."

Sgt. Barry Sadler was hailed as a hero, but in the rush to find a noble advocate for the war, the press failed to look into his background.

"If you didn't know him, you would have gotten the impression that he was an extreme kind of Nazi and anti-Jew," said one of Sadler's friends. "He admired the German soldier mystique and Hitler's use of discipline." As sales of his hit single neared one million copies, Sadler spent his royalties on vintage Nazi memorabilia.

Hollywood cashed in on his popularity. He was cast in the B movie *Dayton's Devils*, a poor man's version of *The Dirty Dozen*. It made money, but Sadler wasn't interested in a film career. "I feel acting for me is pretty much washed up," he said. "Anyway, there's an element in Hollywood, a pinkie, f*ggie element, and I turn 'em off right from the beginning."

As antiwar sentiment grew, Sadler's fame came and went. In the early 1970s, he was performing his one-hit wonder at car dealerships, county fairs, and ribbon cuttings. He was depressed, drinking, and telling his friends, "I wish that I'd never, ever written that stupid song."

Years later his name resurfaced, but it wasn't even on the front page. "Police have charged Barry Sadler, known for his rendition of 'The Ballad of the Green Berets,' with the murder of a songwriter," reported the Associated Press in June 1979. "Sadler, 38, is charged with second degree murder in the Dec. 1 shooting death of songwriter Lee Emerson Bellamy." Eleven years after the murder charge, Sadler was sitting in the back of a taxi in Guatemala when an unknown assailant pressed a gun against his temple and shot him dead.

★

Richard Lester's *How I Won the War* was an antiwar picture starring John Lennon. At a screening in London, the film was interrupted by the League of Empire Loyalists and the British National Party. A man shouted through a megaphone, "We, the National Front, protest this anti-British rubbish!" He led fellow fascists in a chant of "Communist propaganda! Communist propaganda!"

"Stink bombs exploded and a fist fight broke out," reported the Associated Press. "About 20 policemen, warned that there might be trouble, rushed into the Pavilion Theater off Piccadilly Circus and separated several men scuffling and throwing punches."

England and the United States had shifted drastically in a very short amount of time, and some members of the older generation clung to the previous decade. A letter to the editor published in the *Paducah Sun* complained about the proliferation of counterculture guests featured on television: "Talk shows take the refuse of society—hippies, perverts, protesters—clothe them in respectability, and make celebrities out of them." A reader of the *Montgomery Advertiser* wrote, "As for the hippie-peaceniks, the best remedy I can think of is that any time they want to commit suicide I will be delighted to furnish the insect spray. On second thought, why wait until they want to?" A letter published in the *Dayton Daily News* said, "The more I observe the hippie scum, the criminal element, the relief parasites, the campus bums, the militants and the narcotic hopheads that plague our society today, the more I see a need for the extermination ovens of Adolf Hitler's era."

★

Attitudes about war, sex, and censorship had changed, and the influence of the Motion Picture Production Code faltered. Throughout the conservative 1950s and early 1960s, major filmmakers like Otto Preminger, Billy Wilder, and Stanley Kubrick withdrew their compliance and brazenly introduced themes of drug use, sexuality, and politics. Otto Preminger's *The Moon Is Blue* was rejected by the code in 1953 due to "its lecherous tone" and its inclusion of the words "pregnant" and "seduce." The studio, United Artists, ignored the code, released the film without approval from the Motion Picture Association of America, and discovered that nobody really cared. Their open defiance was the first step toward collapse of the code.

Before the code collapsed, however, studios and actors worked hard to get around it. A defining trademark of 1950s showbiz were blonde bomb-shells in bullet bras and tight pants. Marilyn Monroe, Jayne Mansfield, Mamie Van Doren, Diana Dors, Barbara Nichols, and Joi Lansing symbolized the peroxide fast lane. For young women, they provided exciting new fashions to emulate. For male perverts, they provided a release from Atomic Age anxiety. Skin, however, remained taboo.

"Two of the greatest horrors were shots of cleavage and belly buttons," recalled Mamie Van Doren. "Since the censors forbade exposing more than a few centimeters of cleavage, the studios, in their efforts to outdo each other, encouraged their glamour girls to use padded bras, and went for sheer size. Eventually, the padded bras built us out to such mammoth dimensions that we felt a little self-conscious. The bullet-shaped cones under our tight sweaters were just short of becoming hazards to navigation."

Male actors weren't exempt. Chest hair was considered obscene. Actor Jeff Chandler was forced to shave his chest for the swashbuckling movie *Yankee Buccaneer* in order to adhere to the code.

Reverence for Christianity was one of the code's strictest rules. Roberto Rossellini's *The Miracle* was a foreign import that challenged those restrictions. Part of the anthology film *L'Amore,* it told the story of a peasant woman impregnated by a bearded stranger. Holding her newborn, she is convinced it is the Christ child. A minor art film when it was released in 1947, it turned American censorship laws upside down when it played a New York art house in December 1950. Cardinal Francis Spellman, the Roman Catholic archbishop of New York, called it "a vicious insult to Italian womanhood" and a Communist plot to "divide and demoralize Americans."

One thousand members of the Catholic War Veterans marched in protest of *The Miracle* and the theater received so many bomb threats that the New York Board of Regents shut it down as a "menace to public health."

The distributor of *The Miracle* challenged the ban and the case went all the way to the Supreme Court. Judge Tom Clark ruled that motion pictures were a "significant medium for the communication of ideas." Therefore, they were "within the free speech and free press guarantees of the First and Fourteenth Amendments." Local governments could still impose censorship, but now they were more likely to be challenged in court—and lose.

Otto Preminger defied the code again with *The Man with the Golden Arm*, based on Nelson Algren's bleak novel about heroin addicts in Chicago. The movie contradicted the code's ban on drug use. It once again proved that the majority of filmgoers did not give a shit about film code restrictions. "Hollywood's Production Code may be losing a serious amount of its influence," reported *Variety* in December 1955. "Apparently there hasn't been an instance of reluctance among the nation's top circuits to play the film."

Some film censorship was imposed by racist politicians. Stanley Kramer's *The Defiant Ones*, a racial parable starring Tony Curtis and Sidney Poitier, was banned in parts of the South because it "would give moral support and financial gain to subversive propagandists." Darryl Zanuck's *Island in the Sun*, a 1957 film that featured a romance between Joan Fontaine and Harry Belafonte, was suppressed by Southern politicians who accused it of brainwashing the American public "into acceptance of race mongrelization."

Most of Hollywood was appalled by racist censorship, but there were notable exceptions. Charles Coburn was one of the most accomplished actors of classic Hollywood. He won Academy Awards for *The Devil and Miss Jones*, *The More the Merrier*, and *The Green Years*, respectively. But he was not pleased when his movies played desegregated theaters.

"Charles Coburn Joins Segregationist Group," announced the Associated Press in 1959. "Actor Charles Coburn has accepted honorary membership in a White Citizens Council." Coburn lunched with a delegation from the White Citizens' Council of Jackson, Mississippi. They explained their opposition to "race-mixing" and their plan to resist federally imposed integration. Coburn agreed to lend his name to their cause.

By 1964, most film fans embraced new freedoms. *Tom Jones*, a period comedy full of sex references, won four Academy Awards—including Best Picture.

"Although *Tom Jones* ruptured just about every second precept of the Code," recalled film censor Jack Vizzard, "it was clear from the whoops of joy with which it was received by audiences everywhere that the moldy old Code could be [obsolete and] that the American public did not give a damn."

Stanley Kubrick's Cold War satire *Dr. Strangelove or: How I Learned to Stop Worrying and Love the Bomb* made warfare look irrational. The *New York Times* film critic Bosley Crowther disapproved of Kubrick's "contempt for our whole defense establishment" and said "to make a terrible joke of this matter is not only defeatist and destructive to morale, it is to invite a kind of laughter that is only foolish and hysterical." Likewise, Ludwig von Mises, the economic advisor to the John Birch Society, criticized *Dr. Strangelove* for mocking the military rather than the welfare state.

That same year the seventy-year-old head of the Motion Picture Production Code, Geoffrey Shurlock, waged his final fight. He targeted Billy Wilder's *Kiss Me, Stupid*, which featured Dean Martin and Kim Novak in an extramarital affair. "The sanctity of the institution of marriage and the home shall be upheld," said Shurlock. "No film shall infer that casual or promiscuous sex relationships are the accepted or common thing."

The Catholic Legion of Decency was aghast that *Kiss Me, Stupid* was released during Christmastime, accusing Wilder of lacking "respect for the Judeo-Christian sensibilities of the majority of the American people."

Wilder was astounded, "They were just absolutely, totally outraged. I don't know, I never quite could understand what the scream was about."

Geoffrey Shurlock conceded that public opinion had outgrown the code. The month that he retired from the Motion Picture Code, the script for the James Bond film *Goldfinger* landed on his desk. He noticed that one of the characters was named Pussy Galore. "If dogs want to return to their vomit," said Shurlock, "I'm not going to try to stop them."

★

Despite the courts having ruled that motion pictures were a form of protected speech, police departments and their vice squads routinely raided movie theaters, confiscated film prints, and arrested theater employees.

A projectionist at a drive-in theater in Macon, Georgia, was taken away in handcuffs in 1969 during a screening of Russ Meyer's *Vixen!*. Similar arrests occurred around the country. "We should not be arrested in connection with the showing of an 'obscene' film," complained a projectionist facing jail time. "We have no control of what is projected."

A drive-in theater in Delaware was raided for showing a motion picture based on Allen Funt's popular television series *Candid Camera*. *What Do You Say to a Naked Lady?* featured the same type of pranks as the television program, but with the addition of naked women.

"The local sheriff went into the projection booth, watched the movie for about forty-five minutes, then stopped the film and arrested the theater owner," recalled Funt. "The print was seized, and the theater owner briefly jailed."

Between 1968 and 1972, several obscenity laws were ruled unconstitutional. The result was a proliferation of topless dance clubs and adult film theaters. Unwieldy pubes became a familiar sight on both the Broadway stage and the silver screen.

Senator John L. Harmer of California warned, "History attests that societies which tolerate widespread indulgence in deviant sexual practices suffer marked cultural and political decline." He proposed a new obscenity law to replace the old ones, which would "allow local communities to regulate the moral climate [and] allow law enforcement to stop dissemination of harmful matter before the damage is done."

Obscenity laws were overturned so rapidly that it shocked the icons of old Hollywood. Shirley Temple resigned from the board of the San Francisco Film Festival after the Swedish art film *Night Games* was selected. "I am fed up with those medicine-men of movies who pass off hardcore pornography for profit," said Temple. "It's a small band, but noisy and multiplying."

Columbia Pictures president Leo Jaffe promised, "As long as I am president of this company, I cannot have a film that says 'fuck' in it."

Someone asked director John Ford if he had seen the Oscar-winning *Midnight Cowboy*. "No!" shouted Ford. "Especially not that! I don't like porn."

"I don't like to see the Hollywood bloodstream polluted with perversion, and immoral and amoral nuances," said John Wayne. "Filthy minds, filthy words and filthy thoughts have no place in films."

For most of her career, Mae West had been the scourge of church groups, vice squads, and film censors, but she was appalled by the new cinematic freedom. "I guess I'm a bit straitlaced, but I think they go too far these days," she said. "I don't swear and I don't like to hear swearing. I don't tell dirty jokes and I don't like to hear them told in my presence."

Six years after *Kiss Me, Stupid* was condemned as dirty and immoral, Billy Wilder called the modern Hollywood a "whirlpool of filth and dirt."

"I'm totally rattled and, to tell you the truth, also disgusted," said Wilder. "There is a different set of values today. They think it's very romantic. I think it's a lot of shit."

10

WOMEN'S LIB AND GAY LIB
AND THE FRITO BANDITO

Taboos also shifted in terms of what was considered racist. Something not considered racist in the late 1930s could be considered blatantly racist in the late 1960s. There was usually resistance when something was deemed out of line. Older people in particular wondered if it wasn't a problem before, why is it a problem now?

"TV network programmers worry around the clock as they attempt to prune from top-rated laugh shows lines and 'business' that might be labelled offensive to a particular race, creed, color or group," reported the *Des Moines Register* in April 1969. "Material which now arouses stormy complaint would have been shrugged off only a short time back as innocent or harmless fun."

Even though *The Amos 'n' Andy Show* was canceled back in 1953, syndicated reruns aired in various television markets throughout the 1960s. In 1968, at the height of the Black Power movement, CBS Films withdrew the reruns and sent them to the vault. A racist letter to the editor published in the *Corpus Christi Caller-Times* said, "If Negro leaders have such a sensitive inferiority complex over their racial characteristics that such a show as *Amos 'n' Andy* disturbs them, perhaps there is a reason for this complex: inferiority."

As the decade turned, racial stereotypes were purged from established classics. Watermelon stereotypes and the phrase "pickaninny" were deleted from new editions of the book *Mary Poppins. The Travels of Babar*, a popular children's book featuring Babar the Elephant, removed "drawings of fat-lipped, bug-eyed cannibals." Friday night Tarzan movies were pulled from WFMY in Greensboro, North Carolina, because the Black characters were "filled with fear and superstition or [portrayed] as fierce, cruel, or stupid."

Mexican stereotypes were a common trope at the end of the 1960s. A controversial deodorant commercial showed an unwashed Mexican character while a narrator proclaimed, "If it works for him, it will work for anybody."

The Frito-Lay brand of corn chips used an animated mascot designed by Tex Avery and voiced by Mel Blanc. The corn-chip-thieving Frito Bandito wore a sombrero, bandoliers, a big bushy moustache, and had a voice like Speedy Gonzales. A report released by the US Civil Rights Commission called the Frito Bandito a "tool of racist elites."

A civil liberties organization in San Gabriel, California, told Frito-Lay, "We feel that your portrayal of Mexicans as lazy, stupid, and cunning is an insult to all persons, especially to those Mexicans now residing in the United States."

The vice president of Frito-Lay defended their mascot. He said the character had been "carefully focus-grouped among Mexican-Americans in Phoenix, Tucson, Fort Worth, and Waco" and wasn't considered racist. "If we really felt we were offending people of any race," he said, "we would withdraw the advertising."

Some local stations in the Bay Area dropped the ads. "Two of the major VHF stations here [in San Francisco] are dumping Frito Bandito . . . the controversial commercial," reported *Variety*. "In the wake of Mexican-American protests, KPIX-TV and KRON-TV will nevermore air the sight of the fat, mustachioed caricature who ran around extorting corn chips in a whining accent."

The *Washington Post* felt the character shouldn't have been created in the first place: "You just can't imagine a fried chicken restaurant chain trying to sell its product with advertisements featuring a drawling head-scratching Negro chicken thief. Americans are too enlightened to go for that sort of stereotype. Then how in Heaven's name does the Frito-Lay Corp keep getting away with its Frito Bandito ads?"

A letter to the editor published in the *San Antonio Express* said, "It must be painful to be so sensitive as to take offense at such lovable little characters. If these little characters . . . rob the Mexican-American of his dignity, maybe the Anglos should see what is happening to their dignity when Red Skelton appears as Freddie the Freeloader and Clem Kadiddlehopper. What about the re-runs of Laurel & Hardy and Abbott and Costello films—surely such idiocy hurts the Anglo image."

The *Montana Independent Record* wondered, "What's next? Will we be hearing protests from German-Americans, Irish-Americans, Jewish-Americans, Italian Americans . . . ?"

Variety critic Robert J. Landry reminded readers that those protests had already occurred. "German, Irish, Jewish, and Italian Americans protested stereotypes decades ago—and won the war," wrote Landry. "Resentment over the way white fiction and white shows pictured 'darkies' had little outlet for 75 years although at least two largescale protests were organized, first, circa 1915, against the film, 'The Birth Of a Nation' and then, around 1930, against . . . 'Amos n' Andy.' Extensive litigation troubled Griffith's admitted epic. City after city banned the film for fear of riots . . . Hitler finally got the point across that there is a link between racial hatred with extermination in mind and racial humor with protested innocence . . . Show business was rent asunder by quarrels over 'dialect' jokes and many an old-timer refused to concede that his favorite belly laughs were inherently vicious."

Protests occurred in front of Frito-Lay offices in Chicago, Dallas, and Los Angeles in April 1971. An activist named Carlos F. Vela addressed a crowd in front of Frito-Lay's Texas headquarters, "The Mexican-American community has expressed on numerous occasions that the Frito Bandito commercials are perverted, racist, bigoted, demeaning and stereotypic and insulting to the brown community and do irreparable damage to its members." Three weeks later Frito-Lay officially canceled the Frito Bandito.

The movement affected actors like Bernie Kopell, who played ethnic characters in dozens of sitcoms. "I started off in television doing a show called *The Brighter Day* in 1961," recalls Kopell. "I got to CBS Television City and the casting director said, 'Oh, I'm so sorry, Bernie, the part you're up for has already been cast! But since you're here, why don't you read for the part of Pablo?' I was furious. I was so upset about the whole thing that I decided that I'd read for 'Pablo' out of spite—just to waste their time. I read for Pablo without even knowing if I could do that kind of an accent. I didn't care. I was just annoyed. I went in, and I got the part. It changed my life for the next five years. I got cast on television frequently to play Latinos . . .

"Now, I must apologize to all my Latino and Latina friends because this is not the kind of role that should ever go to someone like me, but that's what they did back in the early 1960s. I defer to my Latino friends who, in the late '60s, took a very principled stand: 'Nobody plays Latinos but Latinos.' I agreed. I said, 'You got it.' And I stopped doing those roles."

Comedian Bill Dana created an impish character in the 1950s named Jose Jimenez. He was featured on *The Steve Allen Show* and on a series of bestselling comedy records. Prone to malapropisms, Jose Jimenez transposed the letter *H* with the letter *J*. The character would thumb through the "jello pages" trying to find an instructor of "huhitsu." During a holiday episode, Jose Jimenez came out as Santa Claus and proclaimed, "Jo! Jo! Jo!"

At the height of the Frito Bandito controversy, an activist indicated that Jose Jimenez was next. "We are going to continue the protest of this type and other types of distortions of Mexican-Americans," said the protester. "If nothing else, rip the 'Jello Pages' from the phone book and at an appropriate time we will burn them."

Bill Dana foresaw trouble. The character of Jose Jimenez had made him famous, but he decided to let it go. "The time of the Frito Bandito is out," Dana said in March 1970. "Though Jimenez is not a stereotype of the Latin, I'm trying to faze him out."

Dana's decision was reached after receiving uncomfortable compliments. Dana recalled, "People would come up to me and say, 'I love that dumb Mexican.' Well, I didn't do a dumb Mexican, but if people thought that was all that it was, it was necessary to retire him. A lot of people came to my defense and said what a terrible thing the Mexican-Americans did, but I had to explain it wasn't that way at all."

★

Of the many social movements that arose at the end of the 1960s, women's liberation was the most derided. Comedy referenced the ineptitude of "women drivers" on *The Red Skelton Hour*, *The Flintstones*, *The Jetsons*, and *Rowan & Martin's Laugh-In*. Bob Hope said on his October 1970 television special that the Indianapolis 500 was canceled because "thirty-nine women drivers crashed into the pace car." It was a genre of comedy that had been tolerated for years, but as the decade changed, so did public tastes. "I am not part of women's lib," wrote a viewer of the Hope special, "but I have never felt so insulted nor so infuriated."

Hope was at the Miss World beauty pageant in London in 1971 when he was shut down by an organized protest.

"Shortly after Hope took the stage at the Royal Albert Hall, he was interrupted by a handful of women's liberation activists, who set off noisemakers and smoke bombs, threw tomatoes across the auditorium, and unfurled signs attacking the beauty contest for 'selling women's bodies,'" explained Hope's biographer Richard Zoglin. "Hope, who had braved Vietcong rocket fire in Vietnam, was forced to flee the stage under the feminist barrage."

During a press conference after the event, Hope described it as "the worst theatrical experience of my life." He added, "You'll notice about the women in the liberation movements, none of them are pretty, because pretty women don't have those problems."

Mort Sahl was considered a progressive stand-up comedian in the 1950s, but by the early 1970s he was on a misogyny kick.

"Women lie," complained Sahl. "They say, 'Oh, I wanna do this, I wanna do that.' They don't wanna do that. They are female impersonators. You have to perform when you're a man and it is not in the nature of woman to perform."

Sahl said he received letters accusing him of sexism: "Chicks wrote in to tell me off. But get this—they did so in my terms—using the four syllable words, playing the intellectual. What can I say to them except,

'You've proved yourself as an intellectual—now how do you intend to prove yourself as a woman?"

A few months later he appeared on *The Dick Cavett Show* and went further. "That whole women's liberation thing is really incredible when they equate words like racism and sexism," he said. "I have never met a woman who was an intellectual." The studio audience jeered him.

Sahl had modernized stand-up comedy in the 1950s. His freeform approach broke from the established contrivances of Las Vegas dominant at the time. He influenced a whole new generation of comics, but by the end of the 1960s, they passed him in popularity. As his star power diminished, he turned hostile, storming out of interviews, and the industry abandoned him. Sahl was convinced that his career was faltering not because of erratic behavior, but due to conspiracy.

Sahl was booked at the Redd Foxx Club on La Cienega Boulevard in West Hollywood when nobody else would have him. He ran an ad in *Variety* to promote the engagement:

"An Open Letter to the Establishment. I accuse you of . . . engaging in the conspiracy to silence me by denying me employment in all media . . . for the capital crime of telling the truth. You haven't been successful—I'm back!"

A critic from the *Los Angeles Times* attended opening night:

"A capacity house was on hand to greet Mort Sahl with solid, sustained applause as he began his two-week stand Friday. Sixty-seven minutes later, the applause wasn't quite so enthusiastic . . . The most persistent sound was Sahl's voice, droning on interminable as he trudged back and forth between the comedian's and polemicist's platforms, being neither particularly funny at the former, nor particularly convincing at the latter." Sahl told the audience they "obviously weren't ready" for the truth and stormed off the stage.

★

The gay liberation movement was the next social protest movement, and it too bothered Mort Sahl. Sahl hosted a regional talk show on KCOP-TV in Los Angeles, and one episode featured game-show host Geoff Edwards and two members of the Gay Activists Alliance, Morris Knight and Sharon Cornelison. The episode devolved into a shouting match. GAA member Jinx Beers, who had been in the studio audience, claimed, "Mort Sahl did in fact call for the annihilation of all lesbians and gays . . . Sahl was now attempting to legitimize such action and spur on the perpetrators to lesbian/gay genocide." Unable to be heard over the shouts of the studio audience, Sahl walked off the show, leaving a highly uncomfortable Geoff Edwards to fend for himself.

Motion pictures featured gay subject matter for the first time and some critics were outraged. *Tampa Times* film critic Jeffrey C. Bruce was appalled by William Friedkin's film version of *The Boys in the Band*, a hit play with a homosexual theme.

"The best thing you can say about the 'Boys in the Band,'" wrote Bruce in May 1970, "is that if you're lucky, you might not throw up until after you get outside. How long you are able to tolerate this mess before escaping for some fresh air may well be a mark of your intestinal fortitude . . . It's true, the film is technically sound. The acting is without compare . . . unknown performers are top notch . . . That's the real key to our objection. It is so blatantly real it is disgusting . . . A group of queers barking and clowning around with one another, hugging and kissing and fighting and what not. It just makes you sick. Who in the world wants to see a bunch of queers clowning around with each other?"

Dr. David Reuben's *Everything You Always Wanted to Know About Sex* (*But Were Afraid to Ask)* was one of the bestselling books of the early 1970s. His chapter about "Male Homosexuality" featured a handful of assertions that infuriated the emerging gay liberation movement. Reuben wrote that homosexuals who felt they were born that way were tragic, and could be "cured" if they found a psychiatrist versed in conversion therapy.

The book had been through a remarkable twenty-eight printings by the time Dr. Reuben appeared on a Chicago-based talk show in January 1971. The *Chicago Tribune* reported that Reuben grew nervous during the question-and-answer session with the studio audience:

"The author's sudden reticence to speak on an aspect of his lucrative topic developed when members of a group called the Chicago Gay Alliance tried to take him to task for his treatment [of] homosexuality."

Dr. Reuben "refused to answer questions from homosexuals." Enraged, a member of the Gay Alliance rushed the set and began "shouting at and threatening" Reuben. As ushers tried to remove the man, several more people rushed the stage "and the whole shouting match began again."

The producer, Greg Hoblit, felt the chaos could have been averted if Dr. Reuben had answered the questions posed to him.

"Homosexuals from all over the country have been offended by his treatment of the subject, and I guess he just doesn't want to talk about it anymore," said Hoblit. When the show was over, Dr. Reuben demanded the tape be erased.

The Gay Activists Alliance wrote letters to *The Tonight Show Starring Johnny Carson*, objecting to what they called "bias and bigotry" and the program's "oppressive humor directed at homosexuals." Their tactics were too aggressive for some within the movement who feared the GAA would alienate nongays.

"We watch the activities of the most disruptive gay militants with fascination," wrote the *Advocate*. "We try in vain to detect some rationale in their tactics and philosophy . . . but it becomes more and more apparent that the so-called gay militants are not so much pro-gay as they are anti-establishment, anti-capitalist, anti-society. They lash out in all directions, destroying everything in sight—gay or straight."

Psychiatric meetings were routinely interrupted by gay activists who wanted homosexuality removed from its classification as a mental illness. An episode of the popular medical drama *Marcus Welby, M.D.* featured the lead character reiterating that it was a mental deficiency. The GAA distributed leaflets that said, "Marcus Welby is a quack and a bigot," and staged a sit-in protest at the ABC Television headquarters in New York.

A group called the National Gay Raiders stormed a live broadcast of the *Today* show. Frank Blair was in the middle of reading the news when he was interrupted by a man shouting, "Gay people are sick and tired of NBC's bigotry!" The broadcast went blank as security guards removed the man. After a two-minute lull, Barbara Walters appeared on camera to explain what happened. The National Gay Raiders were upset about an episode of *Sanford and Son* in which Redd Foxx mistakes his son for gay.

Police Woman starring Angie Dickinson was protested in 1974. "NBC
aired a segment of *Police Woman*, entitled 'Flowers of Evil'," explained columnist Frank Swertlow. "It depicted some lesbians as criminals. Following
the telecast, gay groups met with NBC officials to iron out the future of
homosexuality and lesbianism on the network. Ultimately, they want pro-
gay themes aired and offensive ones dropped. Thus, we have the problem
of pressure groups wanting to silence broadcasters."

Public opinion was always split on whether the suppression of bigotry
was good or bad. In theory it sounded reasonable, but it also contradicted
dogmatic interpretations of free speech. Gay activists wanted to suppress
homosexual depictions they considered bigoted or stereotypical. Their
detractors wanted to suppress homosexual depictions they considered
immoral or obscene. "Are we supposed to glorify what isn't the norm?"
asked *Dragnet* creator Jack Webb. "To me, censorship is nothing but instilling good taste in those who don't have it."

11

EXTREMISTS VERSUS COMEDY

Social mores changed rapidly, a fact that was especially evident in comedy. Old comedians condemned young comedians for their subject matter. Young comedians condemned old comedians for being out of touch.

The veteran comedian Red Skelton said, "I don't think comedians should use four-letter words and I don't think they should explain the functions of the body."

Harlan Ellison, a young television critic at the hippie-friendly *Los Angeles Free Press*, reviewed the new season of *The Red Skelton Hour*: "Old, old, incredibly old . . . A half hour appropriately introduced by Spiro [Agnew]—like Skelton, one of the great clowns of our time."

At the start of the 1970s, Red Skelton, Bob Hope, Milton Berle, Jack Benny, and Danny Thomas were among the most common comedians on TV—positions they had held for twenty years. Corporate America loved them because they were predictable company men, but young viewers pined for comedy that reflected the times.

"I am tired of the 'old pros' who should have disappeared a long time ago to make room for some new talent," said a letter published in the *St. Louis*

Post-Dispatch. "Ever since I was young it's been . . . Danny Thomas and a few others hogging the network."

Harlan Ellison trashed Danny Thomas in his review of the new sitcom *Make Room for Granddaddy*: "Mr. Thomas has not been watching the newspapers. He apparently thinks it's 1944."

TV Guide found a television special starring the "tired old timers" George Burns, Jack Benny, and George Jessel downright depressing: "It didn't look so good . . . a valiant try at turning back the clock, but their creaking limbs and croaking tenors were no match for the stubborn trickle of the sands of time."

Meanwhile, old comedians criticized the new comedians poised to replace them. "Most of those fellows just stand there and tell jokes," complained former vaudeville star Ed Wynn. "Simply causing laughter doesn't make anyone a comedian . . . They're not funny men . . . Today, many comedians just stand up and do a monologue."

"Most of the new crop of comedians can do only one thing: stand-up comedy," kvetched Groucho Marx. "All they can do is get up in front of an audience and tell jokes. It's a pity, because this leads to a deadly sameness in comedy style."

"Only Jack Benny and Bob Hope can still make me laugh," said retired radio comedian Bert Gordon. "Comedians today aren't creative . . . they just talk and talk and talk."

The most common complaint was that young comics were vulgar. The old guard was constantly putting new comedians down—and it had a bitter tone. "Many of the young kids today are taking the easy way out," said Danny Thomas. "With filth!"

"I think most modern humor is too dirty," said Steve Allen. "There's far too much what I call 'toilet paper humor,' revolving around sex or drugs, designed to get that kind of silly, high school giggling out of an audience."

"So help me God," said the elderly Jimmy Durante, "I've never seen a comedian be a big success with off-color jokes. I never knew an entertainer or a comedian who ever got anywhere using off-color material."

"I think it's instead of talent," said Mort Sahl. "Cursing instead of humor!"

Some comedians felt certain subjects should be exempt. "I don't believe in comedians making jokes about either their country or the Scriptures," said Red Skelton.

Ridiculing the police was something many law-and-order types frowned upon. The Keystone Cops, revered for their outrageous silent comedy antics in the 1910s, were objected to by law enforcement. Produced by Mack Sennett at the Keystone Studio, the Keystone Cops were an iconic part of the comedy lexicon. "They would probably be going yet," reflected slapstick comedian Edgar Kennedy, "if police departments here and there hadn't been so sensitive."

The Keystone Cops were popular wherever the labor movement was strong. "In their communities the cop on the beat was the flesh-and-blood representative of this higher authority," explains Sennett historian Brent Walker, "and to take him down a peg was a sure laughter tonic for the working class."

August Vollmer, the police chief in Berkeley, California, said the Keystone Cops had damaged the reputation of law enforcement.

"In digging at the roots of crime, modern criminologists find disrespect for the law engendered in the minds of children and adolescents by the comedy motion pictures in which policemen are caricatured," said Vollmer in 1923. "The Keystone Cops, for instance, with their ridiculous antics, and their utter failure to cope with comic screen malefactors, were a nationwide force towards making all guardians of law and order seem absurd and incompetent. When one realizes that over ten million people a day attend movie shows, and in practically any slapstick comedy where policemen figure they are placed in an undignified light, the end result is obvious. Practically all children and many trivial minded adults beget a humorous contempt for the policeman who symbolizes the law . . . Movie comedy producers who make game of the police are . . . enemies of organized society."

In the early 1960s, Fred Gwynne and Joe E. Ross played a pair of dysfunctional police officers in the sitcom *Car 54, Where Are You?* A San Antonio police association said the series made them "look very stupid" and asked NBC to discontinue it. "Being a policeman is a grim and humorless business," they said. "Not at all funny."

TV Guide reported, "A high-ranking New York police official, insisting that he not be identified, said he would like to see *Car 54* cancelled because it makes all policemen appear to be morons."

Footage of real-life policing made them look worse. *Law and Order*, a cinema verité documentary that shadowed police in Kansas City, Missouri, aired on public television in March 1969. A black-and-white precursor to the long-running Fox series *Cops*, its realism was shocking to viewers.

Variety wrote, "Episodic, and abounding in human interest, drama, comedy, and tragedy with everything from the cliché of candy for the lost child to the brutality of a fat vice squad plainclothesman choking a Negro prostitute nearly senseless, the film's overall surface effect was to evoke empathy for the men doing tireless, dirty and dangerous duty among the debris of humanity [but one] could find plenty to criticize in the police attitudes and handling of certain situations . . . A sequence showing the particularly rough arrest of a Negro teenager . . . had nuances of police arrogance, ignorance and prejudice."

In Los Angeles, the LAPD was notorious for corruption. The comedy team of Steve Rossi and Slappy White bantered about their reputation in 1969:

Slappy White: The police out here is as honest as the day is long.
Steve Rossi: Oh, really?
Slappy White: But when it gets dark—watch out!
Steve Rossi: Well, I understand that Los Angeles has a number of honest policemen.
Slappy White: Yes. That number is six.

LAPD police chief Ed Davis was livid that the Smothers Brothers used a policeman for the sake of comedy on their program, writing:

"With the extremely difficult battle the police are fighting to enforce the dope laws, I think it is entirely reprehensible, irresponsible, inconceivable and totally malicious for your network to carry this pro-dope, anti-police theme into the homes of millions of Americans . . . I arrived home early last evening and was shocked to see a representation of policemen on the Smothers Brothers Show which depicted them as a choir . . . It was a very realistic costuming effect; members of my family believed them to be policemen. Part of the dialogue had the leader of the choir stating he had attended the Woodstock Festival and that he smelled something wonderful in the air, and that he hoped whatever it was it would continue to keep growing. He was obviously talking about the growing and the use of marijuana . . . Obviously your network is in sympathy with the American Civil Liberties Union to allow this type of putrid entertainment . . . At a time when the understaffed police forces of American need public cooperation . . . it would appear that you would give greater care in allowing anti-police themes on your network."

Tommy Smothers held a press conference to respond. "I want to tell Chief Davis that Officer Judy was not a real police man and that the officers' choir was not a real police choir," he said. "I also want to tell Chief Davis that the Beverly Hillbillies do not live in Beverly Hills, the Flying Nun does not really fly, and the bear on the Andy Williams Show is not a real bear."

Chief Davis was aggravated. "I think piping dope into the living room and bedroom of American children via television is a pretty serious matter," he told the *Los Angeles Evening News*. "Then when they responded with the 'bear really isn't a bear' routine, I thought that was pretty sick."

★

The boundaries of what network television would and would not allow was tested by Norman Lear. A former writer for Dean Martin and Jerry Lewis, he conceived a sitcom about a bigot named Archie Bunker, who uttered ethnic slurs and sparred with his hippie son-in-law. Lear based his idea on the British sitcom *Till Death Do Us Part*. ABC commissioned a pilot, turned wary, asked for adjustments, and commissioned a second version.

"Both pilots tested poorly and ABC dropped the whole idea," explained TV executive Robert Metz. "Lear and his agent then took the idea to [CBS executive] Robert Wood . . . CBS's censor was horrified; for one thing, 'goddamn' was used several times in the pilot."

"I felt we had to get the network wet completely," said Lear. "Once you're completely wet, you can't get wetter. I wanted the audience to hear all of Archie's epithets, to see his sexual hang-ups, to meet the whole family."

The racist old man was the butt of the joke, but Bunker's language was jarring to those who didn't get it—or didn't want to.

"It had a laugh track," wrote Cynthia Lowry of the Associated Press, "but instead of being funny, it was a half-hour of vulgarity and offensive dialogue."

A letter to the editor published in the *St. Louis Post-Dispatch* in 1971 called *All in the Family* "nothing short of a communist conspiracy to destroy what moral fiber we have left in our nation."

L. Brent Bozell Jr., a former speech writer for Joseph McCarthy, awarded Norman Lear his so-called Shield of Shame for his "tasteless intrusion into American homes . . . whereby he assaults the family's basic sense of decency by advancing coarseness, crudity and a system of moral values which debase the religious principles of millions."

Criticism came from the left as well. The official newspaper of the Teamsters Union called Archie Bunker an insult to blue-collar workers: "For some reason the writers of those shows decided the average worker is a ding-bat, fat, more than a little dumb, a committed racist and most of all, very comical."

Carroll O'Connor's performance was so strong that many people believed that he and Bunker were one and the same. His mother complained, "Everywhere I go, people point me out as Archie Bunker's mother. I hate it. I never raised Carroll to be a bigot and, of course, he isn't in real life. But people now associate him with bigotry."

O'Connor was surprised that *All in the Family* succeeded. "I didn't think we'd get away with it," he said. "I thought that such a storm of protest would go up that we'd be off the air in a couple of weeks."

Red Skelton gave up on watching *All in the Family* after two episodes. "I've seen Archie Bunker's program twice," he said. "I don't look at it because I don't like it . . . I think it's the worst type of program that's ever been on the air. It's out and out Communism from start to finish."

Carl Reiner and Dick Van Dyke were scheduled to follow *All in the Family* in 1971 with *The New Dick Van Dyke Show*. It was an attempt to rekindle the success they enjoyed in the 1960s, but instead of black-and-white New Rochelle, the program took place in sun-blanched Phoenix. Instead of Mary Tyler Moore, there was Hope Lange. Instead of Morey Amsterdam, it was Marty Brill. Instead of being hailed as family-friendly, it was trashed as disgusting and immoral.

"The New Dick Van Dyke show is disgraceful," said a letter to the editor. "I will not allow my children to see it. It is a vulgar show with too many things pertaining to sex. Is there any chance of it being taken off the air?"

Indeed it was pulled off the air—by Carl Reiner himself.

"Curiously, it was sex that contributed to the end of *The New Dick Van Dyke Show*," wrote showbiz columnist Bob Thomas. "CBS refused to carry a show that concerned Van Dyke and his TV wife, Hope Lange, making love in the bedroom when their daughter entered. The show's creator, Carl Reiner, quit in protest over the network censorship."

The New Dick Van Dyke Show was bounced from its post–*All in the Family* timeslot and replaced with a new sitcom called *Bridget Loves Bernie*. Created by the same people as *The Flying Nun* and *The Partridge Family*, it was the quaint story of a Catholic woman, played by Meredith Baxter, falling in love with a Jewish man, played by David Birney. On the surface it seemed innocuous, especially compared to *All in the Family*. Certainly no one anticipated that it would be targeted by extremists and subjected to terrorist threats.

Rabbi Irving Lehrman of Miami Beach's synagogue council wrote to the sponsor, Procter & Gamble, to complain about *Bridget Loves Bernie*: "The program deeply offends the sensibilities of American Jews," he said. "We believe that it is an example of tasteless programming which contributes nothing but mischief and misunderstanding to any consideration of the complex problem of intermarriage." Rabbi Wolfe Kelman of the Rabbinical Assembly of America called *Bridget Loves Bernie* "an insult to some of the most sacred values of both the Jewish and Catholic religions."

In the face of the initial criticism, Rabbi Allen Secher was hired as a program consultant. Secher said he personally considered interfaith marriage "repugnant" but felt it was better to address it than ignore it: "It's better that it doesn't happen, but you can't shove your head in the sand and say it doesn't happen. Anyway, I don't see thousands of Jewish boys running out to chase Catholic girls just because of this show."

CBS held meetings with Orthodox representatives to stave off a sponsor boycott—to no avail. "The program treats intermarriage, one of the gravest problems facing Jews today, not only as an existent phenomenon but one that should be totally accepted," complained Rabbi Balfour Brickner. "This is the sort of thing that goes directly against Jewish teachings, the sort of thing religious Jews consider anathema. Intermarriage to them is a disaster area and works inimically to the future of the Jewish people. The program treats intermarriage in a cavalier, cute, condoning fashion."

CBS was not concerned. The complaints were considered typical special-interest grievances. But when David Fisch and Robert S. Manning of the Jewish Defense League got involved, things went crazy.

Fisch loathed *Bridget Loves Bernie* almost as much as he hated the United Nations. "Anything that brings the UN closer to the grave is very good for the Jewish people," he said. "Demonstrations are nice, but we really feel something much more meaningful would be an act to drive the United Nations out of New York." Fisch and his organization attacked a fleet of Soviet diplomats enroute to the UN in June 1973, dousing their cars with red paint and setting them on fire. Fisch said the paint symbolized "the blood of Soviet Jews that is being spilled in Russia while Brezhnev is being wined and dined in the United States." His next target was *Bridget Loves Bernie.*

"We had bomb threats on the show," recalled Meredith Baxter, who played Bridget. "Some guys from the Jewish Defense League came to my house to say they wanted to talk with me about changing the show."

Robert S. Manning, Fisch's collaborator, had just been arrested for detonating a pipe bomb in East Hollywood. The *Los Angeles Times* received an anonymous phone call: "Take this down carefully. I just bombed an Arab's house in Hollywood. No Arab is going to be safe in this country."

The explosion at 845 N. Harvard Boulevard shattered the windows and blew an eighteen-inch hole in the wall. By the end of the night, Manning and four members of the Jewish Defense League were in LAPD custody. Manning was charged with "intent to injure, intimidate and terrify." The charges did not mellow him any. Eight days later he was on the phone, threatening to murder Ralph Riskin, producer of *Bridget Loves Bernie.*

Fearing further violence, CBS president William Paley told his executives, "Cancel the show—I don't want it on the air."

"We were gone and off," recalled producer Douglas S. Cramer. "Screen Gems wouldn't fight it, they wouldn't take any kind of a stand, didn't offer it to any other network. It was a very strange and, for me, a terribly, terribly, unhappy situation."

After the final episode aired, the LAPD raided the Jewish Defense League's headquarters at 5887 West Pico Boulevard. They found twelve rifles and a machine gun. The FBI eventually classified the JDL as a terrorist organization. Meanwhile, life imitated art as the stars of the program, Meredith Baxter and David Birney, married in real life.

All in the Family, *The New Dick Van Dyke Show*, and *Bridget Loves Bernie* were the first of many sitcoms subjected to protest in the 1970s. Subject matter previously verboten was being introduced in television comedy for the very first time—and many viewers resisted the evolution.

CBS vice chairman Frank Stanton showed up for work one morning and found himself fenced in as his limousine was blockaded by hostile viewers. He was accused of "undeniable malice and a calculated intent to offend the sensibilities and deeply held beliefs of a substantial portion of the American public." In other words, Bea Arthur.

Norman Lear created a spin-off of *All in the Family* called *Maude*. It starred Bea Arthur as Archie Bunker's feminist sister-in-law. Plotlines incorporated controversial subjects including contraception, homosexuality, the Equal Rights Amendment, and abortion.

"I enjoy stirring feelings, even negative feelings, because I think that is what theater is about," said Lear. There were plenty of negative feelings about *Maude*.

"I think Maude is abominable, degrading and disgusting," complained a viewer from Baton Rouge. "I enjoy good comedy, but not that alley talk."

Susan Harris, a staff writer on *All in the Family*, was assigned to develop the episode about abortion. "I thought it was a wonderful idea," said Harris. "I thought it was something that absolutely should be addressed, and I liked tackling issues as well as entertaining . . . I knew it would be an intense reaction. I knew people felt very strongly about it one way or the other—but something like that would never deter me."

CBS ran a disclaimer before the opening credits: "Tonight's episode . . . deals with Maude's dilemma as she contemplates the possibility of abortion. You may wish to refrain from watching it if you believe the broadcast may disturb you or others in your family."

Pepsi, Pharmacraft, and Aqua Velva pulled their commercials and thirty-nine channels refused to air it. WMBD-TV in Peoria ran an editorial explaining their decision—followed by a rerun of *Let's Make a Deal*:

"After screening tonight's episode of *Maude,* we regret that because of the nature of the content of this show, WMBD-TV will not carry it, or the second part, which is scheduled for next Tuesday evening. It is the feeling of the management of this station that the subjects dealt with in this program, namely abortion and vasectomy, are in poor taste when used as the basic theme of a situation comedy show such as *Maude* . . . We feel they are out of place and in bad taste in a comedy format. Again, we regret that *Maude* will not be seen tonight, but we feel that it is the management's responsibility [that] this decision be made."

Maude was used as the example that TV was in the toilet. Cecil Todd of the Revival Fires Ministry in Joplin, Missouri, blamed television for "jamming the minds of the American people [with] foul language, sexual suggestiveness, barnyard humor." Todd was famous for his "revival fires" that were advertised like a wrestling match: "Hear Cecil Todd Blow the Lid on the Horrible Abomination of Little Unborn Babies Being Sold And Processed Into Beauty Products—Documented From His Private Investigation!"

L. Brent Bozell Jr. founded a lobby group called Stop Immorality on Television in November 1973. The former John Birch Society ally sent his spokesman, Paul Fisher, to deliver talking points to the media:

"We conducted a poll recently to ask people what they think of the moral state of television. About 92 per cent of the people felt that TV is more immoral than it was ten years ago; and 91 per cent felt a decline in moral values due to television's influence. And 86 per cent said they would boycott commercial sponsors on shows they deem immoral . . . Times aren't necessarily being changed, they're being tortured and twisted. We want to change the tone of broadcasting and bring it back to where it was in the late 30s."

The board members of Stop Immorality on Television included segregationist congressman Joel Broyhill and evangelist Bob Jones, for whom the university is named. Three celebrities lent their name to the cause: baseball legend Phil Rizzuto, character actor Andy Devine, and Red Skelton.

Speaking in December 1973, a woman from Oklahoma explained why she joined the organization: "We are sick to death of crime, horror, the satanic occult, violence, profanity, a constant barrage of drinking, dirty jokes, homosexuality, adultery and premarital sex practices."

On average, the Federal Communications Commission received around five hundred random letters of complaint every month, but after Stop Immorality on Television came along, the FCC received fourteen thousand. In an attempt to placate the sea of objection, the FCC established something called the "Family Viewing Hour."

The Family Viewing Hour began in February 1975 and imposed restrictions on what subject matter could be featured between 7 and 9 P.M. The FCC announced, "Entertainment programming inappropriate for viewing by a general family audience should not be broadcast during the first hour of network entertainment programming in primetime and in the immediately preceding hour."

Programs that were already on the schedule between 7 and 9, like *All in the Family*, would have to conform to the new rules or lose their position on the network schedule.

"[There was] no way I was going to—or would have any idea how to—change America's most popular show to meet the vague standards of decency that the Family Hour demanded," said Norman Lear. "*All in the Family* was virtually devoid of sex and violence, but its propensity for dealing with topical subjects was evidently deemed equally unfit for children."

CBS president Arthur Taylor believed the Family Viewing Hour was the only solution to the hate mail: "We want American families to be able to watch television in that time period without ever being embarrassed." But what was embarrassing for one family may not have been to another. Lear complained, "The network censor can't tell you what it means. All he knows is that he better not do anything that will get him in trouble."

A handful of people within the industry defended the Family Viewing Hour. "The creative people can't come up with something creative, so they blame the Family Hour," said Bill Cosby. "The hour should be directed toward the family [so it] can sit down together without being faced with some controversial issue or clinical discussion on abortion."

Showrunners ran into problems right away. CBS spent sixteen hours trying to determine whether or not Archie Bunker changing a diaper was obscene. Censors removed the word "sucker" from an episode of *The Jeffersons*. An episode of *Good Times*, written by David Letterman, featured Jimmie "JJ" Walker awaiting a herpes test in a sexual health clinic. It was bounced from its time slot so as not to spread herpes during the Family Viewing Hour.

Even dialogue in shows that had already aired were reedited so as not to violate Family Viewing Hour rules when they were rebroadcast. The sitcom *Barney Miller* was forced to delete "hell" and "damn" from each rerun.

"It's the most ludicrous concept I've ever heard," complained *Barney Miller* producer Danny Arnold. "I don't know of a child in America who doesn't know 'hell' or 'damn.' It's part of the American idiom. I don't see who can be offended, although I realize some people can be offended by chocolate pudding."

The sitcom *Welcome Back, Kotter*, starring Gabe Kaplan and John Travolta, was banned in Boston. "It sounds ridiculous in these days of porno flicks," reported *Variety*, "ABC's *Welcome Back, Kotter* [was] pulled off the schedule in Bean Town because its cast of non-scholastic high schoolers might have an unhealthy influence on local students."

Executive producer James Komack couldn't believe it. "To be banned in Boston is funnier than anything we're doing. This is the first time a tv show has been banned in Boston. We don't quite know why. The ABC local affiliate is very nervous about putting our show on because it feels possibly that we're glorifying school roughnecks, that the Dead End Kids can no longer be funny."

Gabe Kaplan, who played Mr. Kotter on the program, rattled off a list of storylines that were killed by the Family Viewing Hour. "We wanted to do one show where there was someone at the school who had VD. We wanted to do a show where Freddie had to meet a rough basketball schedule and his final exams are coming up at the same time and he starts taking pills and he gets hooked. We also wanted to have a party where everyone got drunk on beer and they wouldn't let us do that."

But even with the Family Viewing Hour in place, detractors of television were not satisfied. The Family Viewing Hour emboldened them, gave them a new sense of power, and led to even more aggressive censorship campaigns.

★

A war on George Carlin and his routine about the seven dirty words you can't say on television was orchestrated by an evangelical lobbyist. The man at the center of the grievance was John H. Douglas of Morality in Media, a group funded by the Coors beer fortune.

Morality in Media ran campaigns to keep *The Godfather* from airing on television and to remove *Playboy* from convenience-store shelves. The group said their purpose was to "prevent American culture from plummeting to the depths of barbarism."

Douglas claimed he was listening to the WBAI program *Lunchpail* on his car radio when host Paul Gorman warned listeners that a George Carlin routine he was about to play was not suitable for all ages. Douglas said he was angry that his "young son" had been exposed to profanity in the Carlin routine—although his "young son" had completed puberty and was already applying for a driver's license.

Morality in Media, the Family Viewing Hour, and Stop Immorality on Television were the result of sustained lobbying by former McCarthyites, Birchers, and old-school segregationists. They directed antagonism toward the biggest comedians of the early 1970s, including George Carlin, Richard Pryor, and Cheech & Chong, all of whom were subjected to harassment or threats of violence.

George Carlin was playing a Playboy Club at a hotel resort in Wisconsin when the audience came after him. After the show, the hotel management called Carlin in his room, "We cannot guarantee your safety. You must leave the premises immediately. People are down here asking what room you're in."

After completing their gig at Curtis Hixon Hall on August 25, 1973, the comedy team of Cheech & Chong were confronted by armed police. "Based on a Tampa city ordinance, Cheech & Chong were arrested immediately after the performance for using obscene words and gestures in public," reported the *Tampa Bay Times*. The duo posted a five-thousand-dollar bond "for simulating a naughty and disgusting act."

After a typical Richard Pryor stand-up performance in Richmond, Virginia, in August 1974, police issued a warrant for his arrest. Pryor was charged with "disorderly conduct" for "failing to clean up his act." He was fingerprinted and released on bail. He was arrested for saying the same words that could be heard in *Blazing Saddles*, a movie which he cowrote that was playing around the country at the exact same time.

Joan Rivers was playing the Deauville Hotel in Miami Beach in January 1974 when she received a telegram from a man upset by a Polish joke:

"Miss Joan Malinsky Rivers: You have managed not only to ruin my Christmas holidays, but you also are making me lose ten days of a sorely needed vacation. I am returning to Miami to put a stop to your Polish 'joke' routine at the Deauville . . . My people will no longer sit back supinely while a human cesspool spews her dirt on them . . . I promise you, you will regret it."

The front desk received a phone call: "There will be a bomb at the Deauville at the Joan Rivers show tonight." The Miami Police Department received a call as well: "The Polish Underground is going to blow up the Deauville Theater in fifteen minutes." The show was canceled, the hotel was swept, no bomb was found, but Rivers was rattled.

★

Saturday Night Live premiered in 1975 and its combination of political satire, drug humor, and references to male prostitution brought complaints. A letter to the editor published in November 1975 criticized the third-ever *SNL* episode, which featured *All in the Family* star Rob Reiner:

"I would like to know who permitted trash like Rob Reiner's Saturday night show to be televised. How low down can anyone get to make jokes about Joe Cocker, Gov. Wallace and President Ford? Is there no respect for anyone anymore? I hated the show."

The complaints continued for years. "Saturday Night Live has gone too far," wrote a reader of the *Arizona Republic.* "May Saturday Night Live, its sponsors and everyone that enjoys this kind of trash rot in hell forever."

A fundamentalist churchgoer from Naples, Florida, founded Clean Up Television (CUT) to combat programs she considered an "immoral insult to decency." CUT listed *Saturday Night Live, Charlie's Angels, Dallas, The Newlywed Game,* and *Three's Company* as "a negative influence on young people."

The movement spread and soon Reverend John M. Hurt of the Tennessee-based Churches of Christ was calling *The Love Boat* a vector for "adultery, fornication and homosexual activity."

The Family Viewing Hour applied in the evening, but even daytime television was considered a corrupting influence. The Church of Christ in Joelton, Tennessee, purchased a full-page ad in *Newsweek* denouncing *The Dating Game* and *The Newlywed Game* and announced a boycott of their sponsors Anacin, Jell-O, Maxwell House, Sani-Flush, Woolite, and Gravy Train dog food.

"The purpose of the campaign is not to take programs off the air," said a Church of Christ spokesman, "but to insist that they be cleaned up so they are no longer an insult to decency. Specifically, companies are being asked to refuse to sponsor programs which depict scenes of adultery, sexual perversion, or incest or which treat immorality in a joking or otherwise favorable light."

General Foods distanced themselves from *The Dating Game* and *The Newlywed Game.* They dropped their ads because the programs had "deteriorated below General Foods' standards of good taste."

Newspaper columnist Frank Leeming complained, "Television, particularly the soap operas and trash like *The Newlywed Game,* use the phrase 'to make love' meaning nothing other than sexual intercourse. The connotation today refers to two people who are not married, at least to each other, doing something once considered illicit or immoral."

Soap operas were accused of encouraging garbage sex. "I would like to know what is happening to *General Hospital,*" wondered a 1976 letter published in the *Indianapolis News.* "The men and women are living together and not married . . . This world is bad enough without showing such garbage. The program needs a house cleaning to get rid of those filthy people."

The game show *Family Feud* was accused of promoting—and spreading—

herpes. *Family Feud* emcee Richard Dawson greeted female contestants with a kiss on the mouth. Several game show fans were repulsed. One viewer complained, "Richard Dawson spreads more bugs every week than a flu epidemic."

"As a physician, I have wondered about the risks Richard Dawson takes in kissing every female contestant on Family Feud," said a letter in the *Philadelphia Daily News*. "The diseases that could be transmitted by promiscuous kissing are too long and too loathsome to recount here. Does Dawson or the producers take any caution to prevent infection? Are none of them informed?"

The *Pacific Daily News* reported that, in response to medical concerns, *Family Feud* instated a new policy: "Contestants, both male and female evidently have to undergo a mouth test with a magnifying glass from medical distaff." A contestant revealed that before her appearance, a *Family Feud* production assistant entered the dressing room with a magnifying glass and a cotton swab and said, "Okay, everybody line up for your herpes test."

The most committed of all TV haters was a Methodist preacher from Tupelo, Mississippi. Reverend Don Wildmon claimed his National Federation for Decency had ten thousand followers—and that he could mobilize their anger within twenty-four hours. He mailed a monthly newsletter to parent-teacher associations, which included a list of shows he claimed promoted "intercourse outside of marriage" and nonreligious use of the word "God." Among the programs Reverend Wildmon denounced as "immoral" were *Barnaby Jones, Fantasy Island,* and *The Six Million Dollar Man.*

Reverend Wildmon was upset when Norman Lear filed a lawsuit against the FCC over the Family Viewing Hour. Lear's legal team argued that it was an unconstitutional attack on free expression. In November of 1976, US district court judge Warren J. Ferguson ruled that "censorship by government or privately created review boards cannot be tolerated" and that the FCC had "violated the First Amendment by threatening the industry with regulatory action if the family hour were not adopted." Norman Lear and his many colleagues were elated, but Reverend Wildmon warned, "There will be hard-core pornography on commercial television within eight years if there isn't an uprising."

The editorial board of the *Herald* in Passaic, New Jersey, accused Reverend Wildmon of mimicking the philosophy of totalitarian countries: "With the rationale used by these groups, some of the most moral, decent television would probably be found in the Soviet Union, Cuba and Iran where strict government control prohibits any true form of entertainment, let alone something along the lines of *Three's Company*."

Three's Company was a popular sitcom starring John Ritter, Joyce DeWitt, Suzanne Somers, and Norman Fell (and later Don Knotts). Ritter played Jack Tripper, a man who pretends to be gay so his landlord won't object to his coed living arrangement. The suggestion of homosexuality, although seldom explicit, made *Three's Company* a bogeyman in the Culture War.

To protest their sponsorship of *Three's Company*, Reverend Wildmon organized pickets at thirty-six Sears outlets. In a highly publicized display, he had members of the National Federation for Decency remove the "Sears cards" from their wallets, cut them up with scissors, and mail them back to the company.

John Ritter defended *Three's Company* on the talk-show circuit, appearing on *The Mike Douglas Show*, *Dinah!*, and the *Tonight Show*. He asked his fans to offset their evangelical critics by supporting the remaining sponsors. "If you like the show," pleaded Ritter, "buy two of everything to counteract these people who hate us."

★

Homosexuality was a Culture War obsession. It triggered passionate emotions that could be exploited for political gain. The leading antigay culture warrior was Anita Bryant. A former band singer whose music made Lawrence Welk seem hip, she appeared on dozens of television variety shows in the 1950s and '60s. She toured Vietnam many times with Bob Hope and became the celebrity spokesperson for Florida orange juice. When an antidiscrimination statute was proposed in Dade County, Florida, in January 1977, Bryant claimed it was a cover for homosexual schoolteachers trying to recruit children into the gay underground.

Bryant became the face of a new organization called Save Our Children Inc., a political lobby group that sought to ban gay people from professional fields of employment. She appeared on sympathetic television programs hosted by preachers Pat Robertson and Jim Bakker, and the Reverend Jerry Falwell offered his support. A promotional flyer with Bryant's photo on the front was sent in the mail: "Dear Friend, I don't hate homosexuals! But as a mother I must protect my children from their evil influence . . . Do you realize what they want? They want to recruit our school children."

Bryant worked with ghostwriters to articulate her position. "There are many things that pose threats to our children and to family life," she wrote in her 1978 book *At Any Cost.* "There's child pornography, child abuse, drugs, alcohol, abortion, and of course, those who would try to foist upon an unsuspecting community what the homosexuals did in Miami. We need to be awakened to these things. Protect America's Children exists to help put a stop to evils in our society that are threatening our children."

She quoted mainstream figures like LAPD chief Ed Davis to bolster her point of view: "There is no question that homosexuals pose a threat to children." She also quoted San Francisco politician Dianne Feinstein: "Gays should not be harassed, but it's reached the point where their lifestyles are imposing on others."

"The attempt by homosexuals to label this a civil-rights issue was nothing but camouflage," said Bryant. "If we as a nation eventually come to the place where this is sanctioned as a legitimate civil-rights issue, then what is to stop . . . the murderer from shouting 'murderer rights'?"

Florida orange juice was subjected to a boycott campaign and there were calls to end her role as spokesperson. The boycott was endorsed by musician Paul Williams, horror legend Vincent Price, and actress Jane Fonda, while Johnny Carson ridiculed her in his *Tonight Show* monologues:

"Anita Bryant was on television last night, I don't know if you saw it or not. She was making a speech . . . I understand now she's going to travel around to supermarkets and get them to remove Froot Loops from the shelves . . . She said she would be happy to come to California and help us. Oh, it's all we need. I think her main objective is to come out here and break up *Starsky & Hutch*."

Television critic Tom Shales wrote of Carson, "In recent months his monologues have grown increasingly audacious and topical, and it's his handling of the Anita Bryant business that has proven most interesting . . . Carson and other comedians have turned her into a new symbolic stock comic figure. Anita Bryant has become the female Archie Bunker, a living caricature of abrasive bigotry."

Anita's husband, Bob Green, believed there was a double standard. "It's fine for entertainers and stars to appear on national TV condemning my wife and satirizing her in the most uncomplimentary ways imaginable; it's fine for the Johnny Carsons, the Carol Burnetts, and others to make her the brunt of their sick jokes; but let word get out that Anita is to appear on a TV program, and the threats of bombings and disruptions cause the network to cancel the show . . . Anita is being denied rights as an American."

"For me, in addition to all of the above, it brought job discrimination and the loss of a lifelong dream of having a television show of my own," said Bryant. "We were cast as bigots, haters, discriminators, and deniers of basic human rights. And all of this happened because we were sincerely concerned for our children and our community."

The New Laugh-In, a 1977 summer replacement featuring a young Robin Williams, featured many jokes at her expense. Bryant said *The New Laugh-In* was "part of the show-biz conspiracy to ridicule and discredit me."

Eventually the jokes gave way to real-life harassment. "One day we opened our post-office box," said Green, "and there was an unmistakable odor . . . How would you have liked to be the person opening the box that contained someone else's excrement?"

Gay activists around the country wore buttons that said, "Anita Bryant Sucks Oranges." A novelty company sold a brand of toilet paper with Bryant's face printed on each square and the slogan "Wipe the Smile off Anita." And at a press conference in Iowa, with television cameras rolling, a prankster hit her in the face with a pie.

Some came to her defense, notably Jesse Helms. The senator objected to a proposed amendment to the "so-called Civil Rights Act of 1964" that would include homosexual protections. Helms opposed all civil rights legislation and the Civil Rights Movement itself.

"She is a lovely person, deeply committed to Christianity," said Helms. "She has warned that unless America returns to basic principles, our freedoms are in jeopardy . . . Here was a fine and decent lady, a dedicated Christian, who had dared to speak out. And because she did, her contract was canceled."

By the end of the decade, Bryant's career was essentially done. Very few in the industry were willing to employ her. Bryant issued a press release: "I have been blacklisted for exercising the right of a mother to defend her children, and all children, against their being recruited by homosexuals. Because I dared to speak out for straight and normal America, because I dared to challenge the immoral influence of homosexual recruiters . . . I have had my career threatened. I have had my First Amendment freedom of speech abridged."

Bob Hope was disturbed by the lengths to which Bryant had gone. He knew the singer well, had done many shows with her over the years, and considered her a friend. "Because of this," said Hope, "it's very hard for me to discuss this subject." Speaking in July 1977, the comedian said Bryant was "going too far. I believe what these people do behind closed doors is their business." Hope said he had known dozens, perhaps hundreds, of homosexuals throughout his long career and they were "nice people, very talented, and have a lot to offer." He watched Bryant's campaign with dismay. "Anita's been around show business long enough that she should know about the contribution homosexuals have made."

Hope made jokes at her expense on his NBC television specials until Texaco, his longtime sponsor, made him stop. Executives met with the comedian and begged, "Please, please lay off the Anita Bryant jokes . . . Customers are tearing up their [Texaco] credit cards and sending them back."

★

Very seldom did sponsors make a decision based on ethics. Sponsors bent to evangelical organizations or civil rights organizations depending on which lobby held the most power at any given time. Sponsors were motivated by a desire to avoid any controversy and all protest.

Comedian David Brenner was cast in a new NBC sitcom called *Snip* in 1976. Loosely inspired by the movie *Shampoo*, the sitcom concerned a hair salon. Despite advance publicity and several episodes being filmed, it never aired.

"They made up all kinds of excuses," said Brenner, "but the reason *Snip* was pulled is we had an actor who was gay and who played a gay part. They were afraid to have a gay on television; this was before *Soap*."

Soap premiered in 1977 with a young Billy Crystal playing a homosexual character. Created by Susan Harris, the writer responsible for *Maude*'s abortion episode, *Soap* was a sitcom with ongoing storylines—like a soap opera.

"I wanted to do a series where you weren't confined to a beginning, middle, and an end in 23 minutes," said Harris. "And that really was the appeal. We would change the storyboard around, we could shift things, kill people, bring them back."

A *Newsweek* story incorrectly suggested that the first episode would feature a priest having sex inside a church. The information was false, but evangelical protest mobilized all the same.

"ABC-TV is counting on our apathy to get away with its immoral television programming," said Harry N. Hollis of the Baptist Christian Life Commission. In an attempt to sidestep a sponsor boycott, ABC withheld the names of the advertisers until the premiere. "Throughout the entire SOAP affair, the American Broadcasting Company has been dishonest with the American people," said Hollis. "They promised SOAP would be a morality play; instead, they are broadcasting an *immorality* play . . . If SOAP dies, the war will not be won, but our message to the networks will be clear: The American people do not want 'entertainment' based on sexual immorality."

The Roman Catholic Church released an official statement condemning the Billy Crystals of the world: "Action is needed to prevent this new debasement of the medium through a contempt for human beings."

ABC executive Herb Jellinek recalled, "What was difficult on the show was to get clearances because the stations were objecting to the show. They were afraid of the FCC, they were afraid of public opinion . . . Stations in the South, you know, huge stations, refused to clear it."

Soap endured, but ABC was annoyed. "The protests may not have derailed the show," said Susan Harris, "but *Soap* was a nonstop source of stress for ABC, causing the network to lose sponsors . . . We got memos all the time."

★

The same week that *Soap* premiered, Richard Pryor caused a near-riot at the Hollywood Bowl. According to comedian David Steinberg, it was the "first benefit supporting the gay community, at a time when Anita Bryant and her anti-gay campaign were making headlines."

Richard Pryor already had a volatile reputation. According to Kevin Cook, Flip Wilson's biographer, Pryor attacked a gay hairstylist on *The Flip Wilson Show* for "what Pryor considered a lascivious look."

"Pryor lashed out," wrote Cook, "poking the stylist in both eyes . . . NBC lawyers made Pryor's attack go away with a settlement and a confidentially agreement."

"Richard practically blinded him," recalled Flip Wilson's son. "They thought the guy was going to lose an eye."

Pryor appeared at the Hollywood Bowl on September 18, 1977, for an event billed as *A Star-Spangled Night for Rights*. It featured performances by David Steinberg, Bette Midler, Lily Tomlin, and Tom Waits. Among the many celebrities on hand were Chevy Chase, Tab Hunter, Julie Kavner, Paul Lynde, Dick Martin, Paul Newman, John Travolta, and Robert Blake.

Pryor walked onstage, scanned the crowd, and said, "While the [N-words] in Watts were out there burning, you guys were up in Hollywood doing whatever you wanted to be doing . . . There are only four [N-words] out there. How can f*ggots be racists? I hope the police shoot your ass accidentally because you motherfuckers ain't helping."

"And from the very top of the Bowl, cascading through the center sections and down into the hotsy-totsy boxes, came a storm of boos and catcalls," reported the *Los Angeles Times*. "Someone shouted, 'Get him off of there.' Pryor pressed on, insulting, goading, looking for reaction. As for the funds being raised he said, 'Give the money to people on welfare.' Angry boos and hisses rained down."

"[N-words] can't deal with the word homosexual," Pryor continued. "There may be a f*ggot in the family but there ain't no homosexual." The booing got louder. "That's what I wanted to hear," Pryor told the crowd. "I wanted to test you to your soul. They're not paying me anything to do this! Where were you f*ggots when they burned down Watts? All of you can kiss my rich black ass!"

Ron Field, the organizer of the event, ran onstage and grabbed the microphone as Pryor walked off, "I want everyone to know this wasn't planned and all of us who are involved in the show are embarrassed over it."

The *Los Angeles Times* received several dozen letters about the incident.

"After having witnessed Richard Pryor's behavior at the Hollywood Bowl Gay Rights Benefit, I can say without hesitation Pryor is the new Florida orange juice of Hollywood," wrote one attendee. "His bigoted presentation was the height of insult thrown at an audience deserving the same respect his black sisters and brothers deserve."

A letter from Pasadena said, "In this country of free speech, presumably anyone has the right to express his hostility toward minority groups. But for Pryor to accept an invitation to perform at a benefit for gay rights and then to *use that benefit* as a forum for expressing his hostility towards gays is the ultimate doublecross."

David Steinberg had known Pryor since the 1960s when they were both new to stand-up. "My guess is, truthfully, that some bad substance was taken that night," said Steinberg. "He was high, he was mad . . . He had lost his humor and was out of control . . . The crowd, which had loved him, now threw chairs at him, got up, and left. He had alienated them . . . It was kind of tragic."

In the late 1970s, there was occasional tension between white gays and Black straights, each vying for equality while sometimes discriminating against each other.

Paul Lynde, the comic actor best known for *Hollywood Squares*, had been present at the Hollywood Bowl event. Three weeks later he stepped into a controversy of his own.

Lynde was flown to Northwestern University in Evanston, Illinois, to serve as the grand marshal in the school's homecoming parade. Drinking heavily throughout the day, Lynde went to a local fast-food joint that night. Standing in line behind the school's Black sociology professor, Lynde shouted belligerently, "Black people are too spoiled!"

He went on a tirade about a new television series he'd been cast in. "There are going to be all these Black people," complained Lynde. "I'm the only white they're having on the show!"

The school paper later said Lynde "kept up a steady chatter, most of it racist comments directed at black people in general and at [the professor] in particular." When the professor turned around to tell him to cool it, Lynde stuck a finger in his face and said, "You've got bad vibes."

Asked to explain himself, Lynde said he was stressed because earlier in the day a Black heckler had yelled, "Hey man, who ever told you you were funny?"

★

Racism was a major discussion in 1977, as Alex Haley's *Roots* became the most-watched miniseries in television history. *Roots* brought the brutal story of slavery into millions of American homes. High school students in Hot Springs, Arkansas, were shown an episode and the following day a brawl broke out between Black and white students. Similar disturbances were reported in Michigan, Mississippi, and Pennsylvania. Things got especially intense in Cincinnati, Ohio.

"Roots, the televised epic inspired by a black man's search for his ancestry, led to Jesse Coulter's rampage says a lawyer for the 42-year-old man accused of taking eight hostages," reported the Associated Press. "During the siege that began Friday night at the Catharine Booth home for unwed mothers, Coulter demanded the return of a son born at the home 20 years earlier." The lawyer explained, "This man sat on this for 20 years, and the dynamite was *Roots*."

Fear consumed the United States in the late 1970s, as serial killers like the Hillside Strangler intimidated Los Angeles and the Son of Sam terrorized New York. They inspired other deranged lunatics, some of whom menaced celebrities. Comedy legend Lucille Ball received a death threat addressed to "Lucille Balls" on August 5, 1977:

Lucille Balls:

When World War III comes there ain't gonna be any more
poor American guys dying for you rich bitches . . . When
the earthquake hits L.A., I will be scouring the obituaries,
expectantly to see your name on it. If you were burning to
death, I wouldn't spit or piss on you to quench the flames.
All there is war, hate, kill, friction, murder, and pressure.

Just call me Mr. Son of Sam Ohio.

Violence flared as religious extremists objected to motion pictures. A
film starring Anthony Quinn led to a hostage taking in Washington, DC, in
March 1977. Armed men identified as "Hanafi extremists" demanded the
cancelation of *Mohammad, Messenger of God* (later retitled *The Message*),
a biopic of the religious prophet. "We're going to kill a lot of people,"
exclaimed a terrorist. "Don't ask me why . . . just listen."

The Associated Press reported:

"In nearly simultaneous invasions, a band of gunmen seized 50 to
100 hostages in the headquarters of a Jewish organization Wednesday,
while another armed man held hostages at a Moslem religious center 10
blocks away. A short time later, gunfire flared at the District Building,
Washington City Hall, and police [had] a report that people may have
been killed there. Mayor Walter Washington was reported barricaded in his
office . . . At the headquarters of B'nai B'rith, at least four invaders armed
with rifles—two of them automatic—commandeered the eighth floor.
They first invaded two lower floors, gathering hostages as they went . . .
At least five persons were injured there. One suffered a gunshot wound
in the arm. Another shooting victim was known to be inside, along with
people injured in beatings."

DC city councilman Marion Barry was shot in the stomach.

Mohammad, Messenger of God was pulled from theaters in Washington,
DC, and New York City, but it eventually played in the rest of the United
States without incident.

A bomb destroyed a theater on the edge of West Hollywood in June

1978. The Jewish Defense League, the same extremist group that had targeted the sitcom *Bridget Loves Bernie*, was responsible.

They resented a documentary called *The Palestinian,* narrated by Vanessa Redgrave. Dore Schary, film producer and former chairman of the Anti-Defamation League, called it "anti-Israel and anti-Zionist," but unlike the JDL, he opposed any attempt to suppress it.

"I feel very strongly against her [Redgrave's] personal political position," said Schary, "but I don't believe in boycotts. I pray there is no boycott or demonstration."

There was no boycott or demonstration—only explosions.

Shortly before 4:30 A.M. on June 15, a bomb tore open the Doheny Plaza Theater near Sunset Plaza. The marquee that advertised *The Palestinian* became a jagged projectile flying over Sunset Boulevard. The roof of the theater caved in, leaving a pile of smoking debris. Two members of the JDL were arrested and sentenced to four years in prison.

★

The decade closed with one of comedy's great controversies.

Monty Python's Life of Brian was an outrageous parody of biblical times. Its wild sight gags, absurd humor, convincing set design, and social commentary delighted Monty Python fans. However, politicians connected to the evangelical movement suggested that the members of Monty Python— John Cleese, Eric Idle, Graham Chapman, Terry Jones, Terry Gilliam, and Michael Palin—be tried for blasphemy.

The idea of a biblical parody made film producers nervous. "Originally, we had the money from EMI for this film," recalled Terry Gilliam. "It was, I believe, the Thursday before the crew was leaving [to start filming], we got the news that EMI had pulled out because apparently [film executive] Lord Bernie Delfont had finally got around to reading the script, decided it was blasphemous, and didn't want his company to be involved in it . . . Everything was canceled."

"Delfont had been approached by certain elements and *leaned on,* and *warned,* that this would be trouble, this film," recalled Eric Idle. "He didn't want to cause offense. Y'know, you can understand it from his point of view, but from *our* point of view, we had already spent about eighty thousand quid on locations and getting things going."

The film was saved by one of Eric Idle's friends—George Harrison. The former Beatle put up four million dollars of his own money and rescued the production.

Investors were right to be cautious. As soon as it was released, *Life of Brian* was besieged by religious fundamentalists. Orthodox rabbis were the first to protest, objecting to a prayer shawl worn by John Cleese at the start of the film.

"It was the first scene to raise any protests," said Terry Jones. "We always thought we were going to get protests from Christians, but in fact the first lot of protests we got [were] from the . . . Rabbinical Association of New York."

Idle said, "The rabbis went away as quickly as they had appeared and were replaced by angry Christians, who picketed the Burbank Studios in L.A., claiming that Warner Bros. were the agents of the devil."

Blasphemy charges were seldom successful in the modern age. Organized evangelical groups figured they'd have better success if they attacked the film on grounds of obscenity. A half-second glimpse of Graham Chapman's penis led to a court order which suppressed *Life of Brian* in the state of Georgia due to "lewd exhibition of genitals."

The movie was banned in Shreveport, Alabama, outlawed in Alexandria, Louisiana, and harassed in South Carolina.

"The film held up to deliberate ridicule my faith in Jesus Christ and made fun of His suffering," said Presbyterian minister William Solomon. "It was cruel and sarcastic, but it was not art." Solomon contacted South Carolina senator Strom Thurmond for help. Thurmond insisted the film distributor withdraw the film, telling them, "My folks take their religion very seriously." The distributor replied, "We take our freedoms very seriously, too."

At a theater in Columbia, South Carolina, protesters distributed leaflets about eternal damnation. Monty Python fans held a counterprotest and carried signs that said, "Strom Doesn't Pay for My Movie Ticket" and "Resurrect Brian, Crucify Censors."

Senator Thurmond inadvertently helped as controversy drove ticket sales. "There was no need for us to fly to the States and do publicity," said Eric Idle. "So, while the movie was being pulled from cinemas across America, people would simply drive across state lines. This pattern repeated itself everywhere."

On an episode of *Friday Night, Saturday Morning* on BBC2, Michael Palin and John Cleese debated a priest and the recently born-again writer Malcolm Muggeridge about the film's merits.

"I would simply point out to you," Muggeridge told them, "that if you care about what constitutes what we call Western Civilization—which now is probably coming to an end—and you were to consider the role that's been played in that by this . . . piece of buffoonery, you would have a certain humility . . . This is such a tenth-rate film . . . and the lampooning of His death, which is the most disgraceful part of the whole thing . . . and all you've done is to make a lot of people on a cross singing a music hall song. I mean, it is so disgusting."

Ironically, Malcolm Muggeridge once contributed an essay to *Esquire* complaining that people were so sensitive you couldn't joke about anything anymore. "The area of life in which ridicule is permissible is steadily shrinking, and a dangerous tendency is becoming manifest to take ourselves with undue seriousness," wrote Muggeridge in 1958. "This decay of humor on both sides of the Atlantic doubtless derives, partly at any rate, from the growing sense of insecurity which haunts the lives of so many today. When institutions and authorities feel themselves to be secure, ridicule and satire are unobjectionable."

Life of Brian was banned in Ireland. It was banned in Norway. And it was suppressed throughout the United Kingdom. Screenings were forbidden in Birkenhead, Brynmawr, Cornwall, East Devon, Haverfordwest, Harrogate, Pontypridd, Swansea, and Whitehaven. The town of Watford allowed it, but only after changing the film's rating to an X. And an advertising campaign in Sweden mocked their neighbor: "Come see *Life of Brian*! A film so funny they banned it in Norway!"

The controversy faded after a year. By the 1980s, the film was syndicated on television and aired on weekend afternoons in several markets—and nobody seemed to care.

"It showed you how much absurd posturing goes on," said John Cleese. "Because people protest and protest and protest and say this is really, really bad. And then two years later the film is shown again and nobody turns out at all. It's about posturing. It's about people feeling they're doing God a favor by going out to protest."

"We were pilloried by religious groups on all sides from Jews to Catholics to Protestants," said Terry Gilliam. "To me, what's important is that we managed to offend a lot of people. But as you notice we were very cautious about offending any Muslims. We would say *nothing* negative about a Muslim, 'cause we'd get a fatwa after us. But your Jews, your Christians, they're easy to push around."

"I was very surprised by the degree to which some people protested," said Cleese, years later. "I did not have an enormous amount of respect for the most vocal people who went out and demonstrated. I had a *lot* of respect for people who came up to me and told me quietly and rationally what bothered them in the film . . . I was also surprised by how many people wrote to me and said, 'I am a Christian and I don't know what this fuss is about. It seemed to me perfectly clear that you were making fun of the way that some people *pretend* they're Christians—when they're not actually following Christ's teachings.'"

Eric Idle said it eventually all came full circle. "One nice footnote to the *Brian* controversy, in our movie, Sue Jones-Davies, a Welsh actress, played Brian's reactionary girlfriend Judith . . . When the movie was first released in her hometown of Aberystwyth in North Wales, the local council banned the film from public screening. Thirty years later she became the mayor of Aberystwyth and overthrew the ban."

12

PAUL WEYRICH: CULTURE WARRIOR

In the late 1970s, Paul Weyrich was far from a household name—and that's the way he liked it. Anita Bryant and Jerry Falwell grabbed the headlines, but it was the tactical support of Weyrich that ensured their political influence.

Few outside of Washington were familiar with Weyrich, but he was connected to every major Culture War controversy. He founded the Heritage Foundation, the Moral Majority, and the American Legislative Exchange Council (ALEC), and assisted the Christian Coalition, all of which coordinated Culture War strategies. Even today, several years after his death, lobbyists and think tank representatives hold a weekly "Weyrich Lunch" to devise Culture War talking points.

Paul Weyrich caused his first big stir in June 1961 in Racine, Wisconsin, at the age of nineteen. A member of the local Young Republicans Club, Weyrich assembled ten people to protest an appearance by Eleanor Roosevelt at Racine's Memorial Hall. He marched with a sign that said, "America Awake—The REDS are among US."

The mayor of Racine ordered increased police protection. When her speech began, Mrs. Roosevelt invited Weyrich inside: "Will someone ask the youngsters to come in and park their weapons at the door. We may disagree, but it is a good thing, in times like these, that young people do voice opinions." The following day, the Young Republicans Club distanced themselves from Weyrich: "We condemn these tactics as do most other responsible young Republicans."

"We have read and heard much lately about the resurgence of the conservative right wing among college students," wrote the *Racine Journal Times*. "If the picketing at Memorial Hall last Friday was an example of this sort of thing, it is not very impressive. The pickets were demonstrating only that they are rather young, rather ill-mannered, and rather silly."

Weyrich responded with a letter to the editor: "The Journal-Times attempted to ridicule the group of pickets . . . Far from being confused, ill-mannered or silly, [we] staged an orderly, quiet, and well-run demonstration against anti-American ideas."

Weyrich developed his political voice writing letters to the editor. Over the course of two years, his letters criticized the separation of church and state, argued Supreme Court justices should pledge a "love of God" or be disbarred, chided the Civil Rights Movement as a Communist conspiracy, and spoke of President Kennedy's "moral bankruptcy."

His sharp tone led to talk radio. He delivered editorials on Wisconsin stations WISN and WFNY and became program director at WAXO. He hosted a show called *Sundial* and complained about "ultraliberals" inside the Republican Party. He was recruited by the American Opinion Speaker's Bureau, an adjunct of the John Birch Society. They sent him to address the Federation of GOP Women in 1965.

"In my estimation his comments were not constructive, but destructive," said one of the Republican women present. "He made derogatory remarks about the state university, its radio stations, the UN, Xerox corp [for sponsoring a civil rights documentary] . . . I firmly believe in freedom of speech, but not freedom of irresponsible speech."

Another attendee complained, "Paul Weyrich, WISN news commentator, made every effort to slander men who the Republican majority have elected to office. Why do we Republican women have to be subjected to this type of program meeting after meeting?" The Federation of GOP Women asked the American Opinion Speaker's Bureau to stop sending "speakers with extremist backgrounds and convictions."

Wisconsin's Republican governor, Warren P. Knowles, agreed with their contempt. "I share your great concern in having such people [Paul Weyrich] using the Republican party as a vehicle for dispensing hate, falsehoods and character assassinations."

The few people who supported Paul Weyrich in the 1960s were fringe extremists like R. J. Rushdoony, an anti-Semitic "Christian Reconstructionist" who wanted the death penalty for children and a federal ban on interracial marriage. Weyrich was also befriended by Samuel T. Francis, the segregationist who coined the term "white pride."

Republican senator Mark Hatfield worried that the Paul Weyrichs of the world would one day seize his Republican Party. "The Far Right has been successfully united by a well-designed, well-financed, and persistent campaign of fear," Hatfield said in 1968. "The continual fanning of this fear . . . has created such a distortion in the perceptions . . . that they can no longer distinguish between fantasy and reality."

But by the early 1970s, Weyrich conceded that his political philosophy was "badly outmatched [and] outgunned by . . . the civil rights movement agenda." He retreated to the shadows and devised a strategy to rebrand extremism for the mainstream.

In 1973, Paul Weyrich met with Joseph Coors, owner of the Coors beer empire. He unveiled a long-term strategy to remake the United States in his image. It so impressed Coors that he gifted Weyrich a multimillion-dollar handout. The generosity was matched by Richard Mellon Scaife, another of the country's wealthiest reactionaries. Together they funded one of the most influential propaganda outfits in modern political history: the Heritage Foundation.

Pretending to be scholarly, the Heritage Foundation released reports to back up outdated John Birch Society philosophy, providing a veneer of respectability for concepts long since discredited by left-wingers and right-wingers alike.

A year after starting the Heritage Foundation, Weyrich took control of the tax-exempt American Legislative Exchange Council (ALEC) with the purpose of rewriting American law. As the book *State Capture* put it, ALEC advocated for the "complete business domination of American public life" with "no regard for the public interest."

The Nation explained, "In the world according to ALEC, competing firms in free markets are the only real source of social efficiency and wealth. Government contributes nothing but security. Outside of this function, it should be demonized, starved or privatized."

Weyrich used a strategist named Richard Larry to structure the Heritage Foundation and to obscure the political lobbying activities of ALEC. Larry did the same for other think tanks including the Hoover Institution, the Cato Institute, and the American Enterprise Institute. Most were funded by the same handful of people.

While lobbying for corporate dominance, ALEC used the Culture War to divide and conquer. Their team of lawyers ghostwrote legislation with the intention of ending abortion rights, civil rights, gun control, and public education.

Paul Weyrich established more think tanks with money provided by Coors, Scaife, Richard DeVos of Amway, and Nelson Bunker Hunt, the son of John Birch Society financier H. L. Hunt. Named the Committee for the Survival of a Free Congress and the Free Congress Foundation respectively, Weyrich drafted a plan "to convert the politically dormant Evangelical Christian constituency to conservative policy positions through new media channels." In doing so, he laid the groundwork for a new voter base which would transform politics.

Among the first Culture War controversies that Weyrich and his associates participated in was the censorship of school textbooks. The Heritage Foundation joined the movement to suppress textbooks that spoke positively about the Civil Rights Movement.

In 1974, a Texas school district was accused of promoting "documented communists" like Charlie Chaplin, Picasso, and Dr. Martin Luther King Jr. A reference to the song "We Shall Overcome" was provided as evidence that Texas textbooks were "furthering Marxism."

Norma Gabler, a housewife who received an influx of cash from Coors, filed over two thousand separate objections with the Texas Board of Education. Her husband, flush with Coors cash, resigned from Exxon to devote himself to full-time censorship. The Gablers wanted to ban a textbook that referred to future presidents as "he or she." They demanded the removal of Edgar Allen Poe because he was "too gruesome." And they objected to math books teaching calculus and trigonometry. Norma Gabler said, "When a student reads in a math book that there are no absolutes, suddenly every value he's been taught is destroyed. And the next thing you know, the student turns to crime and drugs."

The Gablers claimed that history books that covered the Civil Rights Movement would "undermine patriotism." They asked that a history book mentioning the KKK be removed because it lacked balance and failed to mention "the bigotry of African Americans." They spent years fighting their battles in court—with lawyers provided free of charge by the Heritage Foundation.

The Heritage Foundation also sent lawyers to Kanawha County, West Virginia, where local preachers wanted to ban sex education, and the work of e.e. cummings, John Updike, and Mark Twain. A local preacher detonated dynamite at the local elementary school and said, "The only purpose these filthy books have is to degrade your children down to animals."

"The protest was publicly framed as a parents' rights case but, in fact, was focused substantially on books by African-American authors or texts that dealt with the conditions and culture of African-Americans," wrote Russ Bellant, author of *The Coors Connection*. "The Ku Klux Klan was involved in the protest from the start . . . Heritage [Foundation] sent staff counsel James T. McKenna to represent the book protesters."

Meanwhile, Paul Weyrich supported the 1976 presidential bid of Alabama governor George Wallace. He visited with the old segregationist and introduced him to Richard Viguerie, who raised seven million dollars for Wallace's campaign. But the money did little to secure their influence. Frustrated, Weyrich and Viguerie stopped investing in Wallace and focused on an emerging Baptist preacher instead.

"Rise up in arms and throw out every textbook not reflecting our values," exclaimed Jerry Falwell. "Textbooks are Soviet propaganda."

Jerry Falwell met with Weyrich and Viguerie in 1979. Weyrich brought along Howard Phillips, a cohort whose politics were praised by the Ku Klux Klan in the 1960s. Phillips was a convert to "Christian Reconstructionism" and told Falwell it was time for the United States to "resort to biblical law." Phillips, Weyrich, and Viguerie asked Falwell to be their front man in a new organization.

"Weyrich proposed that if the Republican Party could be persuaded to take a stance against abortion, that would split the strong Catholic voting block within the Democratic Party," explained political scientist Sara Diamond. "The New Right leaders wanted Falwell to spearhead a visibly Christian organization that would apply pressure to the GOP. Weyrich proposed that the name have something to do with a moral majority."

The Moral Majority exploited abortion as a Culture War issue. Howard Philips was certain it was their magic bullet for securing political power. Phillips concluded that power came down to who controlled the Culture War talking points: "What is power? It is the ability to tell others what the issues are, what the issues mean, and identify who the good guys are and bad guys are."

Paul Weyrich courted those who remained with the John Birch Society. While the organization was technically still active, its influence, clout, and membership rolls had shrunk to insignificance. Still, Weyrich was loyal to the group. He contributed several editorials to the John Birch Society magazine in 1980 to promote the Moral Majority.

With Jerry Falwell as the face of the operation, the Moral Majority worked full-time to abolish sex education, prevent gay rights, end legal abortion, and repeal civil rights. Paul Weyrich, the Moral Majority, and the Heritage Foundation would have been dismissed as the lunatic fringe in the 1960s, but by the 1980s they had allies inside the White House who could implement their vision.

★

Ronald Reagan was elected president in November 1980. A Warner Bros. movie star in the 1930s, '40s, and '50s, his detractors frequently insulted him as "a failed actor." But his Hollywood filmography was far better than his enemies would ever admit. From glossy blockbusters to marginal B pictures, Reagan's most entertaining films included *Hollywood Hotel, Secret Service of the Air, Dark Victory, Juke Girl, Kings Row, Storm Warning, Law and Order,* and *The Killers.*

Hollywood was notoriously liberal, and so was Ronald Reagan—until the Red Scare of the late 1940s. As president of the Screen Actors Guild during the height of the Cold War, Reagan worked to crush left-wing influence within his union—and impose the wishes of studio bosses. It was his first taste of political leadership, and the invaluable experience eventually led to the governor's house in Sacramento.

Jimmy Stewart, a loyal Republican, was skeptical of Reagan: "He's just a Johnny-come-lately. He'll never get anywhere." Film noir actor Dana Andrews called him "a buffoon." Myrna Loy, costar of *The Thin Man* movies, accused him of "destroying everything now I've lived my life for." *Juke Girl* director Curtis Bernhardt said, "I didn't know about his politics. I only thought he was stupid."

Showbiz columnist Sheilah Graham thought he was strange: "He and Nancy were lunching upstairs at Sardi's restaurant in New York a few years ago and I was rather startled when, after the main course, Ronnie took out his contacts, put them in his mouth, sucked them for a few seconds, and put them back in his eyes."

"This guy was thought to be a company man—and forever a company man," said *Twilight Zone* creator Rod Serling in 1966. "What other qualifications did Ronald Reagan have to be governor of the most populous state in the union? Well, [with] a magnifying glass—I still couldn't discover it. I don't know how the hell this man could run for public office."

Moe Howard of the Three Stooges loathed Reagan, as he held him responsible for cheating elderly actors out of residuals. "A few years after the TV release of our shorts," said Moe, "Ronald Reagan, then president of the Screen Actors Guild, was instrumental in passing a SAG ruling that there would be no residuals for pictures made prior to 1960. This shut us out."

Elected president in a landslide victory in November 1980, Reagan's presidential inaugural gala included performances by actor Ben Vereen and comedian Rich Little. Both were controversial.

Vereen performed a tribute to Bert Williams, the Black star of the 1910s.
However, he did so in blackface, which was considered widely inappropriate for a presidential inaugural. Vereen said ABC Television improperly
edited his routine and that he had been "sabotaged by the network." The
Associated Press explained, "Vereen first danced and sang 'Waiting for the
Robert E. Lee' before a cheering GOP audience, along with the president
and first lady Nancy Reagan. He then stripped the blackface off while singing 'Nobody' to show the pain of blackface and the exploitation of African
Americans. But ABC omitted the second part of Vereen's performance
when airing it, showing only the minstrelsy segment."

Meanwhile, Rich Little told the inaugural crowd that the best way to prevent a Soviet invasion of Poland was to "convince them it was Cleveland."
The joke got a big laugh but angered politicians in Ohio. Congresswoman
Mary Rose Oakar demanded an apology. She got one when Little guest
hosted the *Tonight Show* on February 23, 1981:

"Before we start anything tonight, I would like to personally—
sincerely—apologize to the people of Cleveland for doing a joke at the
inauguration that, uh, heh, stirred up a hornet's nest . . . I got a lot of
letters. Anyway, I apologize. Cleveland: I would like to come back to
your city and do a show. And if I do get a twenty-one-gun salute, please
aim in the air."

The Tonight Show Starring Johnny Carson made fun of politicians frequently, which inevitably led to charges of political bias. Jokes at the expense
of Ronald Reagan were common during the presidential campaign.

"He is probably the most conservative, I guess, of all the Republican
candidates," said Carson. "Ronnie has a bumper sticker that says, 'Honk
if you like using sacred Indian lands for condos.'"

Saturday Night Live ridiculed Reagan, which infuriated a Republican
lobbyist named Jack Abramoff. "Impersonations of Reagan on *Saturday
Night Live*," reported journalist Nina Easton, "prompted Abramoff to
consider launching a boycott of the show."

The Moral Majority galvanized a new base of evangelical voters. As
their influence grew, there was fear that America was about to enter a new
era of censorship.

"The same conservatism that raised Ronald Reagan from the political dead is about to resurrect a handful of old television stars from the grave-yard," reported the Field News Service in September 1981. "At the advent of the new season, we raise our glasses to the Moral Majority and to Jerry Falwell's holy roller gospel . . . Their voice has been heard in the unhallowed halls of ABC, CBS and NBC."

"I object to the networks using my airwaves to make my living room a cesspool," said Falwell. He was referring to Tony Randall.

"I don't give a damn what Jerry Falwell and his so-called Moral Majority think," said Randall. "An ignorant Bible-thumping bastard in Mississippi . . . who cares about them, anyway? I don't think any intelligent person cares what the Moral Majority thinks or says. Personally, I believe whatever influ-ence they now have in the television industry will eventually fade away."

The feud concerned *Love, Sidney*, a TV comedy based on a made-for-television movie. It starred Tony Randall as a gay man renting a room in the home of a straight family. Reverend Don Wildmon, having finished his crusade against *Three's Company*, asked, "Is it necessary to give homosexuals that special recognition?"

It wasn't just evangelical lobbyists who disliked *Love, Sidney*. The sitcom was also condemned by gay activists who felt it was a distortion conceived by straight writers.

"We were attacked by the Moral Majority, we were attacked by the right-wing, we were attacked by the Lubavitcher Jews, and we were attacked by the gay *Advocate*," said Randall. "Gays have never liked it because they say it's an untrue picture of gay life, but the show is not about gay life—it's only about Sidney's life."

Paul Weyrich, riding high with the success of the Moral Majority and the Heritage Foundation, founded the Council for National Policy in 1981. This, his latest think tank, had the same point of view as the others and worked steadily to place its talking heads into the mainstream. The Council for National Policy included Christian Reconstructionist R. J. Rushdoony, Nelson Baker Hunt of the John Birch Society, Richard Shoff of the Ku Klux Klan, and the author of *Communism, Hypnotism and the Beatles*, David A. Noebel.

By the 1980s, Weyrich was considered a mainstream Republican, yet his political philosophy was the same as it had been when Republicans rejected him twenty years earlier. Some of those who knew him back then warned their modern colleagues.

"I am a conservative and I used to be associated with Paul Weyrich in the Capitol Hill 'chapter' of the New Right," wrote attorney Louis Ingram in a letter to the Republican National Committee. "I am convinced that these people put economic and egotistic self-aggrandizement ahead of national interests."

Senator Barry Goldwater, a man who had been endorsed by the John Birch Society, in 1964, distanced himself from Weyrich's influential new movement. "Abortion is a private matter between the woman and her doctor," said Goldwater. "The religious right scares the hell out of me. They have no place in politics . . . Don't try to preach and practice religion in the halls of Congress."

Republican senator Mark Hatfield said of the Weyrich phenomenon: "Isn't it interesting that so much of the support of this New Right comes out of the section of the nation that tolerated and supported slavery? They are substituting the gospel of Christ with a gospel of political conservatism, right-wing conservatism. And in my understanding of Scripture, that's apostasy, that's heresy."

Ethical or not, the Weyrich strategy was effective. Multiple think tanks aimed to manipulate opinion, demonize the opposition, and consolidate political power by spreading panic. Many politicians felt they could overlook Weyrich's more extreme concepts if it meant acquiring political power.

★

"If Ed Asner won't stop aiding the Marxist enemy," said Congressman John LeBoutillier, "then we Americans can retaliate by boycotting those who sponsor his TV show."

Criticism of American foreign policy was relegated to the underground in the 1980s. Whether you were talking about Asia or Cuba, the Soviets or the Middle East, if you criticized the methods of the Pentagon, the CIA, or the State Department, you were not welcome on network television.

Ed Asner starred in *Lou Grant*, a hit drama about a crusading newspaper publisher. He was also the president of the Screen Actors Guild from November 1981 until June 1985. As such, he was invested in political causes. When his program was canceled after its fifth season, he claimed it was because he criticized President Reagan's foreign policy.

Relying on information provided by Amnesty International and Human Rights Watch, Asner accused the State Department of endorsing the executions of Latin American priests. Responding to the criticism, Elliott Abrams, the assistant secretary of state for inter-American affairs, called Human Rights Watch "unpatriotic" and Amnesty International "un-American."

CBS Evening News reported, "Television's Lou Grant, actor Ed Asner, was in Washington today. He led a group of show-business personalities opposed to President Reagan's policy in El Salvador. And they announced a campaign to raise one million dollars as a donation to Salvadoran rebels."

Speaking at a press conference alongside Ralph Waite of *The Waltons*, Penny Marshall of *Laverne & Shirley*, Howard Hesseman of *WKRP in Cincinnati*, and Oscar-winning actress Lee Grant, Asner said, "Today we want to say clearly to President Reagan in the White House and Secretary Haig in the State Department that their enemies in El Salvador are not our enemies."

"Every liberating force is called Communist," complained Lee Grant. She claimed the Reagan administration was doing "exactly the same thing in El Salvador" that the Soviet Union was doing in Poland, namely, "establishing a military dictatorship."

"I wish to state that he [Asner] does *not* represent my views and I resent being spoken for by him," said a dissenting Anthony Hopkins. "His barking, self-important militancy in the name of liberal causes, righteously sheltering behind the name of the Screen Actors Guild, is chillingly reminiscent of East European political debate."

Bruce Herschensohn, an ally of Senator Jesse Helms, delivered an editorial on KABC television. He called Ed Asner a "very dangerous man who consistently shows he knows little about true liberty or threats to liberty."

Asner's lawyer sent a letter demanding a retraction. Instead, the commentator held up the request and waved it in front of the camera. "This letter was designed to make me be quiet about him," said Herschensohn. "To intimidate me and to have a chilling effect—hardly what you'd expect of the man who portrays Lou Grant, representative of the free press."

A campaign to cancel *Lou Grant* was organized by the Council for Inter-American Security (CIAS). Previously, the CIAS published the "Santa Fe document," described by Washington insiders as the "central building block in the construction of Reagan's foreign policy in Central America."

The CIAS established a front called the Congress of Conservative Contributors with the purpose of discrediting Asner. Their byline proliferated in newspapers around the country.

"Asner wants the world to turn its back on democracy," said one of their planted editorials. "He wants the terrorists to win their bloody war. Those opposing the government are terrorists and Communists. There is no middleground."

A collection of leaflets appeared outside the Screen Actors Guild in Hollywood that said, "Ed Asner is a Communist Swine." An anonymous phone call to SAG said a group of "ultra-patriotic marines" was preparing to kill the actor.

One of the sponsors of *Lou Grant* was Kimberly-Clark, the company that made Kleenex tissues and Huggies diapers. They had factories in El Salvador and relied on local dictators to protect their business interests.

Kimberly-Clark concluded that "Asner's activities concerning El Salvador" were against the "national interest" and they sent a letter to Congressman LeBoutillier: "We are pleased to report to you that we are cancelling all advertising on the Lou Grant Show."

Journalist Bruce R. Miller confirmed, "Owning factories in the wartorn country, Kimberly-Clark didn't appreciate the things Asner had to say about El Salvador's volatile political situation."

Lou Grant was canceled in June 1982. CBS denied it was a political decision. "The program was five years old, it had declining ratings and it didn't seem to show any signs of growth for the next year," said a network executive. "If we could have fixed the show, we would have."

Fans of the show believed the very reason the ratings declined was because of the relentless campaign of the CIAS's Congress of Conservative Contributors. "I regret the lack of support," said Asner. "It allows the

Jerry Falwells, the Kleenex people, and the [Congress] of Conservative Consumers [*sic*] to think they can curb freedom of speech at will. The effect of the schnooks is minimal but they will go about crowing over the fact that they achieved what they set out to do."

★

"From Miami to the Pacific Northwest and from New England to the Lone Star of Texas, the '80s are becoming a decade of censorship," wrote the *Miami News* in April 1983. "Since President Reagan was elected in November 1980, censorship attempts have soared by about 300 per cent . . . The complaints come from all points on the political spectrum, as liberals and conservatives fight ideas they think are dangerous."

There were a reported three hundred attempts to censor textbooks, library books, and public-school courses in 1980. Two years later, the number surpassed one thousand.

"In the late sixties we began to receive complaints that we placed in the category of social complaints—mostly racism and sexism," observed Judith Krug of the American Library Association. "But now they're coming from a different direction, focusing on family and religious issues."

Citizens Organized for Better Schools, an evangelical group in Hawkins County, Tennessee, ambushed the local school board and accused them of spreading "secular humanism." In September 1983, they pressured the library to purge *Cinderella*, *Macbeth*, *Rumpelstiltskin*, *The Wizard of Oz*, and *The Diary of a Young Girl* by Anne Frank.

Jerry Falwell and the Moral Majority declared war on children's author Judy Blume in 1984. Her stories were known for earnest teenage emotion and the books were pulled from school libraries around the country.

"Censorship always grows out of fear," said Blume. "But there isn't anything to be afraid of as long as a parent can talk to his child. I can't argue with the Moral Majority about their views. I can only argue that they can't control the rights of all children."

The Zion Christian Life Center of Minnesota burned fourteen hundred vinyl records that same year. Among those burned in a noxious hellscape were James Brown, the Bee Gees, the Moody Blues, Santana, KISS, the Village People, and the Eagles. The church used their newfound notoriety to recruit new members. A magnetic sign on their lawn read, "We're the ones who burned $11,000 in rock music on TV."

Steve and Danny Peters came to prominence during President Reagan's first year in office. Sibling evangelists from St. Paul, Minnesota, they delivered long sermons about the evils of modern music. Their lectures were typically followed by a record burning. The record burning was typically followed by a sales pitch for their six-dollar cassette tape of anti-rock sermons.

The Peters Brothers claimed Simon & Garfunkel's "Bridge Over Troubled Water" was a "paean to heroin." They claimed KISS was an acronym that stood for "Knights in Satan's Service." And they asked their congregation to boycott Captain & Tennille because the duo believed in karma.

"I believe that this is the largest satanic force in the world," said Danny Peters prior to a record burning. "These rock stars are homosexual, bisexual, perverted and involved in drugs, the occult, witchcraft and satanic worship . . . We burn these items in obedience to Jesus Christ."

The Peters Brothers were profiled frequently in the mainstream press and treated as an amusing freak show. The *Lexington Herald* published a lengthy profile on them in February 1981—and interviewed their mother.

"I remember the day Danny brought home a Beach Boys record," said Mrs. Peters. "I sensed it wasn't Christian. The Beach Boys just had a different message than we were used to in this house. We realized that Satan was all around us. Some mothers complain to me about the burnings . . . Some say it reminds them of the burnings in Nazi Germany. I shouldn't say this, but when we were in high school, we thought Hitler had some pretty good ideas."

The *Minneapolis Tribune* arranged a summit meeting between the Peters Brothers and Gene Simmons of KISS. They published the results in February 1983:

Danny Peters: Why should you be so proud of your sexual antics when you know young people, highly impressionable high school kids, are looking for role models?

Gene Simmons: I obviously think there's nothing wrong with it . . .

Danny Peters: We . . . encourage young people to get rid of this material. Some of them break them, some of them burn them . . . To me it's the same with garbage. If you've got garbage in your house and it stinks, get rid of it. If you have stuff in your house that you see no value in, get rid of it. What we're trying to do now, Gene, is to get people to stop listening to you, and instead of buying your records, we're encouraging them to buy guys like Joe English or B.J. Thomas . . .

Gene Simmons: But Dan, they're not cool.

The Peters Brothers were the most notorious of the modern record burners, but there were others throughout the United States.

The Assembly of God Church in Keokuk, Iowa, staged a record burning in March 1981. Church members "lashed out" at the Carpenters, Perry Como, John Denver, Anne Murray, Charlie Rich, Neil Sedaka, the Four Seasons, and the Beach Boys. They smashed their LPs, burned the cardboard covers, and sang hymns around the molten heap.

The Parkdale Baptist Church in Gastonia, North Carolina, staged a record burning in May 1981. "Rock n' roll stars stand for what's ungodly," said the church leader. "The men are wrong, the methods are wrong, and the music is wrong." They burned a pile of 1970s Elvis records and *Red Headed Stranger* by Willie Nelson.

The Religious News Service listed twenty-two "publicized record burnings" in seventeen states between 1982 and 1983. They qualified that the number probably reflected only "one-tenth" of the record burnings in America.

In April 1983, the Santiam Chapel in Lyons, Oregon, burned a collection of Disney "See and Hear" read-along books and records including *Cinderella*, *Peter and the Wolf*, and *Peter Pan*. For no particular reason, they added Jan & Dean's *Surf City* to the fire. Prior to the burning, evangelist Penny Baker said Mickey Mouse encouraged satanic practices in "The Sorcerer's Apprentice," a "See and Hear" record based on *Fantasia*. She criticized the movie *E.T. the Extra-Terrestrial* for "promoting levitation," dismissed *The Love Boat* as the "lust" boat, and called *Laverne & Shirley* "a little perverted."

Nebraska's *Lincoln Star* reported on another record burning that torched everything "from Abba to Zappa." Frank Zappa was fascinated, horrified, and bemused. The rock-music legend was a widely respected cult icon, one of the best guitar players in America, and an accomplished composer. He believed anti-rock hysteria was due to a new television phenomenon: televangelism.

"With the proliferation of video religion in the United States," said Zappa, "and all these fundamentalist organizations gathering up millions of dollars, you're looking at a whole nation full of potential mutants who could be very harmful."

Culture warriors didn't just criticize the music. They accused record labels of including satanic messages that could be heard if records were played backward. Senator Phillip Wyman of Tehachapi, California, claimed there were backward satanic messages on "Snowblind" by Styx and introduced a new law to stop them.

"What the bill would require is a warning," said Senator Wyman, "and this is what it would say: Warning: This record contains backward masking which may be perceptible at a subliminal level when the record is played forward."

James Young of Styx said, "We have never done anything with satanic messages. The whole idea of backward satanic messages is just a bunch of rubbish."

Pastor Jim Brown of the Psalms Ministry in Ironton, Ohio, held a mass burning of *Television's Greatest Hits*, a double album featuring classic theme songs. Pastor Brown claimed that if you reversed one of the theme songs, you could hear Satan himself say, "The source is the devil." The theme song was *Mister Ed*.

13

PUNK ROCK, FRANK ZAPPA, AND THE PMRC

An organization called Back in Control published a twenty-page manual titled *Punk Rock and Heavy Metal: The Problem*, in which they blamed Van Halen, Rush, and the magazine *Hit Parader* for America's supposed decline. Its author was Sergeant Shelton of the Union City Police Department, and he encouraged police officers to use it as a guide for harassing punk and metal concerts.

"You should be concerned over the influence of punk music on your boys," warned advice columnist William D. Brown in 1980. "This latest craze is not only different, something each succeeding generation is called upon to accept, but dangerous in its encouragement of violence . . . Refuse your sons permission to attend punk concerts. You can cast your vote against this reprehensible behavior from the punk music stars by refusing to let your young patronize these happenings described as concerts."

Jazz music, rock music, and now punk. The jitterbug, the twist, and now slam dancing. In each era, young people were blamed by old people for the world going to shit—the very same old people who, when they were young, had been blamed for the same thing.

"To try and write something constructive and positive about punk rock is almost impossible," wrote a music critic in the *South Bend Tribune*. "It's tasteless, talentless and senseless."

MCA Records was set to distribute the Black Flag album *Damaged* until an executive named Al Bergamo intervened. "As a parent with two children, I found it an anti-parent record," he said. "I listened to it all last weekend and it just didn't seem to have any redeeming social value. It certainly wasn't like Bob Dylan or Simon and Garfunkel."

Police temporarily banned punk shows in Baltimore in 1979 because they incited "defecation, fornication and urination." A member of the Vile-tones was arrested in Toronto in 1980 for possessing "a restricted weapon" because he wore a studded collar around his neck.

Undercover police stormed a Milwaukee performance of the Plasmatics in January 1981. Unidentified in plainclothes, the police fought lead singer Wendy O. Williams, who had mistaken them for drunken maniacs storm-ing the stage. When the police began groping her breasts, the Plasmatics' manager, Rod Swenson, intervened. He was beaten to the ground and arrested for "assault on an officer." Williams was charged with "making obscene gestures with a sledge hammer."

"I was so shocked," said Williams. "I turned around to defend myself because I thought I was being sexually assaulted."

She accused the police department of employing "sickies and sadists who hide behind badges to commit crimes against the people . . . My act is not obscene. The obscenity was from the police department here."

Williams told the press, "I was brutally beaten up behind the club . . . Police told me they had seen me on [the ABC television series] *Fridays* the night before and they thought I was an incarnate of the devil. They were waiting there for me. They attacked me and beat me unconscious. They didn't like me because my band was made up of '[N-words]' and 'queers.' That's what they said!"

The Plasmatics were also raided in Cleveland where the police arrested Williams for a "sado-masochistic dance using the microphone." At the subsequent trial, the prosecuting attorney played a Plasmatics music video as evidence of obscenity, but the strategy backfired and the jury acquitted her of all charges.

MTV was dropped from cable packages around the country in 1984 as regional church groups applied political pressure. The elderly wanted censorship. Teenagers wanted their MTV.

A church leader from Hindman, Kentucky, persuaded the local cable company to block MTV after determining it was "not the kind of thing that adds to a community's moral standards." A Hindman high school student complained, "It's all because of the older people around here. One teacher said it promotes Communism."

Access to MTV was blocked at a Mormon student-housing complex in Provo, Utah. The Associated Press quoted a Mormon bishop who claimed MTV promoted "sex, drugs, witchcraft and the bizarre." Angry students draped a large banner over their balcony: "Give Me MTV or Give Me Death." The manager of the building said they would have to choose death, because if you looked at MTV "there are lesbians making love, there is witch-craft, there is sado-masochism."

Frank Zappa warned people about the influence evangelical fundamentalists were having on American politics. "There's a strong possibility that this country is moving in the direction of a fascist theocracy," said Zappa. "Now maybe you feel it is far-fetched that if the extreme elements of the fundamentalist right have political power, that it could come to that. Just remember: they were bombing abortion clinics a little while ago."

The tireless work of Paul Weyrich through his creations ALEC, the Heritage Foundation, and the Moral Majority made it possible. Zappa observed, "The whole business being so tied to . . . vast quantities of money spent behind the scenes . . . and everybody who is involved in politics owing his life to some mysterious unknown force. These forces eventually are going to win out."

★

Zappa was drafted into the Culture War when a group of connected Washington women, many of whom were married to lobbyists and politicians, declared war on modern music.

Tipper Gore, the wife of Tennessee senator Al Gore, founded the Parents Music Resource Center (PMRC) in 1985. "Around that time, my two younger daughters, ages six and eight, began asking me about things they had seen on MTV," said Tipper. "These images frightened my children; They frightened *me*!"

The PMRC included Pam Howar, the wife of a DC real estate mogul; Susan Baker, the wife of Secretary of the Treasury James Baker; Georgia Packwood, the wife of scandalized Senator Bob Packwood; Nancy Thurmond, the wife of segregationist Strom Thurmond; and Sheila Walsh, who cohosted a program with televangelist Pat Robertson.

The PMRC blamed the recording industry for America's woes. Gore said heavy metal was responsible for "devil worship and the occult, sadistic sex, murder, rape, and suicide." As head of the PMRC, she warned parents of records by Cyndi Lauper, Twisted Sister, and Madonna. Gore said an album by Prince left her "appalled and disgusted." Susan Baker said the songs of Sheena Easton were a "contributing factor" in teen suicides. They singled out music videos by Def Leppard, Billy Idol, and Tom Petty.

The PMRC suggested warning stickers on records. They wanted an *X* for sexual lyrics, *D/A* for references to drugs and alcohol, and an *O* for lyrics concerning the occult. Gore asked, "If we have decided it is not in the best interest of society to allow children into X-rated bookstores, why should they be subjected to hard-core porn in the local record shop?"

The PMRC tried to connect Pink Floyd's *The Wall* with a real-life murder. "This woman told me that in the summer of 1980, her sixteen-year-old son went into a trancelike state on a very hot summer night," said Gore. "He was listening to Pink Floyd's album *The Wall* . . . His aunt was asleep on the couch in front of the TV set, which was beaming a violent episode of 'Starsky and Hutch.' . . . The boy suddenly stabbed his aunt to death."

Gore even criticized the names of modern rock bands. "The names of some of these bands imply a fascination with violence and evil," she said. "Venom, The Dead Kennedys, Suicidal Tendencies . . . Judas Priest, Iron Maiden, Warlord, Metallica . . . these heavy metal and punk rock bands make violence, explicit sex, and the power of evil central themes."

Gore claimed the PMRC campaign was "the direct opposite of censorship," but political allies like South Carolina senator Fritz Hollings proposed government intervention if the aforementioned bands were played on the radio.

The PMRC expanded their target to include role-playing games. Gore said Dungeons & Dragons was responsible for "nearly fifty teenage suicides and homicides." She suggested a remedy for parents whose children refused to give up Dungeons & Dragons. "Consider adopting the 'tough love' approach, as depicted in one episode of 'The Cosby Show.' What a great message."

The PMRC was endorsed by James Dobson's Focus on the Family. Focus on the Family opposed sex before marriage, endorsed conversion therapy, and rejected the theory of evolution. The PMRC used Focus on the Family as a source in the reports they issued about rock 'n' roll. Susan Baker sat on the Focus on the Family board of directors.

Other supplemental research was provided by the Victory Christian Church of St. Charles, Missouri. They prepared a rock music research packet in which they denied the Holocaust, condemned Hollywood's "race-mixing," referred to Martin "Lucifer" King, and accused Bruce Springsteen of singing in satanic code.

The PMRC sponsored a senate hearing about lyrics and music videos. Held in September 1985, the hearing was endorsed by only two music industry notables: Mike Love of the Beach Boys and Smokey Robinson of Motown fame. Everyone else rejected the PMRC, including Hall & Oates, John Cougar Mellencamp, the Pointer Sisters, and Donny Osmond. As a child star, his group, the Osmonds, was banned in South Africa for being "drug oriented."

An obscure pastor named Jeff Ling was one of the first to testify. He told the senate committee that Twisted Sister's music video for "We're Not Gonna Take It" was causing chaos in American homes. Ling set up a slideshow to illustrate his testimony, but when the slide projector jammed, the hearing was brought to a halt.

Frank Zappa said the PMRC's arguments were "totally without merit, based on a hodge-podge of fundamentalist frogwash and illogical conclusions." He was the first rock star to testify at the hearing:

Frank Zappa: No one has forced Mrs. Baker or Mrs. Gore to bring Prince or Sheena Easton into their homes . . . they are free to buy other forms of music . . . Bad facts make bad law, and people who write bad laws are, in my opinion, more dangerous than songwriters who celebrate sexuality . . .

Senator Slade Gorton: Mr. Zappa . . . I can only say that I found your statement to be boorish, incredibly and insensitively insulting . . . You could manage to give the First Amendment to the Constitution of the United States a bad name if I felt that you had the slightest understanding of it . . .

Senator Al Gore: I found your [Zappa's] statement very interesting and let me say, although I disagree with some of the statements that you make, and have made on other occasions, I have been a fan of your music, believe it or not. I respect you as a true original and a tremendously talented musician . . . I guess the . . . statement I want to get from you is whether or not you feel that the concern is legitimate.

Frank Zappa: There are too many things that look like hidden agendas . . . I've got four children . . . I want them to grow up in a country where they can think what they want to think, be what they want to be, and not what somebody's wife or somebody in government makes them be . . .

Senator J. James Exon: Mr. Zappa, let me say that I was surprised that Senator Gore knew and liked your music. I must confess that I have never heard any of your music . . .

Frank Zappa: I would be more than happy to recite my lyrics to you.

Senator J. James Exon: Can we forgo that?

Senator Al Gore: You have probably never heard of the Mothers of Invention.

Senator J. James Exon: I have heard of Glenn Miller and Mitch Miller. Did you ever perform with them?

Frank Zappa: As a matter of fact, I took music lessons in grade school from Mitch Miller's brother.

Senator J. James Exon: That is the first sign of hope we have had in this hearing . . .

Congresswoman Paula Hawkins: Mr. Zappa, you say you have four children?

Frank Zappa: Yes, four children.

Congresswoman Paula Hawkins: Have you ever purchased toys for those children?

Frank Zappa: No, my wife does.

Congresswoman Paula Hawkins: Well, I might tell you that if you were to go in a toy store . . . look on the box . . . the box says: this is suitable for five to seven years of age . . . to give you some guidance for a toy for a child. Do you object to that?

Frank Zappa: In a way I do, because that means that somebody in an office some place is making a decision about how smart my child is.

Congresswoman Paula Hawkins: I would be interested to see what toys your kids ever had.

Frank Zappa: Why would you be interested?

Congresswoman Paula Hawkins: Just as a point of interest.

Frank Zappa: Well, come on over to the house. I will show them to you.

Next to testify was singer-songwriter John Denver—a huge mainstream star. Denver's music had a family-friendly reputation and because of that, his testimony had a great deal of impact. He told an anecdote about how one of his songs was defamed by culture warriors in the 1970s.

John Denver: I've had my experience . . . with this sort of censorship. My song "Rocky Mountain High" was banned from many radio stations as a drug-related song. This was obviously done by people who had never seen or been to the Rocky Mountains . . . Mr. Chairman, what assurance have I that any national panel to review my music would make any better judgment? . . . Mr. Chairman, the suppression of the people of a society begins, in my mind, with the censorship of the written or spoken word. It was so in Nazi Germany . . .

Senator Fritz Hollings: . . . They are not all clean-cut John Denvers . . . I think that the . . . atmosphere developing in this particular hearing [is] that the committee is on trial . . . rather [than] back to the original problem: filth, pornography, suicide, all of this other stuff coming out of these records . . .

John Denver: What most concerns me aside from potential legislation . . . is that the whole presentation made by the PMRC comes from . . . a foundation of fear . . . the small percentage of records we're discussing here today, compared to the 125,000 songs that are released every year, is miniscule and is not going to affect our children . . .

Dee Snider's testimony followed. He accused Tipper Gore of misrepresenting Twisted Sister.

Dee Snider: Ms. Gore claimed that one of my songs, "Under the Blade," had lyrics encouraging sadomasochism, bondage, and rape. The lyrics she quoted have absolutely nothing to do with these topics . . . As the creator of "Under the Blade," I can say categorically that the only sadomasochism, bondage, and rape in this song is in the mind of Ms. Gore . . .

The hearings were a media sensation. Frank Zappa fielded hundreds of interviews over the next sixteen months. He criticized the PMRC on the *Tonight Show*, *Nightline*, and *Crossfire*.

"Now, it seems to me that there are a couple of forces at work in American society," said Zappa. "Those two major forces would be the advertising industry and the Republican Party. They have a vested interest in bad schools because the dumber people are, the easier it is for them to work their special magic on the electorate . . . This economy will only work if people are kept sub-stupid and are kept paranoid to the point they will continually invest in weapons."

During a CBS interview, Zappa accused the evangelical movement of being a greater inciter to violence than those they accused of doing the same.

"I think it's inherent in the Christian religion, especially in the fundamentalist branches of it, when they're preaching that fire and brimstone," said Zappa. "So much hate is developed that you take an unstable personality, expose them to that kind of hate, and that kind of rabble rousing, and it causes people to go out and commit violent crimes."

The PMRC did not get everything it wanted, but it scored a victory with the concession of the black-and-white Parental Advisory sticker. Seventy-five albums received a sticker during its initial rollout, including a reissue of 1940s blues music by Sonny Boy Williamson. And while Gore insisted it was a great alternative to censorship, its effects on sales were immediate. Any album with a Parental Advisory sticker was dropped by major chains like Sears and JCPenney.

★

Reverend Don Wildmon returned to oppose a "tide of filth" on American television, including *ALF*; *Murder, She Wrote*; *Perfect Strangers*; and *The Facts of Life*.

"We are in the middle of a spiritual battle," said Wildmon, "that will determine the very destiny of western civilization."

Wildmon's National Federation for Decency joined with the Moral Majority in a campaign to banish *Playboy* and *Penthouse* from the magazine sections of 7-Eleven stores. A protest held in front of the Southland Corporation, the parent company of 7-Eleven, featured speeches by Wildmon and Jerry Falwell. According to Falwell, 7-Eleven was "poisoning" America while Reverend Wildmon said the store fomented "rape and child molestation." Protesters released three thousand helium balloons decorated with the words "No Porn."

Reverend Wildmon was busy. He went after the trading-card phenomenon known as the Garbage Pail Kids (cocreated by cartoonist Art Spiegelman). He convinced CBS to cancel *The New Adventures of Mighty Mouse* because, he claimed, it promoted cocaine use. And he appeared on dozens of news programs criticizing a major motion picture, leading to protests, boycotts, bomb threats, and a full-blown terrorist attack.

★

The Last Temptation of Christ was based on a novel by Nikos Kazantzakis. The premise had Jesus hallucinating on the cross, wondering what life would have been like had he abandoned godliness for a normal human life.

Simon & Schuster published the first English edition in 1960. It was released without much controversy until the Arcadia, California, branch of the John Birch Society demanded its removal. The Birchers of Arcadia formed the Citizens Committee for Clean Books. Their full-page ad in the *Arcadia Tribune* asked, "Are There Any Books Vile Enough Not To Be Acceptable To Our Library?"

The book was optioned by Paramount in 1983, with Martin Scorsese scheduled to direct, but it was quickly aborted. "The Moral Majority picketed Gulf and Western, which owns Paramount," recalled Scorsese, "and the film was dead."

The project was resurrected by Universal in 1986, filmed in 1987, and released in 1988. The Moral Majority ran a campaign to whip up anger and denounce Hollywood as the capital of satanic immorality. Sixty years after the Fatty Arbuckle scandal, the fire-and-brimstone scapegoating of Hollywood remained intact.

"This is Hollywood's darkest hour," said Jerry Falwell. "If we don't speak out, anything goes."

Falwell called for a boycott of all Universal properties including MCA, Motown Records, Universal Studios, G. P. Putnam publishing, and the Universal Amphitheater in Yosemite National Park.

Falwell intended to use the Moral Majority to drive Scorsese's film "out of existence." He predicted, "We're going to bruise him so badly that others are going to pull back and let him die alone."

The Reverend Don Wildmon called *The Last Temptation of Christ* "the most perverted, distorted account of the historical and biblical Jesus I have ever read." He blamed the "pagan" thinking of the "Hollywood elite" and called MCA Universal "a company whose decision-making body is dominated by non-Christians."

MCA Universal's president, Lew Wasserman, was one of the country's leading Jewish businessmen, and Wildmon's statement was widely characterized as anti-Semitic. The Tabernacle Baptist Church of South Los Angeles, an organization that ran an "outreach program" to convert Jews to Christianity, held protest signs in front of Wasserman's house that read, "Wasserman Fans Hatred Toward the Jews" and "Wasserman Endangers Israel." Jerry Falwell said Universal had only itself to blame if there was a "wave of anti-Semitism in this country."

Universal executive Tom Pollock was amazed by the amount of hate mail he received. "Of course, a sizable percentage of them were anti-Semitic hate mail," said Pollock. "Lots of them were death threats. You know, you're going to die, you stupid ignorant Jewish scum."

Universal installed an x-ray machine in the mailroom to check for razors, chemicals, and explosives. The FBI discovered a plot by the Aryan Nations to assassinate Pollock, Wasserman, and fellow executive Sidney Sheinberg.

"It was scary not only for us, but for our children and our families," said Sheinberg. "Bloody pigs were delivered to my house. A dead pig delivered in a package. There were pictures taken of my beach house from the top with telephoto lenses and sent in the mail, saying, 'You may think we don't know where you are at all times, but we always know where you are.'"

Oscar-winning director Franco Zeffirelli reportedly called *The Last Temptation of Christ* a product of the "Jewish cultural scum of Los Angeles which is always spoiling for a chance to attack the Christian world." Zeffirelli later claimed he was misquoted, but he reiterated that it was a "truly horrible and completely deranged" motion picture and asked the Venice Film Festival to ban it. He also confessed that he had not seen the film. Ten years earlier, Zeffirelli had directed a TV miniseries called *Jesus of Nazareth*. He was accused by Protestant ministers of making "a film about Jesus the Man rather than Jesus the God." Zeffirelli was furious that they had condemned his movie "without having seen it."

Reverend Don Wildmon denied there was anything anti-Semitic about the protests, pointing out that they had the support of the Jewish Defense League.

"I was in Los Angeles two weeks ago," said Reverend Wildmon. "Man by the name of Irv Rubin met with me. He's head of the Jewish Defense League in LA. We got together and we talked." Rubin was later jailed for trying to bomb a Culver City mosque.

A huge protest was held in front of the Universal office tower in August 1988. Fifteen thousand people listened to a pro-censorship speech delivered by Dennis Prager, a radio host connected to the Heritage Foundation.

The Last Temptation of Christ opened in Los Angeles, New York, and Chicago. Theater operators in each city received death threats. Security guards were hired to chaperone film prints to and from each venue. Regular sweeps for explosives were paid for by Universal. Some theaters hired their own private security and billed Universal for the expense.

"I can recall areas where we did a tremendous gross," said a Cineplex Odeon theater executive, "and we didn't make a penny because security just ate us alive."

In Paris, a far-right group entered a screening of *The Last Temptation of Christ* at the Saint-Michel theater, attacked a projectionist, and set the building on fire. Ten patrons were injured, and one fell into a coma.

"The situation degraded over the weekend," wrote film critic Thomas R. Lindlof. "In theaters across the country, protesters ripped up and poured acid on seats in theaters, tore movie screens, ransacked foyers and lobbies, threatened employees with physical injury, and called in threats that led to dozens of theaters being evacuated . . . In Marseilles and Lyon, Catholic extremists fired tear gas into theater lobbies and set off stink bombs in the auditoriums, forcing the patrons out into the street, where they were pelted with eggs and pummeled. In Avignon, four moviegoers broke into the projection booth, ripped the film from its reels, and destroyed it. In the town of Besançon, a firebomb ignited a blaze . . ."

Pat Buchanan published an editorial about *The Last Temptation of Christ* titled "Is It Art or Sleaze?":

"We live in an age where the ridicule of blacks is forbidden, where anti-Semitism is punishable by political death, but where Christian-bashing is a popular indoor sport. The reason Universal Pictures and Mr. Scorsese are doing this is because they know they can get away with it."

The controversy frustrated fellow Christians who felt it harmed the reputation of Christianity. Lutheran pastor Charles Bergstrom said, "If the film offends Jerry Falwell's theology it is certainly his right to say so. But he is wrong to suggest that his theology represents the only or true Christian theology." Bergstrom dismissed the Moral Majority as "a narrow group of extremists claiming falsely to represent Christianity."

14

EDDIE MURPHY, SAM KINISON, ANDREW DICE CLAY, AND THEIR HATERS

"Comedy has gotten out of hand in recent years," said Martha Raye, an enormously successful comedian of the 1940s. "The so-called funny people today can't be funny unless they're putting down our government or an ethnic group with dirty, filthy language. Eddie Murphy, Steve Martin, George Carlin—I can't stand any of them."

In the 1980s, Martha Raye was a spokesperson for Polident denture cleaner. Her television commercials featured an onscreen caption that read, "Martha Raye, Denture Wearer." On an episode of *Late Night with David Letterman,* the host joked, "I saw the most terrifying commercial on television last night. Martha Raye: Actress, Condom User."

Raye filed a lawsuit for ten million dollars. She claimed David Letterman "defamed her character" by inferring she "was sexually promiscuous, had loose morals and had frequent sexual intercourse with people she believed to be infected with or exposed to the AIDS virus." Her legal counsel set the record straight: "Ms. Raye, in fact, is *not* a condom user."

Old comedians felt alienated by young comedians.

"I don't think show business can afford comedians who have to use four-letter words to get a laugh," said the elderly Red Skelton. "Sure there's freedom of speech, but why trample it?"

Swearing divided the generations.

"Those four-letter words keep pouring out on the cable stations," complained Lucille Ball. "Inexcusable. Why should we glorify that by watching it? How can we stop it? It's making money, and as long as they're making a buck they don't seem to care. Nobody cares anymore!"

★

Comedian Buddy Hackett first became famous with his Chinese waiter routine. Throughout the 1950s, he used an elastic band to pull his eyes back and spoke in pidgin English, suggesting menu items from "Corumn A" or "Corumn B." It was the basis for his bestselling album *How You Do?* and he performed it on popular programs like *The Steve Allen Show*, *The Ed Sullivan Show*, and the *Tonight Show*. Hackett even reportedly planned a chain of Chinese American restaurants to be named "Buddy Hackett presents the Chinese Waiter." A letter to the editor asked, "Is Buddy Hackett part Chinese?" It was an honest query from a viewer who seldom saw an Asian person on the screen.

As the years went by, the crowds kept calling out, "Chinese waiter! Chinese waiter!" but Hackett grew tired of it. "I don't use the Chinese waiter routine anymore," he said. "Humor has changed."

KTLA television personality Tom Hatten thought it was a shame and brought it up during a 1985 interview. "[The] Chinese waiter routine . . . You can't do it anymore, huh?"

"I just think that nowadays the world is very touchy about stuff like that," said Hackett. "I think a Chinese person could do it. I don't think I could do it."

★

Bob Hope got in trouble in the summer of 1986. Attendees of the Liberty Weekend gala were treated to dinner on a yacht, fireworks along the New York harbor, and a private Bob Hope performance.

"Have you heard?" Hope asked the crowd. "The Statue of Liberty has AIDS. Nobody knows if she got it from the mouth of the Hudson or the Staten Island Ferry."

"Those who did not groan in embarrassment sat silent in dismay," reported the *Los Angeles Times*. "Hope's 'joke' was worse than obscene . . . It is both sad and shameful that a man who many have considered a national treasure should think it would be funny to besmirch Miss Liberty on her 100th birthday with the kind of glibness and vulgarity that, in truth, only brings discredit to him in the evening of his years as an entertainer."

A letter to the editor disagreed: "Bob Hope did not speak indecent language and he is not a vulgar gentleman. It is men like Bob Hope who make our country great. He is above criticism whatsoever."

Hope issued an apology, and he made amends by hosting a series of AIDS benefits with his good friend Elizabeth Taylor. And then he went one step further.

"In what appears to be a gallant effort to make amends for his Liberty-AIDS joke," reported columnist Herb Caen, "Bob Hope has agreed to come out strong against Lyndon LaRouche's initiative, Prop 64."

Lyndon LaRouche was a perpetual third-party candidate who promised to rid America of "evil leftists, liberals, environmentalists, and Zionists." Prop 64 suggested that all HIV-positive employees be fired from their jobs. The proposition was endorsed by Congressman William E. Dannemeyer, a politician who wanted to censor *The Last Temptation of Christ*.

Dannemeyer was connected to Paul Weyrich's Free Congress Foundation, which had a solution for the AIDS crisis. It said the epidemic could be ended overnight by "reintroducing and enforcing anti-sodomy laws."

Meanwhile, in the wake of the Bob Hope controversy, city leaders in West Hollywood and San Francisco proposed a ban on "all AIDS-related jokes." Comedians felt it was one of the dumbest suggestions ever made.

"How can you legislate poor taste?" asked comedian-turned-politician Tom Ammiano. "Homophobic and f*g jokes have always been around."

The *San Francisco Examiner* reported, "Attorneys representing the two cities, which have laws to protect AIDS patients and homosexuals from discrimination, say that in certain circumstances telling AIDS jokes would be illegal."

★

Eddie Murphy was the biggest stand-up comedy star of the 1980s. The opening track on his very first comedy record, made when he was just twenty-one years old, was applauded by fans, but later made him cringe.

The routine opened:

"You be playing with your friends, y'know? Driving around, guys, y'know, you see a f*ggot on the street. You pull up in the car and say, 'Hey, f*ggot! Hey you, f*ggot ass! F*ggot ass, f*ggot!' You forget that this f*ggot is a *guy*, man. They'll kick your ass. That's some embarrassing shit, to get beat up by a f*ggot."

Dressed in a red leather suit a year later, Eddie Murphy opened his HBO special *Delirious* with a similar bit:

"I've got some rules. Straight up. F*ggots aren't allowed to look at my ass while I'm onstage. That's why I keep moving. You don't know where the f*ggot section is, so you keep moving."

He also talked about AIDS:

"AIDS is scary because it kills motherfuckers. AIDS! . . . It petrifies me because girls be hanging out with them. One night they could be in the club having fun with their gay friend, give them a little kiss. And go home with AIDS on their lips!"

A record store in San Francisco removed every Eddie Murphy record and VHS tape from its shelves. "Murphy is basically trying to cause hysteria about AIDS," said the store owner. "I've been in the record business for 20 years, and I've never done anything like this. I hate to do anything that seems like censorship, but what Murphy says is not satire, it's a bad thing . . . There's already too much misinformation about AIDS circulating to the general public without a well-known comedian like Murphy making things worse."

A year passed. Protest came and went. Murphy told a huge crowd in Dallas, Texas, in May 1985, "I did jokes about homosexuals last year. The f*ggots went crazy. If you see any f*ggots picketing outside my show, take the sign and beat their ass with it."

Similar subject matter caused a similar reaction to Sam Kinison, the most bombastic comedian of the decade. Kinison upset "safe sex" advocates with his 1988 comedy album *Have You Seen Me Lately?*

"Safe sex—goddamn these fucking bastards," joked Kinison. "Get off of our back! Because a few f*gs fucked some monkeys? They got so bored, their own assholes weren't enough, they had to go in the fucking *jungle*, grab some fucking monkey, and fuck him in the ass—and bring us back the black plague of the 1980s! Thanks, guys! Because of this shit, they want us to wear fucking rubbers."

When he went on a seventy-city tour in 1989, protesters marched. The *Palm Beach Post* reported on the scene at the West Palm Beach Auditorium:

"As the demonstrators lined the curb in front of the auditorium, they distributed fliers detailing facts about AIDS. Attached to the fliers were blue-wrapped condoms. Most fans attending the performance either ignored the protesters or politely accepted the information."

The *St. Louis Post-Dispatch* chronicled Kinison's gig at the Westport Country Playhouse in Connecticut: "Nearly a dozen AIDS activists picketed Saturday night and claimed that comedian Sam Kinison is sexist, prejudiced toward homosexuals and spreads lies about AIDS."

At a gig in Vancouver, protesters accused Kinison of being "sexist, racist and homophobic." One of those picketing said, "He promotes negative stereotypes against historically disadvantaged groups who don't have much power in society."

The Associated Press reported on a scuffle in Minneapolis: "A performance by comedian Sam Kinison provoked a confrontation between fans and a group of gay and AIDS activists . . . Some fans made obscene gestures and shouted epithets at protesters, and set several of their leaflets ablaze. One picket and a Kinison fan scuffled briefly before university police separated them."

"I think those protesters are embarrassing themselves," said a Kinison fan. "They're taking Kinison way too seriously. He's just a comedian."

Kinison was considered a groundbreaker by many, but some notable comedians didn't like his act.

"They say Sam's comedy is vanguard," said Roseanne Barr. "It's not—it's retro, life-hating, reactionary jive. I got into comedy to counterattack the guys whose whole acts were about homosexual rape or racism. Who cares about the half-baked droolings of that hallucinated toad."

Stand-up comic Bobcat Goldthwait was often confused for Kinison—much to his annoyance. "I'm the one that's not threatened by foreigners or vaginas," said Bobcat. "I'm the one who was not a misogynistic bully."

Kinison was on the defensive when a July 1990 issue of *People* published lurid details about a Sunset Strip scandal that invoked his name.

"For years, primal-scream comedian Sam Kinison has built his act on the elements of psychic terror and sexual violence," wrote *People*. "On the morning of June 21, the themes of his comedy hit Kinison where he lives, and there were no laughs. His dancer girlfriend of two years, Malika Souiri, 25, claims she was raped by Kinison's newly hired bodyguard, Unway Carter, 22, while the comic slept off a long, hard night of drink in another part of his spacious L.A. home . . . On Saturday he performed in Anaheim. Protesters marched in front of the theater, carrying signs opposing the misogynistic rage of Kinison's act. He has made no immediate comment about the alleged rape. Nor did he get in touch with Souiri, who was staying at her mother's, for several days after the incident." As part of the fallout, Kinison was banned from the *Tonight Show* indefinitely.

An all-comedy issue of the *LA Weekly* published in January 1987 said there was more freedom of speech in stand-up than ever before, but also a "disturbing and reactionary trend" featured "within these freedoms [of] male comics who engage in metaphorical but vicious gay-bashing and women battering with seemingly tacit entertainment-industry support." The publication asked a new comedian named Andrew Dice Clay why he chose the subject matter that he did. "Because the audience loves it," he explained.

Wearing a twenty-dollar leather jacket purchased from JCPenney, Andrew Dice Clay adopted the persona of a Brooklyn street tough. He got his first professional bookings in Lake Tahoe in a room booked by Buddy Hackett's son. By day he filmed low-budget sex comedies like *Wacko* and *Private Resort*. By night he brooded onstage at the Comedy Store. "It's not gonna work, Andrew," warned club owner Mitzi Shore. "That character is too tough, too hard-core."

Rodney Dangerfield liked him and helped him secure a spot on the *Young Comedians Special* on HBO in early 1988. The high-profile gig led to more work, and Clay was hired to appear at a Beverly Hills charity banquet. The audience was full of older luminaries including Jack Lemmon, Aaron Spelling, and Sidney Poitier. Instead of tailoring his material to suit the old-fashioned crowd, Clay overwhelmed them with his filthiest material. Emcee Carl Reiner returned to the microphone when Clay finished.

"I don't know what just went on here," said Reiner, "but I'm looking at a bunch of old farts who are laughing—really laughing—for the first time in twenty years. In this room tonight, right before your very eyes, Andrew Dice Clay has become a star."

Clay was signed to Geffen Records, where the roster included Guns N' Roses and Aerosmith. His stand-up persona, like Sam Kinison, embodied the rock star lifestyle. With his connections to the Sunset Strip rock scene, it seemed fitting that Clay was asked to present at the MTV Video Music Awards in 1990.

Clay appeared in a zebra-striped jacket and recited dirty nursery rhymes about Little Boy Blue and Little Miss Muffet. He then went into another dirty rhyme that wasn't cleared ahead of time: "Jack Spratt could eat no fat, his wife could eat no lean. So Jack ignored her flabby tits and licked her asshole clean. Oh!"

MTV was agitated by the insubordination. MTV executive Barry Kluger said, "Andrew Dice Clay did not do this in rehearsal and we were very surprised by it. Based on this experience, Andrew Dice Clay will not be appearing on MTV in the future."

"I felt that MTV can get fucked," said Clay. "Those [music] videos are pushing the line as hard as they fuckin' can with tits and ass. Michael Jackson is grabbing his dick, and Madonna is practically grabbing her pussy. MTV is all about raunchy rock and roll. But if a comic gets on there with some raunchy rock-and-roll humor, that's no good?"

Andrew Dice Clay was enormously popular, and comedians were asked to comment on the phenomenon in nearly every interview.

Comedian Richard Belzer said Clay performed "brownshirt humor" that pandered "to the worst instincts of humanity." Comedy star Bill Murray said, "I think that's just something he's going through. I would predict that he will be a successful actor who will not be doing that act for the rest of his life." The ancient comedian Henny Youngman concluded, "What he needs is an act. Andrew Dice Clay, you're wrong if you think poking fun at helpless people makes you a comedian. My second opinion is that your jokes aren't jokes—they're ugliness."

Larry King asked George Carlin his opinion on a 1990 episode of *Larry King Live*. "The thing that I find unusual, and, y'know, it's not a criticism so much, but his targets are underdogs," said Carlin. "And comedy traditionally has picked on people in power, people who abuse their power . . . Women and gays and immigrants, are kind of, to my way of thinking, underdogs . . . I think his core audience are young white males who are threatened by these groups. I think a lot these guys aren't sure of their manhood. Women who assert themselves and are competent are a threat to these men . . . I think that's what is at the core of that experience that takes place in these arenas . . . a certain sharing of anger and rage at these targets."

Country music legend Johnny Cash was appalled by Andrew Dice Clay's popularity. "There is an undercurrent of violence in this new obscenity," said Cash. "It will shatter the hopes and dreams of many who hoped and prayed for brotherhood and racial tolerance."

Clay's publicist said the reason American soldiers were fighting in the Gulf War was to defend his stand-up act:

"If you don't want to come, you shouldn't come, but the ability for people to watch what they want to watch is one of things that is animating our soldiers 7,000 miles from home."

Clay insisted that the things he said onstage were merely a character and not indicative of his own feelings.

"If the press didn't understand that the Diceman was a character who amplified certain attitudes that millions of people had," said Clay, "not only amplified those attitudes but actually made fun of those attitudes by making fun of himself—then the press had its head up its ass."

He was asked to host *Saturday Night Live* in 1990. Cast member Nora Dunn and musical guest Sinead O'Connor both withdrew. Protesters filled the lobby of 30 Rockefeller Plaza and two gained access to the *SNL* dress rehearsal, sabotaging Clay's opening monologue with shouts of "Clay, Clay, go away."

Protests followed him around the country. Scheduled to perform at the Starplex Amphitheater in Dallas, local politicians threatened legal action if he went through with it. The district attorney of Dallas County warned the comedian that "obscenity laws in Texas were very much alive and would be enforced if any performer crossed them."

Texas was one of the last states enforcing obscenity laws. The group 2 Live Crew had recently been prosecuted for a Texas engagement and comedy team Bowley & Wilson were arrested at a Dallas comedy club for singing a song about farts.

Clay's manager felt it best to cancel the gig. "We fear the possibility," he explained, "that Dice might be subject to arrest, embarrassment and subsequently jailed."

At the height of his fame in February 1990, Clay played two sold-out performances at Madison Square Garden. An edited version was released to theaters. Roger Ebert wrote in his review, "Watching the way thousands of people in his audience could not think for themselves, could not find the courage to allow their ordinary feelings of decency and taste to prevail, I understood better how demagogues are possible. It is eerie, watching the shots of the audience. You never see anyone just plain laughing, as if they'd heard something that was funny. You see, instead, behavior more appropriate at a fascist rally, as his fans stick their fists in the air and chant his name as if he were making some kind of statement for them."

Despite his popularity, Clay was increasingly seen as a burden to the corporations that employed him. Geffen Records cited a difference in "creative philosophy" and cut him loose, and a three-picture film deal was abandoned. Clay was battered, but insisted, "I've created something so unique, so special, people are just going crazy for it. I'm gonna be around for a long time."

15

SHOCK JOCKS, TALK RADIO, AND THE FAIRNESS DOCTRINE

The broadcasting industry went through a monumental shift in the 1980s when the Fairness Doctrine was eliminated. A controversial set of federal regulations first introduced in 1941, its purpose was to prevent radio from devolving into a propaganda medium and to "provide full and equal opportunity for the presentation to the public all sides of public issues."

Since the early days of radio, broadcasters were accused of promoting business interests at the expense of working people. Radio was widely seen as a biased medium which merely reinforced the point of view of its owners. "What radio does [is function] as a major propaganda instrumentality serving the ends of the vested interests of business and finance," concluded former advertising executive James Rorty in 1934.

An NBC executive said the purpose of the national broadcaster was to instill conformity. Radio was a way "to preserve our now vast population from disintegrating into classes. We must know and honor the same heroes, love the same songs, enjoy the same sports, and realize our common interest in our national problems."

Radio personalities like Father Coughlin used the airwaves to spread anti-Semitism, triggering calls for regulated speech in 1938. FCC chairman

Frank McNinch argued, "Should there ever be an attempt here by anyone to so debase radio as to use it as an instrument of racial or religious persecution, the [FCC] would employ every resource it has to prevent any such shocking offense. [We seek] the safeguarding of radio as an instrument of democracy, never to be used to injure any racial, religious or other group."

Robert Landry of *Variety* believed that Americans would favor censorship if its purpose was to diminish bigotry: "In theory if not always in practice everybody accepts tolerance and will therefore not dispute a regulation that outlaws attacks upon other people's religions and racial antecedents. The nature of radio is particularly susceptible to dissemination of wild rumor and inflammatory material and must be guarded more careful on that account."

Regulation was introduced in 1941. Initially known as the Mayflower Doctrine, the laws were opposed by station owners, corporate sponsors, and the National Association of Broadcasters (NAB). The Mayflower Doctrine banned editorializing over the air, and it forbade stations from advocating for specific issues. A station owner in Long Island spoke for many NAB members when he claimed freedom of speech had been "abridged by the Mayflower Doctrine" and was "contrary to the basic embodiments in our laws and their interpretations."

By the late 1940s, the Mayflower Doctrine was rebranded the Fairness Doctrine and amended to apply primarily to election campaigns, but the introduction of television created new concerns. "There is a very real danger in superimposing the methods of show business on politics," wrote television critic Jack Gould in 1952. "Chiefly, these methods can result in misleading oversimplification of vital issues and the substitution of emotion for information, slogans for reasoning and glamour for understanding . . . Now—not tomorrow—is the time to hold the line against television turning politics into a coast-to-coast vaudeville show . . . because if that happens it would be but a short step for video to become the platform of the irresponsible demagogue."

Former president Harry Truman had similar concerns: "I feel that if our constitutional system fails," said Truman in 1960, "it will be because people got scared and turned hysterical and someone in power will demagogue them right into a police state of some kind."

The Fairness Doctrine was amended again in August 1960, this time insisting "both sides" be presented on any "controversial issue." However, what constituted a "controversial issue" was open to interpretation, and that lack of definition was one of the main arguments in favor of its repeal.

During the 1960s, the media was frequently accused of right-wing bias by the left and of left-wing bias by the right. "Liberals in the United States are quite hilarious over the attacks on freedom of speech," said Baptist preacher Billy James Hargis. "With all of their supposed liberalism, they are an intolerant bunch . . . against freedom of speech . . . It began when President John Kennedy entered the White House."

When talk radio first emerged, it was greeted with alarm. The Missouri State Labor Council complained in 1966 that "more often than not these forums accept anonymous calls from irresponsible crackpots or skilled propagandists who attack individuals or organizations seeking to mislead and incite the listeners."

When a talk radio host was sued for slander in 1969, the judge overseeing the case said, "What the people who run these programs have in mind is to get people to call up and then whip them into a frenzy. I'm always amazed by these programs—the people on them don't know anything about the subject."

"Some say that corporate America already controls the airways—it's the nature of the beast," reported *Variety* in January 1968. "Some complain about Bob Hope and flag-waving and network policies that allow the armed services to be glorified at football half-times, but forbid the appearance of peace propaganda. Essentially, the problem is still one of access. As long as the channels are limited, and the owners responsible for what goes out over the air, it would seem unlikely that a fairness doctrine review could fundamentally resolve the controversy."

Lobbyists worked hard to repeal the Fairness Doctrine, but they were generally rebuffed until the 1980s. The think tank infrastructure targeted the doctrine and encouraged each administration to destroy it. In 1987, the FCC voted in a four-to-zero decision that the Fairness Doctrine was unnecessary and "no longer in effect." The balance of opinion tipped in favor of the corporations that owned the airwaves and their vested political interests.

"One of the fantasies that has been created during the Reagan adminis-tration is the myth of the liberal media bias," complained Frank Zappa in October 1988. "Even if you have liberal reporters covering the events—they could be wildly left wing covering the event—the guy who pays the salaries has the right—and usually uses it—to tell the man who does the editing for the television news how it's going to be done."

Zappa added, "If you raise this bogeyman of liberal media bias, it gives you the license under the idea of American fairness to give the people on the other side a little bit more time . . . And what that did was it just swamped the country with conservative propaganda. Except that it *wasn't* conservative propaganda—it was bordering on *fascist* propaganda."

★

The first result of a doctrine-free America was not talk radio or political call-in shows, but the immensely profitable shock-jock phenomenon.

Between 1985 and 1990 there were dozens, perhaps hundreds, of morn-ing radio personalities all trying to outdo each other with sex-related song parodies, racial stereotypes, and fart jokes. The FCC received thousands of complaints as morning deejays talked about their genitals, insulted immigrants, and performed dialect in mockery of African Americans, Arab Americans, and Asian Americans.

The *Orlando Sentinel* reported, "As disturbing as these racial stereotypes and remarks may be, more disturbing still is their acceptance by many radio programmers, listeners and, notably, advertisers. Federal regulation of racial radio humor only threatens to weaken the free-speech protection of valid broadcasters . . . The use of ethnic accents by radio programmers to amuse primarily white listening audiences is only part of the problem . . . It's spreading because they're getting away with it."

On his morning radio program in December 1987, a Boston shock jock named Ken Shelton referred to Jesse Jackson as Sambo. The Boston city council called for his immediate dismissal, but the station stood by him.

Tom Barnard spoke pidgin English in mockery of the local Hmong population on KQRS in Minneapolis. A spokesperson from Twin Cities

Community Action Against Racism complained, "What they're doing in these broadcasts . . . fosters a lot of fear in other communities [and uses] the cover of free speech to hurt minority groups, people of color, people who they feel don't have the power to fight back." The radio personality scoffed, "If they don't like things here [in the United States], then leave."

Florida shock jocks Cleveland Wheeler and Terrence McKeever were described by the *Tampa Bay Times* as "a bigot's dream, playing to almost every stereotypical view of blacks [with] knee-jerk appraisals [that] disparage minorities, women and a host of other people."

The NAACP lodged a formal complaint about their program and the station manager responded, "That's crap, that's really crap. A lot of what you hear is in the ears of the beholder." Wheeler and McKeever claimed their free-speech rights were under attack. The *Tampa Bay Times* reported, "What's fascinating is that, in the midst of all this, Wheeler and McKeever try to pass themselves off as righteous warriors in a quest for truth and justice. To bolster that image, they devote an extraordinary amount of time to attacking their competitors and praising themselves."

Shock jocks were not professional stand-up comics. Most of them were reliant on mimeographed "joke sheets" provided by so-called joke service companies.

"We use several joke services, but we use them—not verbatim," said Doug "The Greaseman" Tracht. "We use them to trigger ideas and stuff like that."

Tracht was booked on a 1987 episode of *Larry King Live* to discuss the phenomenon:

Larry King: Why is there a tendency on these shows—and this has been charged—to make fun of ethnic groups and homosexuals? This is a general pattern of this style of show . . . People who put down *groups*.

Doug "The Greaseman" Tracht: I think if you're doing it just in light fun, and I don't really mean [to put down] ethnic groups, but . . . if you do it, you know, in the spirit that it's meant, not out of hate and bitterness, but out of just, 'Hey, this is going on in the world and it's amusing.' I don't get complaints from any ethnic groups.

Tracht had joined WWDC in Washington, DC, in 1982 as a replacement for the outrageous Howard Stern. Intentionally provocative, Stern tested the boundaries of so-called good taste, essentially daring the FCC to reprimand him for talking about constipation, masturbation, and flatulence. However, it wasn't Stern's subject matter that upset WWDC. His humor made WWDC number one in the ratings, but when Stern criticized his station manager, that was a step too far and Stern was replaced with "The Greaseman."

Speaking on Martin Luther King Jr. Day in 1986, Tracht suggested more Black leaders should be assassinated so there could be more federal holidays. Two hundred students from Howard University marched in front of the radio station for three weeks demanding his removal. Tracht told his critics to relax: "I'm weaving a tapestry of humor."

Tracht bounced from one radio market to another. He got ratings, he got in trouble, he got fired. After several different racial controversies, he joined the police force in Falls Church, Virginia, and worked as a volunteer sheriff. Tracht carried a .40-caliber semiautomatic and transported prisoners to and from court. The local NAACP was astounded: "Someone who is so insulting to African Americans should not be carrying a gun and transporting prisoners, many [of whom] are African Americans."

Eighteen months later, Tracht lost his police gig after he played a song by Black singer Lauryn Hill on his radio program and said, "No wonder people drag them behind trucks."

★

When the Fairness Doctrine was defanged, a still-obscure broadcaster named Rush Limbaugh was at the right place at the right time. A veteran disc jockey, Limbaugh seized on the opportunity to advertise outrageous opinions. The *Sacramento Bee* published the first national profile of Limbaugh in September 1986: "He's the college drop-out who plays the know-it-all. The patriot who never served his country. The man longing for legitimacy, but afraid his product endorsements are creating the image of a huckster."

Limbaugh was hired by radio station KFBK in Sacramento in 1984.

He replaced the outgoing Morton Downey Jr., a combative, chain-smoking broadcaster fired "for using racist language and being less than contrite about it."

On a clear night, KFBK could be heard well into Canada and deep into Mexico. Its powerful signal automatically gave its on-air personalities great influence. Limbaugh stirred emotions and KFBK played it up. The station erected billboards around town with the caption, "Don't you just want to punch Rush Limbaugh?"

The Rush Limbaugh Show held a contract with Premiere On Call, a company that provided actors to phone into the program and agree with the host. The purpose was to create the illusion of consensus. Premiere On Call told its clients, "We supply voice talent [for] your on-air calls, improvise your scenes or deliver your scripts . . . Specify the kind of voice you need, and we'll get you the right person fast. Unless you request it, you won't hear that same voice again for at least two months, ensuring the authenticity of your programming for avid listeners."

The Rush Limbaugh Show went national in 1988, syndicated to radio stations by Premiere Networks. According to journalist Jane Mayer, the company accepted two million dollars each year from the Heritage Foundation in exchange for "push[ing] the think tank's line on issues."

Limbaugh was an entertaining front man for the corporate interests that worked to discredit labor unions, women's groups, minority activists, and anyone who dared criticize Wall Street greed.

Corporate stooges, former segregationists, and evangelical lunatics found a permanent home on talk radio. Frank Zappa sounded the alarm. "As long as there is somebody who has large-scale airtime, doing the kind of bashing that Rush Limbaugh does," said Zappa, "I do think that it is going to be harmful."

Zappa was no partisan. It didn't matter if it was a Republican like Rush Limbaugh or a Democrat like Tipper Gore, he would criticize anyone regardless of party affiliation. His willingness to ridicule both Democrats and Republicans got the attention of the struggling Libertarian movement in 1988.

"I was invited by the Libertarian Party to be a candidate and I didn't know anything about their party, so I asked them for all the documentation," recalled Zappa. "The reason they called me? There were a number of Libertarians who weren't comfortable with Ron Paul [as their leader] because he's not a Libertarian . . . Ron Paul used to be a member of the John Birch Society—probably still is. He was a Republican who decided to call himself a Libertarian."

Zappa looked at their platform and was appalled by their proposal to stop regulating the corporate sector. "They deregulate stuff and what it has proved is, many people in business can't be trusted."

Zappa rejected them, but the Libertarian movement grew thanks to the think tank infrastructure. Charles Koch of the Koch brothers founded the Cato Institute, a think tank which purported to be Libertarian and frequently referenced "personal freedom" and "liberty." However, for the Koch-funded libertarians, the cause of freedom and liberty did not extend to those who opposed "free market" dogma or corporate money in politics. "Their cause, they say, is liberty," concluded Nancy MacLean, a historian of the think tank movement. "But by that they mean . . . a system that would radically reduce the freedom of many."

With the repeal of the Fairness Doctrine, think tanks flooded television and radio with radical ideas opposed by the majority of the population. Opinions were presented as facts and editorials masqueraded as news. Outlandish claims were presented without counterargument. Popular concepts like universal health care, increased funding for public education, and living wages were intentionally skewed or demonized. What had once been the wet dream of the John Birch Society was becoming mainstream reality.

16

NELSON MANDELA, MARTIN LUTHER KING JR. DAY, AND RAP MUSIC

"The worst problems in my life came from a bunch of strangers," said Luther Campbell of 2 Live Crew. "The Moral Majority."

In the late 1980s, the Moral Majority declared war on hip hop just as the John Birch Society had declared war on the Beatles. The playbook had not changed much. The biggest difference between the John Birch Society of the 1960s and the Moral Majority of the 1980s—and the Heritage Foundation which had bridged the two eras—was millions of dollars in funding.

"You had these leftover bigots out there," said Luther Campbell. "The leftover racists, the ones who didn't like Elvis, the ones who didn't like Black singers. These right-wing group people who sent around, 'Don't listen to [N-word] music and do the [N-word] dance and all this."

The leftover bigots. Before zeroing in on the new phenomenon of hip hop, they targeted two significant developments in Black culture: the anti-apartheid movement of Nelson Mandela and a new holiday named in honor of Dr. Martin Luther King Jr.

Massive amounts of cash from the Scaife, Mellon, and Olin fortunes sustained the Culture War. They also sustained the political career of Senator Jesse Helms, one of Dr. King's greatest haters. Helms was elected in

1972 after defeating North Carolina Congressman Nick Galifianakis, the uncle of comedian Zach Galifianakis. Helms's talking points were supplied to him by the Heritage Foundation.

"Dr. King's action-oriented Marxism is not compatible with the concepts of this country," said Helms. He claimed a holiday in his honor would only promote "the official policy of communism."

Evan Mecham, a Mormon extremist with ties to the John Birch Society, became the governor of Arizona in January 1987. During his first week in office, he rescinded Martin Luther King Jr. Day. When the move generated controversy, Governor Mecham blamed homosexuals. In March 1987, he named *The Making of America* by W. Cleon Skousen the official resource for Arizona's Constitutional Bicentennial. The book contained racial slurs and concluded "slavery hurt whites more than blacks."

Skousen opposed all government regulations. At the height of the John Birch Society's popularity, his books were bestsellers in American Opinion bookstores, including the one run by Charles Koch in Wichita. Many years later, he was a political mentor to a young Mormon named Glenn Beck.

★

The Coors beer fortune and the Scaife Foundation funded an organization called Accuracy in Media (AIM), which coined the phrase "liberal media bias." They advocated budget cuts to PBS because the channel aired a documentary about Nelson Mandela, which AIM called a "glorification of an African terrorist." In 1986, Jeffrey Hart, editor of the anti–civil rights periodical the *Dartmouth Review*, dismissed the anti-apartheid movement as "Cultural Marxism." Pat Robertson promoted the South Africa position on television, Jesse Helms accepted payments from a "front for South Africa's white rulers," the John Birch Society called Mandela "a communist terrorist thug," and Congressman Dick Cheney cast a vote opposing his freedom.

"The liberal media has for too long suppressed the other side of the story in South Africa," said Pat Robertson. "It is very important that we stay close enough to South Africa so that it does not fall prey to the clutches of Communism."

Robertson wasn't just the head of the Christian Coalition—he was a broadcasting mogul. Before he got into broadcasting, he was a lobbyist for W. R. Grace, the controversial company that helped Nazi chemist Otto Ambros immigrate to the United States. His father served in Congress for thirty-four years. A signatory to the Southern Manifesto, A. Willis Robertson was opposed to "race mixing" and claimed integration was unconstitutional.

In the 1970s, Pat Robertson purchased property and broadcast licenses with the charitable donations he solicited over the air. He loaned Ted Turner the money to start CNN, and he purchased the rights to *The Mary Tyler Moore Show*. Throughout the 1980s, he became known for outlandish statements. In one of his most famous moments, Robertson called feminism "a socialist, anti-family political movement that encourages women to leave their husbands, kill their children, practice witchcraft, destroy capitalism and become lesbians." Drafted into the political movement by Paul Weyrich, Robertson's cartoonish statements made some old-school conservatives uncomfortable. "Pat has made so many statements that are absolutely wrong and false," said Barry Goldwater. "I'd hate to see him in the White House."

The Christian Coalition, the Heritage Foundation, and the Moral Majority made many inroads in the 1980s, but they were unable to convince Americans that Dr. Martin Luther King Jr. and Nelson Mandela were evil. And so the target changed. Cal Thomas, vice president of the Moral Majority, said, "Rap music pollutes society."

2 Live Crew were the undisputed kings of South Florida party anthems in the late 1980s. They were known for heavy beats, explicit lyrics, and concerts with wild dancing. "Our music is fun entertainment," said Luther Campbell. "Y'know, come in, do some chants, dance—and just have some fun."

The Moral Majority had a different concept of fun. Their ongoing media campaign provided the impetus for police to harass record stores for selling "immoral" and "obscene" records, setting the stage for one of the most high-profile obscenity trials since the days of Lenny Bruce.

A judge halted sales of *As Nasty as They Wanna Be* in South Florida, and when a record store in Fort Lauderdale ignored the ruling, the store manager was convicted of "distributing obscene material."

Luther Campbell didn't think it had anything to do with the music, but everything to do with the need for a political bogeyman. "Every year, if you notice it, with rap, every year is a different thing," said Campbell. "I mean, last year it was Public Enemy. And the year before that, they would say if you go to a rap concert, your kid might get killed. You know? And now, this year, it's 2 Live Crew. Next year it'll be somebody else."

The NAACP rejected the suggestion that the 2 Live Crew controversy had something to do with race. "We are particularly offended by their efforts to wrap the mantle of the black cultural experience around their performances by saying this is the way it is in the black community, and that they are authentic purveyors of our heritage," said an NAACP statement. "Our cultural experience does not include debasing our women, the glorification of violence, the promotion of deviant sexual behavior, or the tearing into shreds of our cherished mores and standards of behavior."

A federal district judge convicted 2 Live Crew of obscenity, but the US Court of Appeals for the Eleventh Circuit overturned the ruling a few months later. Cal Thomas, speaking for the Heritage Foundation complained, "A Fort Lauderdale jury's decision that the rap group 2 Live Crew did not violate local anti-obscenity laws is more a verdict on our own relapse into paganism . . . Every pore of our culture now oozes impurities."

Much of hip hop addressed racism and police brutality, which made it a natural target in the Culture War. The popular song "Fuck tha Police" by NWA was a commentary on corruption, racism, and brutality. It featured the rhyme "So police think they have the authority to kill a minority." An FBI agent considered that a threat.

"A song recorded by the rap group N.W.A. on their album entitled 'Straight Outta Compton' encourages violence against and disrespect for the law enforcement officer and has been brought to my attention," wrote the FBI agent. "Recordings such as the one from N.W.A. are both discouraging and degrading to these brave, dedicated officers."

Police unions around the country asked cities to "help cancel concerts by NWA." Richmond, Virginia, and Kansas City, Missouri, were among the towns that attempted to ban rap. And when NWA arrived in Detroit, the police showed up in force to stop them from playing their most famous song. "We just wanted to show the kids," said one officer, "that you can't say 'fuck the police' in Detroit."

"There were close to two hundred of us," recalled one officer. "We had our marching orders. We were told that under no circumstance that they were to perform that song . . . We immediately jumped on the stage and started taking out amplifiers."

Priority Records, NWA's label, received hundreds of letters of complaint. A reporter with the *Village Voice* tried to determine their origin: "To find out why the letters were so often alike, I called their authors, who came from all over the country. I checked more than 100 letters. Most of the letters claimed that the authors would 'never buy an album from your label again,' but my interviews with their writers indicated that none of them had bought *any* LP, cassette, or CD . . . they'd never heard of N.W.A."

Just as Democrat Tipper Gore had demonized heavy metal, Republican politicians like Oliver North and Dan Quayle demonized rap music. It created fear and helped generate support for politicians with little to offer.

Ice-T was a rapper with a rock-music side project called Body Count. Body Count was actually a hard-core punk band, but politicians referred to it as rap.

Body Count released a song called "Cop Killer." It was a revenge fantasy about police brutality. Ice-T explained, "I grew up threatened by the police. It should be an equal thing. They should know that they can't just step on you and take your life. We're all human beings. I don't care if you got a badge or anything, nobody should be able to treat anybody like they're subhuman."

The song was performed for the first time at Lollapalooza in 1991. It caused no controversy at all. "We figured we played it for seven hundred thousand people during Lollapalooza," said Body Count guitarist Ernie Cunnigan. "No one ever said anything about the song, you know? No complaints."

One year after "Cop Killer" was released, the initial footage of the notorious Rodney King beating aired on the news. While the LAPD defended their actions, the song "Cop Killer" took on new meaning.

"I feel no shame for it," said the officer in charge of the Rodney King beating. "We were doing our job that night . . . The vast majority of the people have listened to the media . . . and what you've seen in this particular case is an electronic lynching . . . They want to make this a racist incident. There's nothing racist about this incident. This is not a case of police brutality."

"The LAPD, they're a different breed," said Body Count's Ernie Cunnigan. "That's what we wrote the song about initially. And it says it in the song. We're specifically talking about the LAPD, because that's what we know."

Time Warner was criticized for having Body Count on Warner Bros. Records. Ron DeLord, leader of a Texas police union, organized a boycott of Time Warner properties, including Six Flags amusement parks and the summer blockbuster *Batman Returns*.

"We want to educate the public there is a trashy side to the company that owns their squeaky-clean theme park," said DeLord. "Time Warner Inc. obviously is a company with no sense of social justice."

Warner executive Howard Klein defended their client: "Ice-T didn't shoot a policeman or beat one into the hospital . . . Something's rotten in the L.A. police force and that's the police force Ice-T and Body Count grew up with. It's a police force that views them differently than they do white people."

Colonel Oliver North, discredited after the Iran-Contra hearings in 1987, staged a post-scandal comeback in 1992, using "Cop Killer" as his main issue. North founded the Freedom Alliance with Jack Thompson, a lawyer who prosecuted 2 Live Crew for obscenity.

The ironically named Freedom Alliance wanted Time Warner executives sent to prison. Oliver North said he wanted "governors in all 50 states to bring criminal proceedings against Time Warner [because they] deliberately stir up hatred and incite violence against the men and women in blue."

Thompson said, "I have advised Colonel North, and he agrees, that the people who run Time Warner are violating state sedition, anti-anarchy, anti-civil disorder and anti-incitement-to-riot statutes." Three years earlier, North had been convicted of obstructing Congress and Thompson was disbarred from practicing law in Florida for "inappropriate conduct, including making false statements."

The *Los Angeles Times* published a letter to the editor in July 1992:

"It is laughable that Oliver North, as president of an organization called Freedom Alliance, seeks to bring criminal proceedings against Time Warner. When North was commissioned as an officer of the U.S. Marines he swore to defend the very Constitution that protects the free speech of Ice-T . . . Like North I am a former Marine officer who believes in law enforcement. Like Ice-T, I am a black male in his 30s who knows that in reality not all cops represent law and order."

Police unions said "Cop Killer" would lead to widespread assassinations. Ice-T laughed at the assertion. "The album has been out since March, we've been performing this album for two years out on the road," he said. "It's stupid. Where are all these dead cops? The people who listen to music *understand* music. And they take it as just that. I think there's a lot of ulterior motives . . . Why are they continually calling this record a *rap* album? This is a *rock* album done by Black guys . . . I think these politicians know that if they use the word *rap*, they can get a lot of people behind them."

Charlton Heston, a Hollywood legend and spokesman for the National Rifle Association, showed up at a Time Warner shareholders meeting to express his contempt. He read the lyrics of "Cop Killer" in his Moses-style delivery. The dramatic rendering made headlines around the country. As a result, sales of "Cop Killer" increased.

"That was just the funniest thing," said Ernie Cunnigan. "He brought people to the album who never would have known who we are."

"Charlton Heston . . . is nothing but a politician," said Ice-T. "He rallies against me, but then at the same time he lobbies to keep a bullet called the cop killer legal because he's spokesperson . . . of the NRA. So, he's got his shit twisted."

The Arsenio Hall Show booked Ice-T as a musical guest in the middle of the hysteria. According to the host, they received menacing messages from off-duty LAPD. "I've gotten a lot of angry and threatening calls today to cancel the appearance," said Hall. "I was even told that if I didn't cancel the appearance, I couldn't depend on getting police response if I ever needed it."

It was reported that low-level Time Warner employees were receiving death threats. Ice-T announced on July 29, 1992, that he was voluntarily pulling "Cop Killer" in order to stop the menacing calls and letters.

"I am going to make the request for Warner Bros. to take the song off the LP," he said, "so that hopefully these gangsters will stop threatening those people's lives."

Politicians obsessed over "Cop Killer." The debate overwhelmed talk radio and cable news, but most of the public hadn't found it to be all that important.

"Over 70 percent of the people we polled disagreed with this call to boycott and over 90 percent have said that the controversy has not stopped them from buying Time Warner products," reported *Entertainment Tonight*. "In fact, over sixty percent of the people we asked, support Time Warner's decision to distribute Ice-T's album."

Americans had been fed another hysteria, but this time refused to swallow.

17

TO HAVE A COW

"There was a time in radio when you couldn't say 'damn' and if you said 'hell,' they'd throw you out of the city," reflected an elderly Bob Hope. "Today, all you get is four-letter words and violence. Have you seen *Goodfellas*? I'd call that an unnecessary picture. It is mostly violence, and they must say the 'F' word one hundred and ten times in the first five minutes!"

Bob Hope had been criticized for being too political in the 1930s and '40s. Steve Allen had been criticized for being an immoral Commie in the 1950s and '60s. Now, all these years later, they lodged similar complaints about the new generation.

Television was still heavily censored despite accusations of immorality and vulgarity. The three-network monopoly of ABC, CBS, and NBC had held firm for decades, but Australian media-mogul Rupert Murdoch had a plan to penetrate the monopoly. His newly established Fox Broadcasting Company attempted to lure viewers away from the big three with "edgier" programming like *The Simpsons* and *Married… with Children*.

Due to the "anti-family attitude" of *Married… with Children*, a sitcom with overtly sexual humor, the network lost major sponsors like Coca-Cola,

General Mills, Johnson & Johnson, and Kimberly-Clark. But controversy was good for the channel overall and established Fox as a legitimate player in network television. By 1991, they had enough credibility to land the broadcast rights to the Emmys.

That year, the category for Outstanding Writing in a Variety or Music Program was presented by comedian Gilbert Gottfried. At the last minute, he decided to ignore the teleprompter and deliver a series of jokes about the recent arrest of Pee-wee Herman in an adult movie theater:

> Y'know, I'll tell you something, ladies and gentlemen, I sleep a lot better since Pee-wee Herman has been arrested.
> [audience laughter]
> Masturbation's a crime—I should be on death row!
> [audience laughter]
> Masturbation's against the law—I should have been sent to the electric chair years ago.
> [audience laughter]
> To think that by age fourteen I was already Al Capone.
> [audience laughter]

Gottfried got big laughs for his spontaneous patter, but producers backstage were "buzzing about the bad taste of it" and the Academy of Television Arts & Sciences—the organization responsible for the Emmys—considered it an affront. "I was angry to no end," said the academy president. "I could have gone on and hung him right there." Kenny Solms, head writer of the Emmy ceremony, said, "We were looking for a bit more decorum and wit. That's not wit."

Newspaper editorials and radio commentaries condemned Gilbert for destroying America. Film critic Michael Medved said Gottfried's performance was indicative of Hollywood's "juvenile addiction to off-color material." And comedy legend Soupy Sales said, "That was in bad taste. There's a difference between being in a club where people are smoking and drinking and a primetime television audience."

Gottfried was astounded that anybody was upset. "What gets me," said Gilbert, "a few months later *Seinfeld* does an episode on masturbation—and it's *Citizen Kane*."

Fox established itself as the controversial channel. And there was one specific show more than any other that sustained the Fox network. It led to school suspensions, merchandise being removed from stores, and a lot of Culture War grandstanding.

The Simpsons was not an instantaneous success. It was initially scheduled on Thursday nights against the highest-rated program on television, *The Cosby Show*. At the start of the season, Bill Cosby said he welcomed the competition, but when *The Simpsons* beat him in the ratings for the first time in April 1991, Cosby criticized *The Simpsons* as an "antisocial" menace that had spiraled "out of control."

"The mean-spirited and cruel think this is 'the edge,' and their excuse is that's the way people are today," said Cosby. "But why should we be entertained by that? TV should be moving in a direction from the Huxtables forward, not backward."

President George H. W. Bush mentioned *The Simpsons* during his keynote address at the annual National Religious Broadcasters convention in January 1992. The president told the assembled crowd, "We need a nation closer to the Waltons—than the Simpsons."

Ironically, *The Waltons* featured Depression-era characters praising the social programs of President Roosevelt's New Deal, and it starred Will Geer, an actor who was blacklisted for being a Communist.

William Bennett, a former member of the Reagan administration, toured a drug addiction treatment center in Philadelphia. As he walked through their common room, he saw them watching Fox and said, "You guys aren't watching *The Simpsons* are you? That's not going to help you any."

First Lady Barbara Bush watched just one episode of *The Simpsons*. Despite having raised future president George W. Bush, she called *The Simpsons* "the dumbest thing I had ever seen."

The show was immensely popular, but an anti-*Simpsons* crusade spread through the country. A letter to the editor published in the *Detroit Free Press* complained, "This so-called comedy exploits so many negative things that children do not need to be exposed to: violence, vandalism, disrespectfulness, lying, cheating, bad language, and all-around negative attitude toward life."

"Bart is an outgrowth of the trend in popular culture to depict violence solely for the sake of violence, depriving it of meaning and making it an end in itself," wrote a *Simpsons*-hater to the *Los Angeles Times*. "This gratuitous expression of violence has now filtered its way into the pre-pubescent realm . . . I am a sixth grade teacher . . . 10% of our students wear Bart shirts. Drawings of Bart flourish on blackboards and on hundreds of papers . . . precisely the kind of 'anti-hero' these students don't need."

A merchandising blitz of *Simpsons* toys, clothes, and posters ensued. Bart Simpson T-shirts became the decade's most popular schoolyard fashion statement. But the popularity of the impudent "underachiever" who was "proud of it" disturbed teachers and school boards. "To be proud of being an incompetent is a contradiction of what we stand for," said a high school principal in Ohio. "It teaches the wrong thing to students."

Clothing that featured *The Simpsons* was banned throughout the country. A school principal in Kentucky explained, "We feel like the Bart Simpson show does a lot of things that do not help student self-esteem, such as saying it's okay to be stupid." A wave of hostility greeted companies that heavily invested in *The Simpsons* merchandise trend. The Associated Press reported that JCPenney, after establishing "Simpsons boutiques" in its many stores, was forced to remove "any Bart Simpson t-shirt that might encourage juvenile delinquency."

A pair of Catholic nuns from Miami Shores, Florida, pretended to condemn *The Simpsons*, but actually cashed in. "I don't think Bart is helping us," said a nun. "We hope in some way to balance out Bart." The nuns copied *The Simpsons* shirt design and released a new clothing line featuring "colorful decals of popular saints."

★

While the president attacked *The Simpsons*, the vice president blamed the 1992 LA riots on the sitcom *Murphy Brown*.

"I believe the lawless social anarchy which we saw is directly related to the breakdown of family structure, personal responsibility, and social order in too many areas of our society," said Vice President Dan Quayle.

"It doesn't help matters when primetime TV has *Murphy Brown*—a character who supposedly epitomizes today's intelligent, highly paid, professional woman—mocking the importance of fathers, by bearing a child alone."

In the storyline referenced by Quayle, the newswoman protagonist played by Candice Bergen decides to raise a child alone—after the father walks out on her. Real-life news personalities Katie Couric and Joan Lunden played themselves in a baby shower scene, which Quayle said "appalled" him. David Letterman joked that the real reason Dan Quayle was upset was that *Murphy Brown* "didn't feature enough positive portrayals of really dumb guys."

White House spokesman David Beckwith confessed that the vice president invoked *Murphy Brown* to further the Culture War. "He has never seen the whole show," said Beckwith. "They don't watch television in their house . . . the Vice President knew that to make a speech on the subject [of single parenting] more relevant, an example was needed."

Political observers from outside the United States were contemptuous. German correspondent Mario Dederichs said, "The discussion here [in America] is so shallow that sometimes Europeans really feel that there is a loss of reality here in the whole political discussion." BBC reporter Gavin Esler explained, "When you have a campaign in which people can take comments about Murphy Brown, a fictitious character's pregnancy seriously—they *seriously* discuss this—it strikes most Europeans as utterly bizarre."

Dan Quayle claimed that the majority of Americans agreed with him. "I'm sure the media elite and Hollywood didn't like the speech that I gave, but the American people support what I'm talking about."

They didn't.

"Dan Quayle is crazy," said Nikki Giovanni, a single mother who became a famous poet. "I get so sick of listening to white people talk about the erosion of the family. They sold men, women and children away from each other [into slavery]."

Controversy could lose a program its sponsors and it could lead to political demonization, but it also led to increased curiosity—and larger ratings. After George H. W. Bush and Bill Cosby criticized *The Simpsons*, the Fox network was riding high. When the new Fox sketch-comedy series *In Living Color* debuted, the network was well versed in hysteria.

In Living Color featured several comedians who became household names, including Keenen Ivory Wayans, Damon Wayans, Jamie Foxx, and Jim Carrey. The program often made fun of old-fashioned stereotypes, but at the same time it was accused of furthering new ones. A recurring sketch about two Black youths selling stolen products on the "Homeboy Shopping Network" was criticized behind the scenes.

"Homeboy Shopping Network divided the staff," said *In Living Color* writer Rob Edwards. "That one seemed to come from a different point of view where the people being made fun of were poor Black people. For us Black writers . . . it seemed like making fun of people who didn't need to be made fun of."

After viewing initial episodes with trepidation, white executives at Fox arranged advance screenings with the NAACP. Keenen Ivory Wayans, creator and star of the program, was insulted.

"At one point, Fox brought this old Black man that they wanted to hire as a consultant to the show," recalled Wayans. "They told me how he'd marched with Dr. King and had a lump on the side of his head from when he got beat up. I said, 'I respect all he has done, but if he ain't got no jokes, I don't need him. He's no blacker than me. I don't need him to validate me."

"Men on Film" was one of the early recurring sketches. It featured David Alan Grier and Damon Wayans as a pair of gay film critics who saw a gay inference in every movie they viewed. The sketch was "among the most criticized, and not without some justification," writes *In Living Color* historian David Peisner. "Their flamboyant wardrobes and effeminate manner indulged persistent gay stereotypes, and some gay rights organizations complained."

"The sketch is not a *bashing* sketch," insisted Wayans. "We don't do jokes about any issues related to gay people. It's really a play on the extremes of the stereotypes and that's it."

"All those stereotypes are truth," said cast member Jamie Foxx. "Stereotypes come from something [but] no one should be discriminated against because of a stereotype."

At the height of *In Living Color*'s popularity, the cast appeared on an episode of *Donahue*. The daytime talk show host baited them by comparing their gay characters to Lightnin' on the old *Amos 'n' Andy Show*.

Keenen Ivory Wayans: *Amos 'n' Andy* . . . didn't at all have any validity or authenticity. It was not even exaggeration. It was someone else's creation . . . In any sketch-variety format, you're gonna make fun of stereotypes . . .

David Alan Grier: A caricature is a drawing of something that is based in reality, but you stretch it and you exaggerate it. That's what it is.

Phil Donahue: As Lightnin' was.

Keenen Ivory Wayans: No. Lightnin' had no validity. Lightnin' was someone else's idea . . . There was no authenticity with him . . . We get letters every day from homosexuals that ask us to never stop doing it.

There was only one target Wayans considered off-limits. According to Peisner, the program had a "hands-off policy" when it came to Bill Cosby. An anonymous *In Living* Color writer said Wayans instructed the staff "not to do a sketch about a well-traveled rumor that Cosby had gotten caught getting a hand job under a table."

★

Sometimes material was purged from television to placate complainers on the left, and sometimes material was cut to placate complainers on the right. In either case, censorship was imposed to avoid offense.

Comedian Bill Hicks did stand-up on the *Late Show with David Letterman* on October 1, 1993. The studio audience laughed, applauded, and enjoyed the routine:

"You know who's really bugging me these days? These pro-lifers . . . You ever look at their faces? [Hicks scrunches up his face like a prude.] 'I'm pro-life! I'm pro-life!' Boy, they look it, don't they? They just exude joie de vivre. You just want to hang with them and play Trivial Pursuit all night long. You know what bugs me about them? If you're so pro-life, do me a favor—don't lock arms and block medical clinics. If you're so pro-life, lock arms and block cemeteries! I want to see pro-lifers at funerals opening a casket, 'Get out!' Then I'd really be impressed by their mission."

The audience applauded and Letterman's staff praised him, but two hours later Hicks got a phone call from Letterman's producer, Robert Morton. Morton informed him that his entire routine had been cut from the program and would not be broadcast.

"Bob, they're just jokes," protested Hicks. "I don't want to be edited by you or anyone else. Why are people so afraid of jokes?"

"Bill, you've got to understand our audience," said Morton.

"Your audience! Your audience is comprised of people, right? Well, I understand people, being one myself. People are who I play to every night, Bob. We get along just fine. We taped the show at 5:30 in the afternoon, and your audience had no problem with the material then. Does your audience become overly sensitive between the hours of 11:30 P.M. and 12:30 A.M.? And by the way, Bob, when I'm not performing on your show, *I'm* a member of the audience of your show. Are you saying my material is not suitable for me?"

Bill Hicks did a number of interviews in the months that followed, and he complained about the state of network television. "Comedy in the States has been totally gutted," he said. "It's commercialized. They don't have people on TV who have points of view, because that defies the status quo, and we can't have that in the totalitarian mind-control government that runs the fuckin' airwaves. I can't get a shot there. I get David Letterman a lot. I love Letterman, but every time I go on, we have tiffs over material." And yet, despite all his frustration, Hicks said the controversy gave him "more attention than my other eleven appearances on Letterman" combined.

★

As each hysteria faded, another was quick to take its place. By the fall of 1993, *The Simpsons* was established as part of the mainstream cultural fabric, and another satirical cartoon replaced it as the scourge of America.

Beavis and Butt-Head concerned two moronic, antisocial metalheads who hated school, loved music, and liked to break things out of sexual frustration. Mike Judge's creation went over the heads of politicians, but it was embraced by people in comedy. It became a phenomenon and merchandise followed in *The Simpsons* tradition. *Beavis and Butt-Head* apparel was banned in schools around the country and Walmart announced a new "chainwide ban on Beavis and Butt-head merchandise."

A factory worker in Greenville, Pennsylvania, said he was concerned *Beavis and Butt-Head* would "lower the morality" of his town. "We may just keep pushing our standards a little further and further in the wrong direction and not even realize it," he said. "One day we'll say, 'Why didn't we do anything when we could?'"

On the program, Beavis would occasionally shout: "Fire! Fire! Fire!" The mantra was blamed for a real-life disaster when five-year-old Austin Messner burned down his family's trailer home in Moraine, Ohio—a tragedy in which his little sister was killed.

"The mother says he had never played with matches or lighters prior to witnessing 'Beavis and Butt-Head' and laughing about fire being fun," said the fire chief. "The mother told our investigator that Austin watched 'Beavis and Butt-Head' all the time and became obsessed with playing with fire. We're going to ask MTV to remove those segments—and if they won't do it voluntarily, we'll go through the powers that be and force pressure on them."

Politicians led the charge for cancelation. MTV refused to end the program but did delete certain antisocial segments and put the kibosh on lighters, matches, and the shouting of "Fire! Fire! Fire!" The controversy consumed the news for months.

But years later, when Messner was a grown man, he claimed his mother fabricated the story so she wouldn't be blamed. "I literally *never* saw the cartoon," said Messner. "How could I? We couldn't afford cable!"

★

Just as it had been in the days of Mae West and *Amos 'n' Andy*, the majority of protest dealt either with sexuality or stereotypes. *Basic Instinct*, the 1992 blockbuster starring Sharon Stone, was the subject of protests from right-wing evangelicals who objected to its overt sexuality *and* protests from left-wing activists who considered it homophobic.

"It is yet another movie which pits lesbian and gay characters against heterosexuals and makes the lesbian characters into the villains," concluded the Gay and Lesbian Alliance Against Defamation after previewing a draft of the script. "Hollywood never seems to come up with a realistic depiction of lesbians and gays."

"Not unless the script is completely rewritten and the premise changed, will we stop demonstrations," said a spokesperson from the militant organization Queer Nation. While the crew was filming, protesters sabotaged production by blowing whistles and blaring car horns. Nearly one hundred police in riot gear positioned themselves around the crew to protect them and disperse the protesters.

Screenwriter Joe Eszterhas met with gay advocacy groups and said he "understood their concerns and would make some revisions." Director Paul Verhoeven was annoyed because he didn't think Eszterhas could do so "without destroying the structure of the movie, which has already been in production for three weeks."

When the film was released, Sharon Stone hosted *Saturday Night Live*. While she delivered her opening monologue, six protesters outside the studio were arrested for "disorderly conduct and harassment."

The action film *True Lies* starring Arnold Schwarzenegger and Jamie Lee Curtis was protested in 1994. Arab American film historian Jack Shaheen called it "one of the most racist movies Hollywood has ever produced" for portraying "Palestinians as dirty, demonic, and despicable peoples."

Casey Kasem, the beloved disc jockey who voiced Shaggy on *Scooby-Doo, Where Are You!*, wrote to studio executives to complain, "In the future, I hope you'll aim for balance in your depictions. I presume it was inadvertent or unintended racism, but believe it: that's what it was—racism."

Hollywood movies were banned or denounced for various reasons throughout the 1990s. *Executive Decision* starring Kurt Russell and *The Siege* starring Denzel Washington were denounced as racist by Arab American civil rights groups. VHS copies of Oliver Stone's *Natural Born Killers* were banned from Kmart, Walmart, and Blockbuster. *Exit to Eden* starring Dan

Aykroyd was banned in the Canadian province of Saskatchewan. Children were banned from seeing *Teenage Mutant Ninja Turtles II: The Secret of the Ooze* in Germany. *The Naked Gun 2½* was banned in Turkey. *Schindler's List* was banned in Malaysia.

Hollywood's greatest adversaries, however, were not foreign governments but their own. Senator Bob Dole wasn't much interested in film or TV, but in preparing for a presidential bid, he attacked Hollywood for its "nightmares of depravity."

"America's long-running romance with Hollywood is over," claimed Michael Medved, the film critic turned Rush Limbaugh guest host. "As a nation, we no longer believe that popular culture enriches our lives . . . Instead, tens of millions of Americans now see the entertainment industry as an all-powerful enemy, an alien force that assaults our most cherished values and corrupts our children. The dream factory has become the poison factory."

Medved said Mel Brooks was a typical example of "the loony left" because he named a recent movie *Life Stinks*. "When an industry attempts to market a Mel Brooks comedy with a title that conveys a grim, pessimistic view of human existence," said Medved, "then it's safe to say that industry has lost touch with the public."

Accusations that Hollywood was out of touch were frequently issued by politicians who themselves seemed out of touch with the needs of average Americans.

Burton Yale Pines, vice president of the Heritage Foundation, complained that Hollywood unfairly maligned big business. "Not only did TV criminalize businesspersons in 1992," said Pines, "it trivialized them." Pines criticized *Matlock* for featuring a criminal banker, *A Different World* for a storyline about sexual harassment in the workplace, and *Picket Fences* for a scene in which a real estate developer bribes a politician.

Reverend Don Wildmon returned in 1993. Steven Bochco's *NYPD Blue* was an ABC drama that tested the limits of what the FCC would allow. It intentionally included curse words—and Dennis Franz's hairy ass. In doing so, it moved the needle ever so slightly about what was considered acceptable.

Reverend Wildmon purchased a page in the major newspapers: "A Petition Asking ABC Not To Show Softcore Pornography And To

Show Respect For Our Families—We Are FED UP! Will Steven Bochco's upcoming ABC cop show, NYPD Blue, become the first 'R-rated' series to feature softcore pornography? USA Today said the pilot had A SEX SCENE THAT SHOWS A WOMAN'S BREASTS AND INCLUDES RAW LANGUAGE . . . Is this what you want TV teaching your children?"

The bottom of the ad included a prompt to send Reverend Wildmon money:

"Yes, I am fed up with ABC's plans to show the 'R-rated' program NYPD Blue, and their desire to show nudity, more extreme violence and more profane language. I agree it is time to draw the line . . . I am enclosing a tax-deductible contribution of $_____ to help pay for this ad and to get more parents, grandparents and concerned individuals involved."

Bill Cosby agreed with the sentiment. "I've always had a problem with these new shows using that kind of language," said Cosby in reference to NYPD Blue. "That's a problem. We have to understand that there's a point where the producer is using you, the audience, to satisfy some sort of adolescent immaturity."

The Southern Baptist Convention called for a boycott of the corporation that owned ABC: the Walt Disney Company. NYPD Blue was bad enough, but when Disney announced they were extending worker benefits to include same-sex partners, the SBC staged a series of protests. A spokesman said, "In recent years, the Disney Company has given the appearance that the promotion of homosexuality is more important than its historic commitment to traditional family values."

A Disney spokesperson responded, "We find it curious that a group that would claim to espouse family values would vote to boycott the world's largest producer of wholesome family entertainment. We question any group that demands that we deprive people of health benefits."

The anti-Disney campaign continued when an ABC sitcom starring Ellen DeGeneres announced a special episode. Originally titled These Friends of Mine, the comedy struggled to find an audience. The title was changed to Ellen. The cast was replaced. The premise was changed. And it was moved to a different time slot. Nothing worked. ABC executives were desperate, and at one point someone suggested Ellen's character "get a puppy" to increase ratings. In a shameless ploy to boost viewership, the writers decided to have Ellen's straight character come out as gay. In mockery of ABC executives, they called it "The Puppy Episode."

When word got out, the Christian Coalition purchased a full-page ad in *Variety* to denounce it, and Jerry Falwell appeared on *Larry King Live* calling for a sponsor boycott. Wendy's and JCPenney pulled their ads from the program, and a petition delivered to the network was signed by Watergate coconspirator Chuck Colson and Colonel Oliver North.

An unlikely comedy legend aligned himself with evangelical culture warriors at the time. Steve Allen had been threatened by the John Birch Society in the early 1960s, but by the mid-1990s he joined former Birchers in a critique of Hollywood content.

Steve Allen disapproved of the Austin Powers title *The Spy Who Shagged Me*. He criticized director Betty Thomas for including "components of sleaze" in her 1995 feature *The Brady Bunch Movie*. And he called the Farrelly brothers, the men who made *Dumb and Dumber*, the "sickest" people in Hollywood. A longtime fan of comedy and tireless advocate for comedians, Steve Allen could no longer defend his genre. He rejected the comedy of the 1990s and said he'd much rather listen to *Amos 'n' Andy* because they "never depended on shock to get laughs."

Allen became the spokesman for an evangelical censorship group called the Parents Television Council, founded by Brent Bozell III, son of L. Brent Bozell Jr., who founded Stop Immorality on Television in the 1970s.

During a speech sponsored by the Heritage Foundation, Bozell III said that liberal views needed to be counteracted in the press "in equal measure with no regard for their veracity."

Bozell III had just finished working on Pat Buchanan's presidential campaign when he recruited Steve Allen as the face of the Parents Television Council. Bozell ran an ad in thousands of newspapers featuring a large photo of Steve Allen above the text:

TV is Leading Children Down a Moral Sewer

Are you as disgusted as I am at the filth, vulgarity, sex and violence TV is sending into our homes? Are you fed up with steamy unmarried sex situations, filthy jokes, perversion, vulgarity, foul language, violence, killings etc.? Are you as outraged as I am at how TV is undermining the morals of children . . . encouraging them to have pre-marital sex . . . [sending] our country down to the lowest standards of decency? Well now you and I can end it. Yes we can, actually and literally. We can do it by reaching the TV sponsors whose ad dollars make it possible.

Below was a clippable form for sending financial donations to Bozell III. Steve Allen went on the lecture circuit where he connected the television "sewer" with societal downfall. He said *Just Shoot Me*, a popular sitcom starring David Spade, was "beyond the boundaries of even the overly permissive standards that have prevailed in recent years." He came down hard on *Dawson's Creek* for promoting "moral disorder." And he was appalled by *The Tonight Show*, a show that he himself started back in the 1950s, because of Jay Leno's "sex-oriented jokes."

"The producers," Allen lectured, "incapable of creating actual wit . . . decide to go with the current flow, despite the fact that the flow is carrying us all along right into the sewer."

But of the many things that drove him crazy, none bothered him more than the "morally hopeless" Howard Stern. Stern was frequently sexist and racist in the 1980s and '90s, but Allen fixated on his most benign aspects. When the celebrity gossip program *Extra* ran a piece about Howard Stern's new movie, Allen wrote a letter complaining about its title: *Private Parts*.

Brent Bozell III appeared regularly on C-SPAN during the late 1990s and early 2000s. During an episode of C-SPAN's *Washington Journal*, a viewer phoned in and accused Bozell III of obsessing over meaningless television shows while ignoring a far more harmful aspect of the broadcast medium:

"Thank you for taking my call. It seems to be a superficial argument. I'm more offended by untruths than I am by specific words. And I don't find that particularly regulated by *anyone*—the untruths and lies on our public airwaves."

18

ENDLESS CULTURE WARS

"[If the] public did not trust the information it got from the professional media, the Right could win more influence." So said a professional polemicist and career politician named Newt Gingrich. In the early 1980s, Gingrich learned the art of political warfare from his mentor, Paul Weyrich. Gingrich was one of many political operatives whose career was sustained by the think tank universe.

The Heritage Foundation had been tremendously successful in repackaging discredited John Birch Society concepts for the mainstream. Throughout the 1990s, dozens of representatives from the Heritage Foundation appeared on television news described as "senior fellows." The euphemism gave an illusion of credibility and scholarship. Very rarely did anyone on the news explain exactly what "senior fellow" was supposed to mean, nor clarified what the Heritage Foundation was, nor who funded it, nor who founded it.

In the late 1980s, Paul Weyrich coauthored a number of books and articles with William Lind, an articulate writer who became Weyrich's primary collaborator. Lind delivered speeches at the Heritage Foundation, in which he argued African Americans were better off when they were enslaved and that America was in decline because of desegregation. When his critics accused him of spreading hate, he proudly agreed.

"In fact, if we are going to rescue our culture we need a lot more hate," said Lind. "We need hate of the very things Cultural Marxism most strongly promotes, including loose sexual morals, feminism and bad behavior by certain racial and ethnic groups."

The term "Cultural Marxism" had been used intermittently in the race-baiting periodical the *Dartmouth Review* and by third-party candidate Lyndon LaRouche in the 1980s. Lind and Weyrich repeated the term throughout the 1990s as a euphemism for "political correctness."

Lind and Weyrich were determined to demonize the college campus and replace the curriculum with one that would serve corporate interests. As the lobbyist Jack Abramoff explained, "It is not our job to seek peaceful co-existence with the Left. Our job is to remove them from power permanently . . . This means removing Leftists from positions of power and influence in every area of student life: student newspapers and radio stations, student governments . . . and academia. We are replacing these Leftists with committed conservatives."

Charles Koch was increasingly active in the 1990s. The billionaire oil tycoon and former John Birch Society bookstore manager said college campuses were "a great investment" for a "significant competitive advantage" in the body politic.

According to investigative reporter Jane Mayer, donations from the Charles Koch Foundation "corrupted academia, sponsoring courses that would otherwise fail to meet the standards of legitimate scholarship." At several schools, Koch turned the campus into "a delivery system for the donors . . . a long-range strategy to change the country's political makeup."

Politicians who rose to power with Koch money "sought to slash their states' public university budgets while simultaneously raising tuition, ending need-based scholarships, limiting or curtailing tenure protections, reducing faculty governance, and undermining support for the liberal arts curriculum." George Mason University was used as a model, and the result was "a steady stream of academic research intended to support widespread deregulation of federal and state governments."

The Bradley Foundation, a powerful and ubiquitous far-right piggy bank, provided grants to cash-starved schools in exchange for mandatory courses about Ayn Rand. The Bradley Foundation had come a long way since the 1950s when the Allen-Bradley company was merely running advertisements in John Birch Society newsletters. While journalists occasionally chronicled the Bradley Foundation methods, their roots in the old John Birch Society were seldom mentioned.

One student attending a school funded by the Bradley and Koch foundations said, "We learned that Keynes was bad, the free-market was better, that sweatshop labor wasn't so bad, and that the hands-off regulations in China were better than those in the U.S." When teachers and students objected, Koch-funded "senior fellows" accused the campus of being opposed to free speech.

William Lind had been Paul Weyrich's obscure ghostwriter, but he got his chance in the spotlight when Weyrich unveiled a new cable channel in 1993 called National Empowerment Television. NET focused on many of the same Culture War topics that Fox News would eventually cover. Weyrich pledged, "We will no longer allow the Cultural Marxism of an elite few to dictate words, language and opinions." NET was funded by Coors, Philip Morris, and the National Rifle Association, and it featured "paid programming" from preacher Pat Robertson and the Cato Institute. Burton Yale Pines of the Heritage Foundation was named the channel's chief executive officer and Lind was named its editorial advisor.

Lind hosted a weekly program called *Next Revolution*. He sat in an easy chair, puffed on a pipe, and spoke as he stared directly into the camera. He denounced the state of the college campus and argued that America would have been better off if the South had won the Civil War:

"Critical Theory is the basis for gay studies, Black studies, women's studies, and various other *studies* departments found on American university campuses today. These departments are the home base of political correctness . . . Given how bad things have gotten in the old USA, it's not hard to believe that history might have taken a better turn [had the South won]. It is highly unlikely that the Confederacy would have embraced the Cultural Marxism of political correctness."

The terminology hatched in the think tank laboratories inevitably ended up on the political stage. On the campaign trail, presidential candidate Pat Buchanan said, "The violence of this political correctness is nothing less than Cultural Marxism."

Buchanan had been part of the Culture War for decades. As a young newspaper editor in St. Louis, Buchanan opposed the Civil Rights Movement, as a strategist for Richard Nixon he coined the term "silent majority," and as a speechwriter for Spiro Agnew, he composed a famous attack on the media. Buchanan was an editor at *TV Guide*, an on-air personality on CNN's *Crossfire*, and a staffer in the Reagan White House until the administration concluded he was a liability.

"I hadn't encountered anyone like Pat since I had to deal with the White Citizens Councils in my days as a Mississippi news editor," said Ronald Reagan's press secretary, Larry Speakes. "Pat caused more trouble than anyone else who worked closely with Reagan in the first six years."

Buchanan believed that in order to earn attention, discredit opponents, and secure power, conservatives should be bombastic. "There is a genuine question whether any conservative politician can rivet the camera's attention without ceasing to be, strictly speaking, a conservative," he said. He concluded, according to his biographer, "The only way to get noticed was to float conservative ideas in a radical, noisy way."

Buchanan ran for president in 1992. His campaign was distinguished from those of Bill Clinton, Ross Perot, and George H. W. Bush with its focus on race. "The African Americans of the 1990s demand racial quotas and set-asides," Buchanan said on the campaign trail. "Who speaks for the Euro-Americans who founded the United States?"

During his campaign, Buchanan stood beneath a Confederate flag and shared the stage with an elderly Lester Maddox. Buchanan referred to the Voting Rights Act of 1965 as "an act of regional discrimination against the South." And he blamed the LA riots on Latino immigrants who "ransack and loot the apartments of the terrified old men and women." He promised that, if elected, he would "build a massive wall along the border to keep them out."

David Duke, the former Ku Klux Klan leader, was also running for president, but his followers abandoned him in favor of Buchanan. "I will always be a David Duke supporter," said a New Orleans police officer, "but come election day I'm going to cast my ballot for Pat Buchanan. Pat Buchanan has a better chance of winning than David Duke."

At the Republican National Convention in 1992, Buchanan invoked the Culture War in a speech that upstaged the event. He ended his campaign and threw his support behind George Bush in exchange for a choice timeslot to deliver his speech:

"George Bush is a defender of right-to-life, and a champion of the Judeo-Christian values and beliefs upon which America was founded. Mr. Clinton, however, has a different agenda. At its top is unrestricted abortion on demand. When the Irish-Catholic governor of Pennsylvania, Robert Casey, asked to say a few words on behalf of the 25 million unborn children destroyed since *Roe v. Wade*, Bob Casey was told there was no place for him at the podium at Bill Clinton's convention, no room at the inn. Yet a militant leader of the homosexual rights movement could rise at that same convention and say: 'Bill Clinton and Al Gore represent the most pro-lesbian and pro-gay ticket in history.' And so they do."

Buchanan warned that if Bill Clinton were elected, Hillary Clinton would be part of the package. "This, my friends, is radical feminism. The agenda that Clinton and Clinton would impose on America—abortion on demand, a litmus test for the Supreme Court, homosexual rights, discrimination against religious schools, women in combat units—that's change, all right. But it is not the kind of change America needs. It is not the kind of change America wants. And it is not the kind of change we can abide in a nation that we still call God's country . . .

"My friends, this election is about more than who gets what. It is about who we are. It is about what we believe, and what we stand for as Americans. There is a religious war going on in this country. It is a cultural war, as critical to the kind of nation we shall be as was the Cold War itself, for this war is for the soul of America."

Buchanan's biographer said the speech marked a new stage in the Culture War: "The Republicans wouldn't be content to call Democrats dumb anymore. They were going to call them sacrilegious perverts as well."

Many Republicans objected to the Buchanan speech. Rudy Giuliani and Rush Limbaugh believed it would harm their cause. Republican senator

Richard Lugar said, "You don't build majorities by excluding whole groups of people and you don't have to be nasty to be conservative."

But a new era of nastiness was about to emerge with the help of a new technological advancement. The writer Harlan Ellison took note of this evolution in June 1994:

"What I don't like are the hairbrained idiots who get on these computer bulletin boards and spend all night long bad-mouthing people with impunity, spreading gossip, and doing ugliness. What bothers me about the information superhighway is that it is going to be traversed by the same imbeciles who are walking around *without* an information superhighway."

The Republican Party swept the midterms on November 25, 1994. The victories of Newt Gingrich and his allies were celebrated by the think tanks, which claimed responsibility. "In news stories that day, the Heritage Foundation was mentioned fourteen times, the Cato Institute seven times, the American Enterprise Institute seven times, the Manhattan Institute twice," reported the *Columbia Journalism Review*. The number of think tanks operating in Washington had grown, but their wealthy funders remained the same. Former Heritage Foundation employee David Brock said, "While it may appear to readers and viewers that they are hearing hundreds of independent conclusions, they are really hearing from a handful of right-wing multimillionaires like Richard Mellon Scaife, whose money has gone into more than one-third of the think tanks, and from a few dozen corporations."

Charles Koch and his "foundations" funded dozens of front groups with deceiving, euphemistic names. Among them were the American Future Fund, Americans for Prosperity, Center for Shared Services, Club for Growth, Citizens for a Sound Economy, the Competitive Enterprise Institute, Concerned Women for America, the Foundation for Individual Rights in Education, FreedomWorks, Generation Opportunity, the George C. Marshall Institute, the Hoover Institution, the Institute for Humane Studies, the Leadership Institute, Libre Initiative, the Mercatus Center, and the Tax Foundation. Every single one existed for the purpose of political propaganda, to protect the wealth of Koch Industries, and to discredit those who might stand in their way.

The Bradley Foundation, the Scaife Foundation, the Olin Foundation, the Heritage Foundation, the Heartland Institute, the American Enterprise Institute, the Cato Institute, the Claremont Institute, the Discovery Institute, DonorsTrust, the Federalist Society—all of them were funded by the vast wealth of Koch, Olin, Scaife, Bradley, and DeVos. Nearly all started out assisting the John Birch Society in the 1960s. As the millennium approached, hundreds of "senior fellows" appeared on talk radio, cable news, and even some late-night comedy shows. They published hundreds of newspaper editorials, toured the lecture circuit, and conformed to identical talking points.

"The news business has changed so radically," reported the *Columbia Journalism Review*, "groups like Heritage, Cato, and Citizens for a Sound Economy can now help define the news, and influence and shape public opinion."

FreedomWorks, one of the groups operated by Charles Koch, paid radio personality Glenn Beck to integrate their talking points into his commentaries. "For an annual payment that eventually topped $1 million, Beck read 'embedded content' written by the FreedomWorks staff," explained journalist Jane Mayer. "They told him what to say on the air, and he blended the promotional material seamlessly into his monologue, making it sound as if it were his own opinion." Meyer said the purpose was to "balance" factual news with "fraudulent research" in order to "deceive the public about pressing issues in which their sponsors had financial interests."

The success of the strategy was dependent on repetition. According to the "senior fellows," America was always at the precipice of disaster—unless the corporate wish list was immediately implemented. Catchphrases such as "weapons of mass destruction," "ACORN," "fiscal cliff," and "Cultural Marxism," became common parlance, paving the way for a new generation of buzzwords like "critical race theory." The think tanks turned obscure terms into American obsessions, inciting large segments of the population to turn against anything standing in the way of corporate dominance.

A spokesman with the Heritage Foundation gloated, "It doesn't take a rocket scientist to figure out that the millions spent by conservative think tanks have enabled them virtually to dictate the issues and terms of national debates."

"They understand the propaganda potential," observed one journalist. "Viewers are confused about what's hard news and out-and-out propaganda. They can't tell the difference between Paul Weyrich and Dan Rather."

Paul Weyrich warned his allies that they risked losing the Culture War if they didn't double down. In April 1999 he said:

"The ideology of Political Correctness, which openly calls for the destruction of our traditional culture, has so gripped the body politic, has so gripped our institutions, that it is even affecting the Church. It has completely taken over the academic community. It is now pervasive in the entertainment industry, and it threatens to control literally every aspect of our lives. Those who came up with Political Correctness, which we more accurately call 'Cultural Marxism,' did so in a deliberate fashion . . . Suffice it to say that the United States is very close to becoming a state totally dominated by an alien ideology, an ideology bitterly hostile to Western culture . . . If you say the 'wrong thing,' you suddenly have legal problems, political problems, you might even lose your job or be expelled from college. Certain topics are forbidden. You can't approach the truth about a lot of different subjects. If you do, you are immediately branded as 'racist,' 'sexist,' 'homophobic,' 'insensitive.' . . . Cultural Marxism is succeeding in its war against our culture . . . We will be lucky if we escape with any remnants of the great Judeo-Christian civilization that we have known down through the ages."

A decade later, ten days before his death, the Heritage Foundation hosted a salute to Paul Weyrich. Guests included the Reverend Don Wildmon, Indiana senator Mike Pence, and billionaire think tank funder Richard Mellon Scaife. Conservative columnist George Will told the assembled crowd, "Someone once said the history of philosophy is nothing but a series of footnotes to Plato. Well, the last forty years of Washington politics is, in a sense, a series of footnotes to Paul Weyrich. He's been on the front lines of the Culture Wars—as well he should be—because he started a number of the skirmishes."

★

The White Citizens' Councils that had opposed the Civil Rights Movement had been defunct for decades. But as Y2K approached, they reemerged under the name the Council of Conservative Citizens. According to the president of a Mississippi chapter, they used the "old White Citizens Council mailing lists to set up the new organization." The Council of Conservative Citizens said they were tired of the culture of "political correctness," which derided them as racists simply because they were racist.

"Racism, sexism and chauvinism are powerful weapons in the Marxist psychological warfare against traditional American values," said Gordon Lee Baum, the president of the Council of Conservative Citizens. "Political correctness, the product of critical theory, is really treason against the U.S. Constitution and against America. We at the council indeed speak out for white European Americans, their civilization and faith, and the U.S. Constitution. We are indeed pro-white, but we are not racist." Previously, Baum was employed as David Duke's personal assistant.

Pat Buchanan ran for president one more time in the year 2000. He warned that the United States was operating "under a form of Cultural Marxism" in which immigrants promoted a "moral decadence" that threatened "to radically change the nation's composition." At one campaign stop in August 2000, Buchanan said, "We must take out country back . . . cleaning up what I think is the dismal swamp, draining that swamp."

Mel Gibson hosted a fundraiser for Buchanan, but overall he was not taken seriously as a candidate. Real estate mogul Donald Trump said, "He's anti-Semitic. He's anti-Black. He obviously has been having a love affair with Adolf Hitler."

Between October 2001 and March 2003, the multitude of "senior fellows" representing think tank interests proliferated in American broadcasting. One of the mantras repeated over and over was that the United States needed to immediately invade the country of Iraq before America was annihilated. Those who opposed the war were dismissed as anti-American, and those who warned that it would destabilize the Middle East were dismissed as fools.

"Just so you know, we're ashamed the president of the United States is from Texas," Natalie Maines told a London audience. The lead singer of the Dixie Chicks was referring to President Bush and the invasion of Iraq. The majority of the world's population was opposed to the war, but in the United States, think tank propaganda convinced many that Iraq posed an imminent threat to America.

When a journalist from the *Guardian* quoted Maines, American news outlets seized on it, and the Dixie Chicks were dragged into the Culture War.

"We've been overseas for several weeks and have been reading and following the news accounts of our government's position," said the Dixie Chicks in an official statement. "The anti-American sentiment that has unfolded here is astounding. While we support our troops, there is nothing more frightening than the notion of going to war with Iraq and the prospect of all the innocent lives that will be lost."

Their clarification did not mollify Americans who were consuming a daily dose of talk radio and cable news. When the Dixie Chicks appeared in Greenville, South Carolina, a large group of detractors picketed the concert. "I wonder if their attitudes would change," asked one protester, "if they were gassed by chemicals the way the Iraqis were! What if they got shot in the head and put in a factory?"

Their music was pulled from dozens of country music stations throughout the United States. The radio station WTDR in Talladega, Alabama, polled its listeners as to whether or not the Dixie Chicks should stay on their playlist. "The phone just went ballistic," said one of the disc jockeys. "I've been doing radio for twenty-eight years, and I've never seen anything get that kind of response."

Glenn Beck, then a morning radio host at WLAC in Nashville, said Natalie Maines deserved "a shove into an airplane propeller." Beck conceived a series of pro-war rallies in which Dixie Chicks compact discs were melted on portable barbecues.

Beck's radio program was syndicated by Clear Channel Worldwide, a company that owned 1,233 different stations, reaching over one hundred million listeners. "Some of the biggest rallies this month have endorsed President Bush's strategy against Saddam Hussein, and the common thread linking most of them is Clear Channel Worldwide Inc., the nation's largest owner of radio stations," reported the *Chicago Tribune*. "In a move that has raised eyebrows in some legal and journalistic circles, Clear Channel radio stations in Atlanta, Cleveland, San Antonio, Cincinnati and [fourteen] other cities have sponsored rallies attended by up to 20,000 people . . . Clear Channel is by far the largest owner of radio stations in the nation. The company owned only 43 in 1995, but when Congress removed many of the ownership limits in 1996, Clear Channel was quickly on the highway to radio dominance."

The music of the Dixie Chicks was banned by Clear Channel stations, and their largest competitor, Cox Broadcasting, canceled a program because the host refused to stop playing them. KRMD in Bossier City, Louisiana, staged a stunt in which listeners were invited to bring their Dixie Chicks records to the station "to be smashed by a tractor." WDAF in Kansas City, Missouri, arranged garbage cans for its listeners to discard their albums during a massive "chicken toss." Nashville radio host Phil Valentine said, "We're looking at the logistics of doing a Dixie Chicks skeet shoot."

Dan Whitney, a stand-up comedian who was gaining traction under the name Larry the Cable Guy, was fuming: "How dare this first hippo of country music go to a country whose support we're trying to get for a possible war and then attack our president in that country. It's a shame [the] good-looking Dixie Chicks gotta put up with this singing sow's ridiculous rants."

Natalie Maines's aunt worked as a news anchorwoman in Lubbock, Texas, but she quit after death threats were sent to the station. Lipton, sponsors of the Dixie Chicks national tour, removed their banners, broke their contract, and said the Dixie Chicks did not reflect the values of chicken soup.

"I think it will go down in history as an example of what was happening during this time," said Dixie Chicks singer Emily Robison. "Everyone's just being scared right now—scared to speak up, scared to question. And that's unfortunate, because I think our country's based on asking questions."

Facebook, Twitter, and YouTube did not yet exist, but there were reportedly thousands of anti–Dixie Chicks posts on an AOL forum.

"What a sickening disgrace and slap in the face to every military family in the country," wrote an AOL user. "My best wishes for the bitch traitor is that their sales go in the toilet, the public throws out their records, public outcry makes CMA take back the awards, and the lousy bitch never gets to sing in public again and her ass gets shipped to Baghdad before the bombs fall . . . It is time for America to return to the days when the people were proud and the scumbag traitors and enemy sympathizers were put on trial or turned over to military tribunals."

"In these [internet] forums, they're talking about manipulating radio," said Dixie Chicks manager Simon Renshaw. "It's sinister to me how in this communications age certain people intentionally aim to affect the media's perception of the mood of the country. It's the great thing about the Internet and the bad thing about the Internet. All of a sudden it becomes very easy for individuals and small groups to start manipulating public opinion."

EPILOGUE

Robert M. Berger was a police officer with the Baltimore Police Department. Joining the force in 1972, he was a white cop who patrolled a Black neighborhood. On his nights off, he liked to sing, and he had a passion for Al Jolson songs. Out of uniform, Berger developed an act, which the NAACP called "socially and racially reprehensible."

Officer Berger performed in blackface throughout the 1970s and 1980s. His superiors at the Baltimore Police Department told him blackface was unbecoming to an officer and sent him a memo: "This activity has become the subject of tremendous negative reaction from members of the public who perceive this to be demeaning to the Black race."

"They pay you for eight hours a day and tell you what you can do with the other sixteen," complained Berger. He said he was being discriminated against simply because he loved doing blackface. Berger hired a lawyer from the ACLU to defend his right to burnt cork.

The *Baltimore Sun* reported, "A city policeman whose performances in blackface makeup drew protests from the NAACP has accused the police department in a U.S. District Court law suit of violating his right to free speech by ordering him to stop performing in public." The BPD disagreed, arguing that "performances in blackface are not the kind of expression by a public employee that the Constitution's guarantee of free speech protects."

Berger was painting his skin as he told a journalist, "There's nothing racial involved in it. I still don't understand what the beef is. I'm just a guy singing a song."

Officer Berger staged a night of blackface at the Baltimore Hilton in 1982. The local NAACP staged a large protest, while the ACLU came to Berger's defense. "I would hate to think we live in such dangerous times that . . . we have stop other people from . . . entertaining," said Barbara Mello of the ACLU. "That's Germany in 1939." Officer Berger solicited donations from supporters and handed out buttons that read "Justice for Jolson."

Officer Berger kept doing blackface for the rest of his tenure. The police department concluded that Berger's "blackface performances were fostering racial confrontation and threatening hard-won relations with the black community." It was a public relations disaster for the BPD.

"A city police department trial board yesterday recommended firing singing policeman Robert M. Berger for disobeying recent orders that he not continue his performances of Al Jolson routines in blackface," reported the *Baltimore Sun* in 1984. "Following a disciplinary hearing yesterday morning, the board ordered Officer Berger, 35, suspended . . . The hearing was conducted after Officer Berger disobeyed another of several orders the department has issued over a two-year period that he not perform in blackface. He recently lost a civil suit in federal court against the police department over the earlier orders, which he claimed violated his right to free speech."

Officer Berger sued for unlawful dismissal and violation of his constitutional right to blackface. And the US Court of Appeals for the Fourth Circuit in Richmond, Virginia, ruled that his blackface shtick was indeed protected by the First Amendment. One week later, however, the ruling was overturned by a district court, which concluded the police had every right "to protect its relations with the Black community." The court ordered Officer Berger to "undergo psychological evaluations, which concluded he was unfit for police duty."

Retired from the force, he opened a blackface-themed nightclub called Berger's Colonial Inn. It operated in rural Baltimore from 1988 until 1996. The year it went out of business, Berger performed blackface at a retirement dinner for a white police officer. Black officers with the Baltimore Police Department protested. Officer Debbie Pridgen explained, "For them to be members or former members of the Baltimore County Police Department, and for me as an officer to know that this is how they feel about Blacks, I just think it's a shame."

As far as Officer Berger was concerned, blackface would never die. In the year 2015, he was back in the news. Now a senior citizen, he resurrected his old blackface act one more time, at a fundraiser for the five police officers implicated in the death of Freddie Gray.

ACKNOWLEDGMENTS

Judd Apatow, Dan Aykroyd, W. Kamau Bell, Jerry Beck, Michael Bonfiglio, Neal Brennan, Albert Brooks, Kelly Carlin, Ernie Chambers, Frank Conniff, Mario Diaz, Illeana Douglas, Wayne Federman, Dara Gottfried, Gilbert Gottfried, Daniel Greenberg, Caroline Hirsch, Norm Macdonald, Mark Malkoff, Merrill Markoe, Marc Maron, Steve Martin, Katie Mears, Bob Odenkirk, Dan Pasternack, Steve Randisi, Michele Reiner, Rob Reiner, Kathryn H. Fuller-Seeley, Jamison Stoltz, James Urbaniak, Valentina, Robert Weide, Fred Willard, Jordan R. Young, Alan and Robin Zweibel. Last and certainly least, the members of the secret clubhouse: Scott Alexander, Craig Bierko, Dan Clowes, Drew Friedman, Dana Gould, Larry Karaszewski, Richard Kind, Leonard Maltin, Michael McKean, Matt Oswalt, Patton Oswalt, Frank Santopadre, Ben Schwartz, Cris Shapan, Jimmy Vivino, Steven Weber, Terry Zwigoff, and President Theodore Roosevelt.

NOTES

v   **"If you want to get comedians"**: Radio KPFK comedy panel with Groucho Marx, Steve Allen, Carl Reiner; April 2, 1962.

v   **"We have created a marketplace"**: Council on Foreign Relations, "A Conversation with Ted Koppel," November 12, 2019.

INTRODUCTION

2   **"The central image"**: Richard Hofstadter, *The Paranoid Style in American Politics and Other Essays* (New York: Alfred A. Knopf, 1965), 3–5, 26–3.

2   **"mistook change for decline"**: Fritz Stern, *The Politics of Cultural Despair: A Study in the Rise of the Germanic Ideology* (Berkeley: University of California Press, 1961), xxvii.

2   **"Nothing short of a great"**: Michael Medved, *Hollywood vs. America* (New York: Harper Collins, 1992), 23.

2   **Throughout the 1960s:** Robert W. Whitaker, ed., *The New Right Papers* (New York: St. Martin's Press, 1982), 59–60.

4   **"I think the people today"**: *Man of the Year*, NBC Television, January 1, 1955.

4   **"If you want to ascertain the liberal"**: Joseph Keeley, *The Left-Leaning Antenna Political Bias in Television* (New Rochelle, NY: Arlington House, 1971), 39–41.

5   **"The fact that Americans are losing"**: *Boston Globe*, March 10, 1968.

5   **"The PC movement is really the first"**: Ralph Wilson and Isaac Kamola, *Free Speech and Koch Money: Manufacturing a Campus Culture War* (London: Pluto Press, 2021), 95.

6   **"You can joke"**: "Please stop saying 'You can't joke about anything anymore'. You can. You can joke about whatever the fuck you like. And some people won't like it and they will tell you they don't like it. . . .": Ricky Gervais (@rickygervais), Twitter, December 31, 2018, 11:59 A.M., https://twitter.com/rickygervais/status/1079784120945967104.

6   **"This atmosphere of fear"**: *Pittsburgh Press*, January 31, 1954.

6   **"There's this wild lunatic fringe"**: Rod Serling, interview by Mike Wallace, CBS, September 22, 1959.

6   *The Smothers Brothers Comedy Hour* **was:** David Steinberg, *Inside Comedy: The Soul, Wit, and Bite of Comedy and Comedians of the Last Five Decades* (New York: Alfred A. Knopf, 2021), 28.

6   **"My husband and I were shocked"**: *St. Louis Post-Dispatch*, November 17, 1968.

7   **"The CBS switchboards"**: Robert Metz, *CBS: Reflections in a Bloodshot Eye* (Chicago: Playboy Press, 1975), 300–301.

7   **CBS received a letter addressed:** Metz, *CBS: Reflections*, 299.

7   **CBS forced:** Metz, *CBS: Reflections*, 296.

7   **"There's no question"**: Ernest Chambers, interview by the author, January 2022.

1

9   **"Public amusements were"**: Armond Fields, *Eddie Foy A Biography*, (Jefferson, NC: McFarland & Company, Inc., 1999), 1.

9   **The original blackface craze:** Jim Haskins and N. R. Mitgang, *Mr. Bojangles: The Biography of Bill Robinson* (New York: William Morrow and Company, Inc., 1988), 31.

10   **"scrambling-looking man"**: Dale Cockrell, *Demons of Disorder: Early Blackface Minstrels and their World* (Cambridge, UK: Cambridge University Press, 1997), 63.

10   **"It seemed as though"**: Mel Watkins, *On the Real Side: A History of African American Comedy* (Chicago: Lawrence Hill Books, 1994), 87.

10   **As early as 1848:** William Barlow, *Voice Over: The Making of Black Radio* (Philadelphia: Temple University Press, 1999), 6.

10   **"filthy scum of white society"**: *North Star*, October 27, 1848.

10   **"brickbats, fire-crackers and other missiles"**: R.J.M. Blackett, ed., *Thomas Morris Chester, Black Civil War Correspondent: His Dispatches from the Virginia Front* (New York: Da Capo Press, 1989), 7.

10   **"in a vision"**: J.C. Furnas, *Goodbye to Uncle Tom* (New York: William Sloane Associates, 1956), 6.

10   **"her readers into deepening"**: Furnas, *Goodbye to Uncle Tom*, 48–50.

11   **"proslavery and antislavery"**: Barlow, *Voice Over*, 6.

11   **"From about 1853"**: Watkins, *On the Real Side*, 94–95.

11   **"White southerners had no sympathy"**: Haskins and Mitgang, *Mr. Bojangles*, 33.

11   **"Hitherto . . . the form of amusement"**: *Brooklyn Daily Eagle*, October 21, 1877.

11   **"A conspiracy exists"**: Richard Hofstadter, *The Paranoid Style in American Politics and Other Essays* (New York: Alfred A. Knopf, 1965), 19–20.

11   **"long-haired, wild-eyed"**: Higham, *Strangers in the Land*, 55.

12   **"thousands of idle"**: Higham, *Strangers in the Land*, 71.

12   **"The more conservative religious groups"**: Arthur Frank Wertheim and Barbara Bair, eds., *The Papers of Will Rogers*, vol. 2, *Wild West to Vaudeville, April 1904–September 2008* (Norman, OK: University of Oklahoma Press, 2000), 304.

12   **"rigorously forbidden"**: Irving Wallace, *The Fabulous Showman: The Life and Times of P. T. Barnum* (New York: Signet Classics, 1962), 35.

12   **Vaudevillian Sam Devere:** Trav S.D., *No Applause—Just Throw Money: The Book That Made Vaudeville Famous* (London: Faber & Faber, 2006), 43.

12   **Vaudeville comic Eddie Foy:** Wertheim and Bair, eds., *The Papers of Will Rogers*, vol. 2, 304.

12   **"Ladies and Gentlemen":** *San Francisco Examiner*, March 7, 1895.

13   **"It is not unusual":** *Tampa Times*, June 22, 1920.

13   **"If there is one objectionable":** *Topeka Daily Capital*, April 5, 1903.

13   **"If almost all of America's young":** Hallie Lieberman, *Buzz: The Stimulating History of the Sex Toy* (New York: Pegasus Books, 2017), 31.

13   **"It breeds lust":** Heywood Broun and Margaret Leech, *Anthony Comstock: Roundsman of the Lord* (New York: The Literary Guild of America, 1927), 80.

14   **"I have destroyed 160":** Stephen Stiff, *Acid Hype: American News Media and the Psychedelic Experience* (Champaign, IL: University of Illinois Press, 2015), 19.

14   **"too obscene to be placed":** Broun and Leech, *Anthony Comstock*, 87.

14   **Police reports:** Ernst and Seagle, *To the Pure*, 75.

14   **"Many passages are expressed":** Ernst and Seagle, *To the Pure*, 54.

14   **"an Irish smut dealer":** Broun and Leech, *Anthony Comstock*, 18.

14   **"Inevitably Comstock was the":** Broun and Leech, *Anthony Comstock*, 189–191.

14   **"to investigate a complaint":** Broun and Leech, *Anthony Comstock*, 18–19.

14   **"The blow was instantly repeated":** *Brooklyn Daily Eagle*, November 2, 1874.

14   **began in 1876:** *Marion Star*, November 24, 1879.

14   **"contamination of the youth of the country":** *Lima Clipper*, March 6, 1896.

15   **"Do these people need":** *Lucifer, the Light Bearer*, April 24, 1891.

15   **"sexual and moral pervert":** Ernst and Seagle, *To the Pure*, 76.

15   **"suitable only for slums":** *Decatur Daily*, September 4, 1955.

15   **The federal government banned:** *Brooklyn Times Union*, December 10, 1932.

15   **It increased demand:** Ernst and Seagle, *To the Pure*, 41.

15   **"The morals of the youth":** Broun and Leech, *Anthony Comstock*, 223–224.

15   **"The whole World's Fair"; "During many centuries":** Ernst and Seagle, *To the Pure*, 227–228, 268–269.

15   **"lowering the standards of thinking":** *St. Mary's Star*, January 1, 1904.

15   **Lighthearted references:** M. Bennett, *The Champions of the Church: Their Crimes and Persecutions* (New York: Liberal and Scientific Publishing House, 1878), 1009.

16   **"A sacrilegious comedian":** *Maysville Evening Bulletin*, April 17, 1894.

16   **"the morals of the young people":** *Long Branch Daily Record*, November 19, 1912.

16   **"ordered out of town":** *Fort Wayne News*, January 21, 1898.

16   **"Some of the jokes":** *Valley Spirit*, August 3, 1910.

16   **"as a lawless creature":** Higham, *Strangers in the Land*, 55.

16   **"a letter threatening his life":** *Democrat and Chronicle*, August 3, 1904.

16   **the Clan na Gael:** *Pittsburgh Post-Gazette*, March 8, 1915.

17   **"Hammerstein had agreed":** *Washington Evening Star*, January 25, 1907.

18   **"Sensitiveness under such":** *Brooklyn Daily Eagle*, January 26, 1907.

18   **"This may well worry the playwrights":** *Topeka Daily Capital*, April 5, 1903.

18   **"As a whole the show":** *Indianapolis Freeman*, March 30, 1901.

18   **"protested against cheap and vulgar":** *Placer Herald*, June 4, 1910.

19   **"The hue and cry":** *Pittsburgh Daily Post*, May 8, 1910.

19   **"critics of acting contend":** *Pittsburgh Post-Gazette*, November 23, 1910.

19   **"Racial Caricature Out of Date"**: *American Israelite*, April 21, 1910.

19   **"The stage loses nothing"**: *Tonopah Daily Bonanza*, December 15, 1911.

20   **"A number of years ago the Irish"**: *New York Tribune*, April 30, 1913.

20   **"Taking his cue from other races"**: *Tonopah Daily Bonanza*, December 15, 1911.

21   **"Let our humorists try fresh fields"**: *Pittsburgh Post-Gazette*, March 8, 1915.

21   **"Certainly our ideas of what is funny"**: *New York Times*, April 25, 1915.

21   **"There is to be no more offensive"**: *South Bend Tribune*, July 17, 1922.

21   **"The bill forbids"**: *Variety*, April 9, 1915.

21   **"All that sort of"**: *South Bend Tribune*, July 17, 1922.

21   **"A near-riot"**: *Variety*, February 16, 1927.

22   **"dope fiend"**: *Variety*, December 3, 1915.

22   **"All references to Prohibition"**: *Vancouver Sun*, August 12, 1922.

22   **"I had a line here but the President"**: *Pittsburgh Press*, March 22, 1953.

22   **"a rule similar to the federal"**: *South Bend Tribune*, July 17, 1922.

23   **"While working this date, they booked me"**: Bill Smith, *The Vaudevillians* (New York: Macmillan Pub Co., 1976), 90.

23   **"Wouldn't it be a blessing"**: *Moline Dispatch*, November 17, 1915.

23   **"bare knees on the stage"**; **"moral pervert or sex degenerate"**: *Variety*, April 15, 1921.

23   **"The trouble with profanity"**: Herbert Lloyd, *Vaudeville Trails thru the West* (Philadelphia: Herbert Lloyd, 1919), 29.

24   **A clampdown**: *Variety*, September 6, 1932.

2

25   **"outrage to public"**; **"as immoral places"**: Richard S. Randall, *Censorship of the Movies: The Social and Political Control of a Mass Medium* (Madison: University of Wisconsin Press, 1968), 11.

25   **Thomas Edison's film:** Thomas Cripps, *Slow Fade to Black The Negro in American Film, 1900–1942* (New York: Oxford University Press, 1993), 12.

25   **The Biograph:** Brent E. Walker, *Mack Sennett's Fun Factory: A History and Filmography of His Studio and His Keystone and Mack Sennett Comedies, with Biographies of Players and Personnel* (Jefferson, NC: McFarland & Company Inc., 2013), 40.

25   **And an early Mack Sennett:** Cripps, *Slow Fade*, 37.

25   **"In this film Arbuckle":** Walker, *Mack Sennett's Fun Factory*, 40.

26   **"into a possible beast":** Mel Watkins, *On the Real Side: A History of African American Comedy* (Chicago: Lawrence Hill Books, 1994), 188.

26   **"to denounce me":** Raymond Allen Cook, *Fire from the Flint: The Amazing Careers of Thomas Dixon* (Winston-Salem, NC: John F. Blair, 1968), 119–121.

26   **"an atrocity":** Kevin Brownlow, *Hollywood: The Pioneers* (New York: Alfred A. Knopf, 1979), 65.

26   **"to create a feeling":** NAACP, *Fighting a Vicious Film: Protest Against "The Birth of a Nation"* (Boston: NAACP, 1915), 5.

26   "During this period": *Rock Island Argus*, April 17, 1906.

26   "To claim that it is"; "For God's sake": Cripps, *Slow Fade*, 44, 143.

27   "We shall be agreeably surprised": Cook, *Fire from the Flint*, 142.

27   "It has been found necessary": *Chattanooga Daily Times*, November 13, 1905.

27   "How the mind of a man": Cripps, *Slow Fade*, 144.

28   "We protest against this play": *The Broad Ax*, November 10, 1906.

28   "From the evidence that": Cook, *Fire from the Flint*, 149.

28   "While the author may": *The Broad Ax*, November 10, 1906.

28   "They had a farm": Frank Manchel, *Every Step a Struggle: Interviews with Seven who Shaped the African-American Image in Movies* (Washington, DC: New Academia Publishing, 2007), 174.

28   Thirty thousand African Americans: NAACP, *Fighting a Vicious Film*, 15.

28   "pamphlets by the thousands": Cripps, *Slow Fade*, 52.

29   "deliberate attempt to humiliate": *Photoplay*, September 1924.

29   "to have all": NAACP, *Fighting a Vicious Film*, 5.

29   "They would have none"; "For them it was": Cripps, *Slow Fade*, 52-55.

29   Actors posing: Philip Dray, *At the Hands of Persons Unknown: The Lynching of Black America* (New York: Modern Library, 2003), 202–204.

29   At the Atlanta: Brownlow, *Hollywood*, 65.

29   "He is yellow because": Cook, *Fire from the Flint*, 174.

30   "If it be true": Cripps, *Slow Fade*, 55.

30   "The *New York Evening Post*": Cook, *Fire from the Flint*, 169-175.

30   The movie was banned: *Variety*, October 1, 1915; Cripps, *Slow Fade*, 47.

30   "For eight long weeks": *Motion Picture World*, June 19, 1915.

30   Five hundred Black protesters: Cripps, *Slow Fade*, 59.

30   Twenty-five thousand: Dray, *At the Hands*, 202.

30   Governor David Walsh: Cripps, *Slow Fade*, 60.

30   "then there is no room": David Wark Griffith, *The Rise and Fall of Free Speech in America* (Los Angeles: self-published, 1916), unnumbered.

31   "a fight for the whole": *Photoplay*, September 1924.

31   "Today the censorship": Griffith, *The Rise and Fall*, unnumbered.

31   "could not afford the economic costs": Ernest Freeberg, *Democracy's Prisoner: Eugene V. Debs, the Great War, and the Right to Dissent* (Cambridge, MA: Harvard University Press, 2010), 263.

31   "preached hate against America": Freeberg, *Democracy's Prisoner*, 215.

31   "sly and crafty eyes"; "unmistakable criminal": Freeberg, *Democracy's Prisoner*, 219.

31   "The recent decision prohibiting men": *Variety*, May 25, 1917.

31   Cartoonist Art Young: *Chattanooga News*, April 23, 1918.

31   "satanic bloodbath": Freeberg, *Democracy's Prisoner*, 80.

32   "broke through the crowd": *Selma Enterprise*, May 19, 1921.

32   "with the possible exception": Freeberg, *Democracy's Prisoner*, 284.

32   "Are you losing your sense": Cripps, *Slow Fade*, 139–140.

32   **A minor scandal ensued:** *Moving Picture World*, December 18, 1928.

32   **"Too many women are screened":** *Exhibitor's Trade Review*, October 28, 1922.

33   **"Hays had been":** Jack Vizzard, *See No Evil: Life Inside a Hollywood Censor* (New York: Simon & Schuster, 1970), 36–44.

33   **"ridicule of public officials":** John Billheimer, *Hitchcock and the Censors* (Lexington: University Press of Kentucky, 2019), 11.

33   **"Are We To Have Immoral":** *Grand Junction Daily Sentinel*, April 14, 1922.

33   **The Keith vaudeville chain:** *Times Herald*, September 15, 1922.

33–34 **"As long as the man"; "showing of Arbuckle"; "The decision is a complete";** **"Fatty Arbuckle is still":** *Moving Picture World*, April 29, 1922; January 20, 1923; April 29, 1922; October 13, 1923.

34   **"I found God":** *Exhibitor's Trade Review*, June 1924.

34   **"He stepped into a two-minute":** *Variety*, June 11, 1924.

34   **Throughout the year:** *Variety*, October 18, 1923; *Film Daily*, November 2, 1924.

34   **"The custard pie":** *Kansas City Kansan*, October 5, 1921.

35   **"The day of the slapstick":** *Great Falls Tribune*, February 25, 1923.

35   **"In 1910 the first":** *Mountaineer Courier*, December 1, 1921.

35   **"Indulgence in the turkey trot":** *Marysville Evening Democrat*, May 12, 1913.

35   **"These dances are a reversion":** Emily Wortis Leider, *Becoming Mae West* (New York: Farrar Straus Giroux, 1997), 54.

35   **"anti-waltzing party":** Harper's Bazaar, May 1912.

35   **"Do not wriggle the shoulders":** Wortis Leider, *Becoming Mae West*, 83.

35   **"unladylike":** *Variety*, July 11, 1919.

35   **"shameless evidence of debauchery":** Wortis Leider, *Becoming Mae West*, 107.

36   **"shoulder movements":** Wortis Leider, *Becoming Mae West*, 107.

36   **"The so-called jazz music":** *Greeley Daily Tribune*, March 4, 1920.

36   **"It is a sort of musical hysteria":** *Charlotte News*, December 17, 1922.

36   **"Jazz bands are an abomination":** Matthew Murray, *Broadcast Content Regulation and Cultural Limits* (Madison: University of Wisconsin, 1997), 71.

36   **"Music should be censored":** *Variety*, September 10, 1924.

36   **"Jungle music, our American":** *Houston Post*, August 10, 1924.

37   **"Jewish Jazz":** *Dearborn Independent*, August 6, 1921.

37   **"bleating and whining":** Robert Pondillo, *America's First Network TV Censor: The Work of NBC's Stockton Helffrich* (Carbondale: Southern Illinois University Press, 2010), 4.

37   **"I desire to speak":** *Hamilton Journal News*, January 21, 1932.

37   **The National League:** *Heinl Radio Business Letter*, May 17, 1935; *Variety*, September 11, 1935.

37   **"sex delinquency and moral perversion"; "The only solution":** Michele Hilmes, ed., *Radio Reader: Essays in the Cultural History of Radio* (New York: Routledge, 2001), 147.

37   **Some of America's:** John Crosby, *Out of the Blue: A Book about Radio and Television* (New York: Simon & Schuster, 1952), 279–280.

38   **"Psychologists and doctors"**: Dan Gilbert, *Movieland's Madhouse* (San Diego, CA: The Danielle Publishers, 1943), 39–41.

38   **Adeline Leitzbach**; *Sex* **was an action-comedy; "disgrace to all"; "Monstrosity Plucked"**: Wortis Leider, *Becoming Mae West*, 137, 143, 150.

39   **"Wipe Out Those Evil"**: Wortis Leider, *Becoming Mae West*, 155.

39   **"giving an immoral"**: *New York Daily News*, February 16, 1927.

39   **"corrupting the morals"**: *New York Daily News*, February 10, 1927.

39   **stage manager faced; "widely viewed"; "Standards of today"**: Wortis Leider, *Becoming Mae West*, 167, 163–164.

39   **"This show must be judged"**: *Variety*, March 30, 1927.

39   **The next night**: Wortis Leider, *Becoming Mae West*, 166–168.

39   **"to jail, and release"**: *The Pittsburgh Press*, March 3, 1929.

39–40 **Between her arrest; "I want to be filthy"; "No play of our time"**: Wortis Leider, *Becoming Mae West*, 165–166, 178–179, 6.

40   *Pleasure Man: New York Daily News*, December 14, 1928; *Charlotte Observer*, December 16, 1928; *Kenosha News*, December 7, 1928.

40   **"If the shutting down"**: Wortis Leider, *Becoming Mae West*, 209.

40   **"It's the queerest"**: *Variety*, September 19, 1928.

40   **It failed to make it**: Wortis Leider, *Becoming Mae West*, 158.

40   **"It was about homosexuality"**: Charles Higham, *Celebrity Circus* (New York, Dell Publishing, 1979), 37.

40   **"They flaunt"**: *Variety*, September 5, 1928.

41   **"a three-ring circus"**: Wortis Leider, *Becoming Mae West*, 229.

41   **"objectionable intermingling"**: Wortis Leider, *Becoming Mae West*, 232.

41   **When a Forty-Second Street**: *Brooklyn Times Union*, September 29, 1927.

41   **"Electric light bulbs"**: *Escanaba Daily Press*, August 26, 1927.

41   **"the picture would be barred"**: *Variety*, August 15, 1928.

42   **"Whereas *The Birth*"**: Carlton Jackson, *Hattie: The Life of Hattie McDaniel* (Lanham, MD: Madison Books, 1993), 40.

42   **Margaret Mitchell, the novelist**: Malcolm Vance, *Tara Revisited: The Inside Story of What Really Happened to the Stars of* Gone with the Wind (New York: Award Books, 1976), 209.

42   **"I was practically raised"**: Thomas Cripps, *Making Movies Black: The Hollywood Message Movie from World War II to the Civil Rights Era* (New York: Oxford University Press, 1993), 19.

42   *The Nation* **and** *New Republic*: David Thomson, *Showman: The Life of David O. Selznick* (New York: Alfred A. Knopf, 1992), 216.

42   **"glorifies the"**: Susan Myrick, Richard Harwell ed., *White Columns in Hollywood: Reports from the GWTW Sets* (Macon, GA: Mercer University Press, 1982), 213–215.

42   **Screenwriter Ring**: Ring Lardner Jr., *I'd Hate Myself in the Morning: A Memoir* (New York: Thunder's Mouth Press, 2000), ix.

42   **"These are no times"**: Jackson, *Hattie*, 40–43.

43 **"I personally feel quite strongly"**: Rudy Behlmer, ed., *Memo from David O. Selznick* (Hollywood, CA: Samuel French, 1989), 62.

43 **"Hattie McDaniel is not"**; **"She lacks"**; **"teaching Negro talk"**: Myrick, Harwell ed., *White Columns*, 11, 49–50, 65.

43 **"It is with decided relief"**: Myrick, Harwell ed., *White Columns*, 214.

43 **"The Negro press has"**: Myrick, Harwell ed., *White Columns*, 215.

43 **"mockery of civil liberties"**: Charlene B. Regester, *African American Actresses: The Struggle for Visibility, 1900–1960* (Bloomington: Indiana University Press, 2010), 149.

43 **"pus oozing"**: Regester, *African American Actresses*, 149.

44 **"It's resurrecting"**: Jackson, *Hattie*, 51.

44 **Among the protesters**: Michael Rosenthal, *Barney: Grove Press and Barney Rosset, America's Maverick Publisher and His Battle against Censorship* (New York: Skyhorse Publishing, 2017), 14.

44 **"I hope my winning"**: Jackson, *Hattie*, 54.

44 **"And where does this"**: Cripps, *Slow Fade*, 364.

3

45 **Charles Correll's father**: *Wilkes-Barre Record*, April 15, 1930.

46 **Gosden and Correll performed**: William Barlow, *Voice Over: The Making of Black Radio* (Philadelphia: Temple University Press, 1999), 36–37.

46 **"the biggest and best"**: *New York Age*, October 21, 1915.

46 **They authored**: *New York Age*, May 3, 1930.

46 **"We recall having seen"**: *Pittsburgh Courier*, May 10, 1930.

46 **"the white comedians"**: *Pittsburgh Courier*, May 10, 1930.

46 **The case was thrown out**: *Press-Forum Weekly*, May 17, 1930.

46 **"Mark Twain of the air"**: *Wilkes-Barre Record*, April 14, 1930.

46 **The NAACP pointed**: Mel Watkins, *On the Real Side: A History of African American Comedy* (Chicago: Lawrence Hill Books, 1994), 31.

46 **"moronic" and "dangerous"**: Barlow, *Voice Over*, 42.

46 **Gosden and Correll**: *Pittsburgh Courier*, September 19, 1931.

47 **To demonstrate**: Barlow, *Voice Over*, 43.

47 **"post slavery tales and jokes"**: Watkins, *On the Real Side*, 31.

47 **"Yes, I have been called"**: *Pittsburgh Courier*, May 2, 1931.

47 **"They are a shame"**: *Pittsburgh Courier*, May 2, 1931.

47 **"Amos 'n' Andy must go"**: *Pittsburgh Courier*, September 19, 1931.

47 **"A Nation-wide Protest"**: Andrew Buni, *Robert L. Vann: of the Pittsburgh Courier; Politics and Black Journalism* (Pittsburgh: University of Pittsburgh Press, 1974), 228–229.

47 **"I think that all the members"**: *Pittsburgh Courier*, October 3, 1931.

47 **"It seems to me"**: Monroe N. Work, ed., *Negro Year Book: An Annual Encyclopedia of the Negro 1931–1932* (Tuskegee, AL: Tuskegee Institute Press, 1931), 18.

47 **"What is the damage"**: Buni, *Robert L. Vann*, 228.

48 **"There is little doubt"**: Barlow, *Voice Over*, 40–43.

48 **They never:** Buni, *Robert L. Vann*, 229.

48 **Eight songs were removed:** *Variety*, December 4, 1935.

48 **"The guys that run radio":** Irving Brecher with Hank Rosenfeld, *The Wicked Wit of the West: The Last Great Golden Age Screenwriter Shares the Hilarity and Heartaches of Working With Groucho, Garland, Gleason, Burns, Berle, Benny, and Many More* (Teaneck, NJ: Ben Yehuda Press, 2009), 43.

49 **Even innocuous political:** Harrison B. Summers, ed., *Radio Censorship* (New York: Arno Press, 1971), 264.

49 **"We are getting many protests":** NBC internal telegram, November 19, 1940.

49 **"This country is in a state":** *Broadcasting*, March 15, 1933.

49 **The Chase and Sanborn Hour:** Michele Hilmes, ed., *Radio Reader: Essays in the Cultural History of Radio* (New York: Routledge, 2001), 140.

49 **"She said to Charlie":** Edgar Bergen, interview by Chuck Schaden, February 20, 1975.

49 **"a quality of humor":** *Variety*, December 22, 1937.

49 **"offensive to the great mass"; "to prevent the recurrence of such broadcasts.":** Emily Wortis Leider, *Becoming Mae West* (New York: Farrar Straus Giroux), 341.

49 **"After listening to radio":** *Pittsburgh Press*, December 19, 1937.

50 **"It was like a great wave":** Credo Fitch Harris, *Microphone Memoirs of the Horse and Buggy Days of Radio* (New York: Bobbs-Merrill Co., 1937), 114

50 **"We got into all kinds":** Edgar Bergen, interview by Chuck Schaden, February 20, 1975.

50 **After the hysteria:** Hilmes, ed., *Radio Reader*, 138.

50 **Radio censors forced:** John Crosby, *Out of the Blue: A Book about Radio and Television* (New York: Simon & Schuster, 1952), 272–273.

50 **He would censor comedians:** Robert Pondillo, *America's First Network TV Censor: The Work of NBC's Stockton Helffrich* (Carbondale: Southern Illinois University Press, 2010), 11.

4

51 **The Nazi politicians:** *Broadcasting*, March 15, 1933; *Louisville Courier Journal*, August 29, 1937; *Washington Evening Star*, March 5, 1933; *Lima News*, June 4, 1932.

51 **A comedian named:** *Detroit Free Press*, April 16, 1978.

51 **"You know, it's funny":** *Reading Times*, February 6, 1939.

52 **Nazi propaganda:** *Nevada State Journal*, February 4, 1939.

52 **"Comedians have no right":** Nevada State Journal, February 4, 1939.

52 **Warner Bros. pulled:** Alan K. Rode, *Michael Curtiz: A Life in Film* (Lexington: University Press of Kentucky, 2017), 198.

52 **"Americans should accept":** John Billheimer, *Hitchcock and the Censors* (Lexington: University Press of Kentucky, 2019), 79.

52 **Films starring:** Derek Jones, ed., *Censorship: A World Encyclopedia* (New York: Routledge, 2001) 1,916.

52 **"cheap Hebrew"; "I congratulate you":** *Wisconsin State Journal*, February 14, 1938.

52 **Father Charles Coughlin of Michigan:** Charles J. Tull, *Father Coughlin and the New Deal* (Syracuse: Syracuse University Press, 1965), 197–198.

53 **He referred to:** Erik Barnouw, *The Golden Web: A History of Broadcasting in the United States, 1933–1953* (Oxford, UK: Oxford University Press, 1968), 221–224.

53 **Father Coughlin's program:** Tull, *Father Coughlin*, 193; 6–7; 198; 202.

53 **"Freedom such as we":** *Reading Times*, December 28, 1938

53 **"Father Coughlin is a great":** Michele Hilmes, ed., *NBC: America's Network* (Oakland: University of California Press, 2007), 103.

53 **"If you believe":** *Medford Mail Tribune*, October 21, 1936; *Salem Capitol Journal*, October 21, 1936.

54 **"Tell Cantor to get out":** *Cedar Rapids Gazette*, March 31, 1938.

54 **"One of the most momentous":** *Variety*, September 14, 1938.

55 **"song parodies":** *Motion Picture Daily*, September 12, 1939.

55 **The novelty song:** *Variety*, March 31, 1939.

55 **Criticism of Hitler:** *Variety*, June 26, 1941.

55 **Charlie Chaplin's:** *Independent Film Exhibitors Bulletin*, February 6, 1961.

55 **Chicago's Police:** *Motion Picture Herald*, November 16, 1935; *Variety*, September 25, 1940; *Variety*, April 3, 1940; *Variety*, February 7, 1940.

55 **"Racial equality forms":** Kirstin Downey, *The Woman Behind the New Deal: The Life and Legacy of Frances Perkins, Social Security, Unemployment Insurance, and the Minimum Wage* (New York: Anchor, 2010), 273.

55 **"May I express my":** Miranda J. Banks, *The Writers: A History of American Screenwriters and Their Guild* (New Brunswick, NJ: Rutgers University Press, 2015), 74.

55 **His father was elected:** William Gellerman, *Martin Dies* (New York: The John Day Company, 1944), 17–23.

55 **"Every true American,":** *The Charlotte Observer*, April, 4, 1965.

56 **"Hollywood has a":** Dan Gilbert, *Hell Over Hollywood: The Truth About the Movies* (Grand Rapids, MI: Zondervan Publishing House, 1943), 13.

56 **"I am unalterably opposed":** *Variety*, April 3, 1940.

56 **"Before the war":** *Montreal Gazette*, February 12, 1947.

56 **"I saw comedian Alan":** *New York Worker*, July 18, 1946.

57 **"snoopery, meddling":** *Variety*, May 13, 1946.

57 **"We are now in the midst":** *New World A'Comin'*, radio station WMCA, February 4, 1945.

57 **"distinct dissatisfaction":** *Pittsburgh Courier*, October 7, 1944.

58 **"all clichés and racial":** *Variety*, August 2, 1944.

58 **"Feeling has long been manifest":** *Variety*, August 2, 1944.

58 **"Comedians persist":** *Variety*, July 11, 1945.

58 **"had shown a lack":** Philip Dray, *At the Hands of Persons Unknown: The Lynching of Black America* (New York: Modern Library, 2003), 369.

58 **"Even before the soldiers":** Dray, *At the Hands*, 378.

58 **And when the vocal:** Dray, *At the Hands*, 381.

58 **Black celebrities were not immune:** *New York Worker*, December 25, 1945.

59   **Hired by a labor:** Dray, *At the Hands*, 390–392.

60   **"their flying nightsticks":** *Pittsburgh Courier*, September 10, 1949.

60   **"Several personalities":** Maurice Zolotow, *No People Like Show People* (New York: Random House, 1951), 218.

60   **Speakers included:** *New Masses*, January 15, 1946.

61   **"I'm not suggesting":** *Montreal Gazette*, February 12, 1947.

61   **"The classic vaudeville dialecticians":** *Commentary*, August 1952.

61   **"Let me start":** *Montreal Gazette*, February 12, 1947.

61   *The Jack Benny Program* **also:** Kathryn H. Fuller-Seeley, *Jack Benny and the Golden Age of American Radio Comedy* (Oakland: University of California Press, 2017), 156.

61   **"I believe those who have shown":** Estelle Edmerson, "Descriptive Study of the American Negro in the United States Professional Radio 1922–1953" (master's thesis, University of California, August 1954).

62   **"Negro delegates spoke":** *Pittsburgh Courier*, October 11, 1947.

5

63   **In 1946:** John E. O'Connor, ed., *American History/American Television: Interpreting the Video Past* (New York: Ungar Pub. Co., 1983), 96; Erik Barnouw, *The Golden Web: A History of Broadcasting in the United States, 1933–1953* (Oxford, UK: Oxford University Press, 1968), 286.

63   **"Abnormalities are":** *Rochester Democrat and Chronicle*, October 24, 1951.

64   **"Berle started to do":** Irving Brecher with Hank Rosenfeld, *The Wicked Wit of the West: The Last Great Golden Age Screenwriter Shares the Hilarity and Heartaches of Working With Groucho, Garland, Gleason, Burns, Berle, Benny, and Many More* (Teaneck, NJ: Ben Yehuda Press, 2009), 45.

64   **"Milton Berle's show has":** *TV Forecast*, December 6, 1952.

64   **"I think Milton Berle":** *TV Forecast*, March 8, 1952.

64   **"Why station WNBC":** *The Tablet*, January 3, 1948.

64   **NBC censors complained:** Robert Pondillo, *America's First Network TV Censor: The Work of NBC's Stockton Helffrich* (Carbondale, IL: Southern Illinois University Press, 2010), 82–83; Pondillo, *America's First Network TV Censor*, 96.

64   **On an episode:** Michele Hilmes, ed., *Radio Reader: Essays in the Cultural History of Radio* (New York: Routledge, 2001), 149.

64   **"effeminate gentlemen":** Pondillo, *America's First Network TV Censor*, 4.

64   **"It is about time":** *Boston Globe*, January 17, 1951.

64   **"It is shocking":** *Cincinnati Enquirer*, June 9, 1956.

65   **"I don't like the way":** *Cincinnati Enquirer*, April 14, 1956.

65   **"Television, popular magazines":** *Dayton Daily News*, March 28, 1950.

65   **"In boxing":** *New York Daily News*, June 4, 1952.

65   **"I am glad to see someone":** *Muncie Star Press*, June 1, 1952.

65   **Senator E. C. Gathings:** *New York Daily News*, June 4, 1952.

65   **"Barnyard and bathroom":** *Mount Vernon Register News*, June 4, 1952.

66   "to outlaw suggestivity": *Newsday*, June 6, 1952.

66   "Television is the greatest": *Great Falls Tribune*, June 6, 1952.

66   "It's terrible to flick": *Variety*, February 25, 1959.

66   "We have waited for TV": *Baltimore Sun*, March 1, 1951.

66   A Chicago archdiocese: Pondillo, *America's First Network TV Censor*, 28–29.

66   He proposed: *Pottsville Republican and Herald*, April 12, 1952.

66   "I was disappointed": *Cincinnati Enquirer*, February 18, 1956.

67   "down the home": *Cincinnati Enquirer*, January 21, 1956.

67   The general contempt: *Odessa American*, August 12, 1954.

67   *Lassie*, the popular family: Viewer, "The Mike Wallace Interview of Rod Serling," CBS, September 22, 1959.

67   Arnaz hired priests: Desi Arnaz, *A Book* (New York: Warner Books, 1977), 277–282.

67   "We are not the only ones"; "I did not find them": *TV Forecast*, February 14, 1953.

68   "If we want to know": *TV Forecast*, February 21, 1953.

68   Sid Caesar abandoned: *Minneapolis Star Tribune*, October 27, 1957.

68   *Variety* reported: *Variety*, April 1, 1959.

68   "You crack a joke about lawyers": *Saturday Evening Post*, September 20, 1958.

68   "The few comedians": Steve Allen, *Mark It and Strike It: An Autobiography* (New York: Hillman Books, 1960), 254.

68   "In television everything known": *Arizona Republic*, April 21, 1954.

69   "Profanity and Obscenity": Nathan Godfried, *WCFL: Chicago's Voice of Labor, 1926–78* (Champaign: University of Illinois Press, 1997), 209.

69   As the NAB deliberated: Kay Mills, *Changing Channels: The Civil Rights Case that Transformed Television* (Jackson: University Press of Mississippi, 2004), 66.

69   "Good taste alone": *Binghamton Press & Sun-Bulletin*, January 6, 1952.

70   In his early days: Mel Watkins, *On the Real Side: A History of African American Comedy* (Chicago: Lawrence Hill Books, 1994), 226.

70   Eventually, he teamed: *New York Age*, October 8, 1914.

70   "The words on paper": Robert Justman, interview at the Academy of Television.

70   "He was the funniest man": *The Steve Allen Show*, NBC Radio, 1988.

71   "Of all the comedians": Nipsey Russell, *Mo' Funny: Black Comedy in America*, HBO, 1993.

71   The old radio theme song: John E. O'Connor, ed., *American History*, 39–40.

71   "consultant on racial": Elizabeth McLeod, "Some History of *Amos 'n' Andy*," archived at jeff560.tripod.com/amos.html.

71   A columnist: J. Fred MacDonald, *Blacks and White TV: African Americans in Television Since 1948* (Chicago, IL: Nelson-Hall Publishers, 1988), 27–28.

71   The Committee: John E. O'Connor, ed., *American History*, 49.

71   "What is needed": *Variety*, August 8, 1951.

72   The makers of Blatz: John E. O'Connor, ed., *American History*, 41.

72   A joint statement: *Variety*, August 8, 1951.

72   James Edwards: *Alabama Tribune*, August 17, 1951.

72   **In the daytime I played:** Nick Stewart, interview at the Archive of American Television, June 20, 1997.

73   **"It's all part of the segregation issue":** *Variety,* June 20, 1956.

73   **"Gosden and Correll are millionaires":** Nick Stewart, interview.

73   **"In Virginia":** Nancy MacLean, *Democracy in Chains: The Deep History of the Radical Right's Stealth Plan for America* (New York: Viking, 2017), xiii.

73   **Phil L. Ryan:** *Variety,* December 3, 1954.

73   **"Until they know":** *Variety,* December 6, 1954.

74   **"The best pictures I did":** Ezra Goodman, *The Fifty-Year Decline and Fall of Hollywood* (New York: Simon & Schuster, 1961), 1–13.

74   **"We fail to see how":** *Cincinnati Enquirer,* April 17, 1954.

74   **The songs of Stephen:** *Variety,* May 8, 1956.

75   **Frank R. Crosswaith, the:** *Pittsburgh Courier,* July 17, 1954.

75   **"They have no more right":** *Variety,* August 28, 1957.

75   **"The American people":** *Variety,* July 2, 1958.

75   **The Florida Association:** *Miami News,* July 25, 1957.

75   **Former president:** *New York Daily News,* November 15, 1957.

75   **"Action is a direct result":** *Variety,* August 27, 1957.

76   **Some liberal:** *Variety,* February 8, 1956.

76   **NBC executive Harry Ward:** Pondillo, *America's First Network TV Censor,* 150.

76   **"We deleted":** *Variety,* May 8, 1956.

76   **The ongoing controversy:** Pondillo, *America's First Network TV Censor,* 106.

76   **"A motorist was about":** *New York Times,* November 9, 1951.

76   **Columnist Erskine Johnson:** *Pittsburgh Press,* January 18, 1960.

77   **"Slowly but surely":** *Saturday Evening Post,* September 20, 1958.

77   **"Americans are losing":** *Louisville Courier Journal,* July 27, 1954.

77   **"As an old-time amateur":** *New York Daily News,* January 12, 1964.

77   **"full of racial jokes":** *Victoria Times Colonist,* September 10, 1949.

77   **"Dialect jokes are taboo":** *Los Angeles Times,* September 16, 1958.

77   **"Now you can't kid":** *Fort Worth Star-Telegram,* June 22, 1962.

77   **"We're losing our sense":** *Saturday Evening Post,* September 20, 1958.

78   **Popular comedian Danny:** *Shamokin News Dispatch,* December 23, 1958.

78   **"The area of life":** *Esquire,* April 1958.

78   **Comedian George Gobel:** *Minneapolis Star Tribune,* October 27, 1957.

78   **"Is American Humor":** *Lake Charles American Press,* October 11, 1961.

78   **"I'd like to do a definitive":** *Show Business Illustrated,* November 28, 1961.

78   **"The Citizens' Council is the":** George Thayer, *The Farther Shores of Politics: The American Political Fringe Today* (New York: Simon & Schuster, 1967), 108.

79   **"The doctoring":** *Alabama Tribune,* May 11, 1956.

79   **Rod Serling; "Till was changed"; "a nice guy who":** *Charlestown Courier,* July 18, 1957, and *Alabama Tribune,* May 11, 1956; Rod Serling, interview by Mike Wallace, CBS, September 22, 1959; *Variety,* October 9, 1957.

79   **Prior to his concert:** *Variety,* August 7, 1957.

79 **"I can't understand it"**: Brian Ward, *Just My Soul Responding: Rhythm and Blues, Black Consciousness and Race Relations* (Oakland: University of California Press, 1998), 131.

79 **"It's not the people"**: *Variety*, September 4, 1957.

79 **Other major celebrities**: *Philadelphia Inquirer*, February 25, 1957.

80 **Lena Horne was not**: Lena Horne and Richard Schickel, *Lena* (Garden City, NY: Doubleday & Co, 1965), 273.

80 **"My anger is directed"**: *Miami News*, February 21, 1960.

80 **When legendary comedian**: *Virginia-Pilot*, February 3, 2009.

80 **"The Kingfish told me"**: *Reno Post-Gazette*, July 23, 1971.

80 **"He can't talk directly"; "See, the white boys"**: Timmie Rogers, *Mo' Funny: Black Comedy in America*, HBO, 1993.

80 **"Boy, you trying to do"**: Timmie Rogers, *Mo' Funny: Black Comedy in America*, HBO, 1993.

80 **"The sight of a"**: *Sydney Sun-Herald*, November 23, 1969.

81 **"go down in theatrical"**: *The California Eagle*, October 12, 1950.

81 **Among those**: *Jet*, July 13, 1987.

81 **The *Pittsburgh Courier* reported**: *Pittsburgh Courier*, August 16, 1958.

81 **"inflicting grievous bodily harm"**: *Pittsburgh Courier*, October 4, 1958.

81 **After much press**: *Pittsburgh Courier*, October 11, 1958; *New York Age*, November 1, 1958.

82 **"Man, the jury"**: *Jet*, July 9, 1959.

6

83 **"Alaska is coming into"**: *New York Daily News*, November 30, 1958.

83 **In the mid-twentieth century**: *Linton Daily Citizen*, November 13, 1953; *Newport News Daily Press*, August 7, 1954; Jane Mayer, *Dark Money: The Hidden History of the Billionaires Behind the Rise of the Radical Right* (New York: Doubleday, 2016), 53; Kim Phillips-Fein, *Invisible Hands: The Businessmen's Crusade Against the New Deal* (New York: W. W. Norton, 2010), 58; Erik Barnouw, *The Golden Web: A History of Broadcasting in the United States, 1933–1953* (Oxford, UK: Oxford University Press, 1968), 275; Phillips-Fein, *Invisible Hands*, 170–171; Phillips-Fein, *Invisible Hands*, 59; *Arizona Republic*, March 1, 1961.

84 **"nightmarish fears"**: Phillips-Fein, *Invisible Hands*, 60–66.

84 **Advertising agencies like**: Gerald Nachman, *Raised on Radio* (New York: Pantheon, 1998), 497.

84 **BBD&O crossed**: Barnouw, *The Golden Web*, 282.

84 **One sponsor**: *Sponsor*, June 17, 1963.

84 **"There is not one"**: International News Service, February 6, 1956.

84 **The American Gas Company deleted**: Eugene Paul, *The Hungry Eye* (New York: Ballantine Books, 1962), 257.

85 **"It mattered little to these guys"**: Rod Serling, interview by Mike Wallace, CBS, September 22, 1959.

85   **"save our 'Christian-style' civilization":** Edward Cain, *They'd Rather Be Right: Youth and the Conservative Movement* (New York: The MacMillan Company, 1963), 77.

85   **His parents:** Edward H. Miller, *A Conspiratorial Life: Robert Welch, the John Birch Society, and the Revolution of American Conservatism* (Chicago, IL: University of Chicago Press, 2021), 10, 23.

85   **But for Welch, it was *The Decline*:** Kurt Schuparra, *Triumph of the Right: The Rise and Triumph of the California Right, 1945–66* (Armonk, NY: M.E. Sharpe, Inc., 1998), 51.

85   **In the late 1940s:** Miller, *A Conspiratorial Life,* 171; 45.

85   **"a massive Communist conspiracy":** *Kansas City Times,* August 15, 1961.

85   **"Civil Rights is a perfect":** *Bismarck Tribune,* August 19, 1965.

85   **"In 1930, his company":** Jane Mayer, *Dark Money: The Hidden History of the Billionaires Behind the Rise of the Radical Right* (New York: Doubleday, 2016), 31.

86   **Koch defended:** Mayer, *Dark Money,* 27–31.

86   **Oliver's anti-Semitism:** *Birmingham News,* April 2, 1961.

86   **The John Birch Society received support:** Mayer, *Dark Money,* 307.

86   **An early Bircher was:** Morrie Ryskind with John H. M. Roberts, *I Shot an Elephant in My Pajamas: The Morrie Ryskind Story* (Lafayette, LA: Huntington House Publishers, 1994), 198–200.

86   **Two weeks later, while Robert Ryan:** *Daily Standard,* February 14, 1962.

87   **"We had round-the-clock police":** Lisa Ryan, interview by Conversations at the Cinematheque, November 11, 2019.

87   **The disarmament group:** George Thayer, *The Farther Shores of Politics: The American Political Fringe Today* (New York: Simon & Schuster, 1967), 478.

87   **"You . . . have a queasy smell":** Steve Allen, FBI file, letter dated March 13, 1961.

87   **"I have nothing to lose":** Steve Allen, FBI file, memo dated October 16, 1960.

87   **Initially the former *Tonight Show*:** Steve Allen, interview by the Archive of American Television, December 15, 1997.

87   **"I'm not quite certain just":** Steve Allen, FBI file, memo dated October 16, 1960.

88   **"You have committed":** Steve Allen, FBI file, memo dated October 16, 1960.

88   **"There could be only one":** Steve Allen, FBI file, memo dated October 21, 1960.

88   **"Dear Editor, I just got":** Steve Allen, FBI file, memo dated November 1, 1960.

88   **"Here's sincere[ly] hoping":** Steve Allen, FBI file, memo dated November 17, 1960.

88   **"In the name of God":** Steve Allen, FBI file, memo dated November 4, 1960.

88   **Soon the hostility:** Steve Allen, FBI file, memo dated January 12, 1961; *Vancouver Province,* January 17, 1961.

89   **Fagan had a grudge:** Deborah Del Vecchio, *Beverly Garland: Her Life and Career* (Jefferson, NC: McFarland and Co., 2012), 32; *Variety,* September 23, 1953.

89   **Fagan wrote Richard:** Donald T. Critchlow, *When Hollywood Was Right: How Movie Stas, Studio Moguls, and Big Business Remade American Politics* (New York: Cambridge University Press, 2013), 113.

89   **Fagan believed:** Myron C. Fagan, *Red Stars in Hollywood* (St. Louis, MO: Patriotic Tract Society, 1950); *Sponsor,* June 17, 1963; *Millville Daily,* September 2, 1964.

89   **Koch opened the store:** *Wichita Eagle,* July 15, 1965, and April 30, 1978.

90 **Among the available titles:** Grove, *Inside the John Birch Society*, 119.

90 **"Behind his façade":** Earl Lively Jr., *The Invasion of Mississippi* (Belmont, MA: American Opinion, 1963), 25–26.

90 **Republican senator Thomas Kuchel criticized:** *Shreveport Times*, May 3, 1963.

90 **Fred Hall, president:** *Santa Rosa Press Democrat*, February 20, 1963.

90 **"a horde":** Thayer, *The Farther Shores*, 183.

90 **Arranged in a series:** *Bedford Times-Mail*, September 25, 1965.

91 **"Thanks very much":** George Carlin and Merv Griffin, *The Merv Griffin Show*, November 16, 1965.

91 **"At times our":** Brooks R. Walker, *The Christian Fright Peddlers: The Radical Right of the Churches* (Garden City: NY, Doubleday & Company, Inc., 1964), 151.

91 **"He was one of the":** *Critic's Corner with Jack O'Brian*, Radio 710 WOR, May 29, 1979.

91 **From the sides of the bus:** *Fort Worth Star-Telegram*, May 24, 1961.

92 **A man named Speros:** *Hartford Courant*, July 25, 1963.

92 **"Dylan went through it":** John Moffitt, interview by the Author.

92 **"The hazards":** *Variety*, May 2, 1962.

92 **"Those satires on American":** *Variety*, February 14, 1962.

93 **"Freberg was given the freedom":** *Variety*, June 15, 1959.

93 **"I've become":** *Variety*, May 10, 1961.

93 **But thanks to the:** *Tampa Tribune*, July 2, 1961; NY Herald Tribune Service, May 17, 1961.

93 **"not up to programming standards":** NY Herald Tribune Service, May 17, 1961.

93 **Seven independent:** *Tampa Tribune*, July 2, 1961.

93 **One of its members:** *Pittsburgh Press*, May 14, 1961.

94 **"What they're trying to say":** NY Herald Tribune Service, May 17, 1961.

94 **Booked on *The Tonight Show*:** Freberg, *It Only Hurts When I Laugh* (New York: Times Books, 1988), 208–209, 211.

94 **"We commend the use":** NY Herald Tribune Service, May 17, 1961.

7

95 **In the 1950s:** *Napa Valley Register*, September 19, 1952.

96 **Early R&B stations:** Erik Barnouw, *The Golden Web: A History of Broadcasting in the United States, 1933–1953* (Oxford, UK: Oxford University Press, 1968), 289; William Barlow, *Voice Over: The Making of Black Radio* (Philadelphia: Temple University Press, 1998), 207, 170; Barnouw, *The Golden Web*, 289; Barlow, *Voice Over*, 207

96 **Church leaders:** *Cincinnati Enquirer*, August 22, 1959.

96 **"Rock 'n' roll music is the most barbaric":** *New York Daily News*, February 29, 1956.

96 **"The rhythm in blues called rock":** *New York Daily News*, March 18, 1955.

96 **"The people of this country":** *Detroit Free Press*, June 14, 1958.

97　"Rock n' roll is lewd": James L. Neibaur, *The Elvis Movies* (Washington, DC: Rowman & Littlefield Publishers, 2014), 53.

97　"I find Elvis Presley": *Cincinnati Enquirer*, June 16, 1956.

97　"Mr. Presley has no": Lewis L. Gould, ed., *Watching Television Come of Age: The* New York Times *Reviews by Jack Gould* (Austin: University of Texas Press, 2002), 129.

97　"Creep!!! Goon!!!": *Cincinnati Enquirer*, July 6, 1957.

97　Radio KWK: *Variety*, January 22, 1958.

97　A man poured gasoline: *Variety*, February 27, 1957.

98　"into a bonfire": *Rochester Democrat and Chronicle*, January 20, 1958.

98　"A disc jockey was stabbed": United Press International, December 16, 1960.

98　Wisconsin radio station: *Variety*, September 5, 1956.

98　Dick Clark's *American Bandstand* was: Dick Clark, FBI file, September 1962.

98　A letter to the editor asked: *St. Louis Dispatch*, February 4, 1962.

98　When Dick Clark brought: *Variety*, October 21, 1959.

98　Colombian dictator: United Press International, February 8, 1957.

98　Rock 'n' roll was against the law: *Cincinnati Enquirer*, February 17, 1957.

99　The Batista regime: *Des Moines Register*, February 14, 1957.

99　Rock concerts were against the law: *Daily News*, April 11, 1956.

99　Bobby Darin's: *Cincinnati Post*, October 12, 1959.

99　*Blackboard Jungle*: *Green Bay Press Gazette*, November 29, 1955; *Variety*, February 1, 1955.

99　A police chief in Santa Cruz: *South Bend Tribune*, June 5, 1956.

99　He canceled a scheduled: *Variety*, June 12, 1956.

99　"Man, I could not go": *Pittsburgh Courier*, August 25, 1956.

100　"Beer bottles, beer cans and pitchers": *Freeport Journal Standard*, September 19, 1956.

100　"Planted upstairs early morning": *Variety*, July 22, 1953.

100　"From puritanical Boston": *Daily News*, April 11, 1956.

100　When they arrived in Birmingham: *Fort Myers News-Press*, May 24, 1956.

100　Carter said of rock 'n' roll: *Tampa Tribune*, March 30, 1956.

101　The City of Tampa outlawed the twist: *Berkshire Eagle*, January 4, 1962.

101　The Texas Liquor Control Board: *Eureka Humboldt Standard*, May 28, 1964.

101　A civic official in Huntington: *Cincinnati Enquirer*, November 17, 1961.

101　The manager of the Roseland: *Eureka Standard*, October 21, 1961.

101　The twist was banned: *Lancaster Intelligencer Journal*, November 27, 1962; Associated Press, January 18, 1962; *Richmond Palladium-Item*, March 25, 1962; *York Dispatch*, January 26, 1963.

101　"The Twist is far too": *Montana Standard*, January 6, 1962.

101　A twist club in Madeira Beach: *Tampa Bay Times*, May 25, 1963, and June 6, 1963.

101　"Chubby Checker, given": *Variety*, January 8, 1964; *Los Angeles Times*, March 21, 1963; *Hackensack Record*, March 16, 1963.

102　"It was not only trash": Billy James Hargis, FBI file, undated.

102 **The Beatles were blamed:** *Waukesha Daily Freeman*, September 10, 1965; *St. Joseph News-Press Gazette*, October 30, 1964; *Newport News Daily Press*, July 28, 1966.

102 **"Communist scientists":** *Variety*, September 7, 1966.

102 **"These Beatle lovers should secure":** *Fort Myers News-Press*, July 25, 1965.

103 **"I'm glad to see the boycott":** *Princeton Daily Clarion*, August 5, 1966.

103 **The Beatles were banned:** *Ottawa Journal*, August 5, 1966; *San Bernardino County Sun*, April 3, 1966; *Longview News-Journal*, July 5, 1965; *Pittsburgh Press*, August 9, 1966; *Variety*, August 31, 1966; *Terre Haute Star*, August 11, 1966; *Indianapolis Star*, August 10, 1966.

103 **"Should not on principle":** *Variety*, September 7, 1966.

103 **"The Beatles, judged by":** David A. Noebel, *Rhythm, Riots and Revolution* (Tulsa, OK: Christian Crusade Publications, 1966), 98.

104 **"Throw your Beatle and rock":** David A. Noebel, Rev., *Communism, Hypnotism, and the Beatles* (Tulsa, OK: Christian Crusade Publications, 1965), 14–15.

8

105 **"Any other teleseries":** *Variety*, July 24, 1963.

105 **"Not only the FCC":** *Variety*, November 17, 1965.

105 **"The average":** Nick Stewart, *The Joe Pyne Show*, May 6, 1966.

106 **Luther James:** *Variety*, November 17, 1965.

106 **The Farmer's Daughter:** *Hanford Sentinel*, October 1, 1963; *The Mike Douglas Show*, July 27, 1970.

106 **"I must reiterate":** *Variety*, September 10, 1969.

106 **General Motors tried to kill:** *Variety*, April 1, 1964.

106 **"General Motors last week":** *Variety*, April 22, 1964.

107 **"This is no time":** *Mobile Beacon and Alabama Citizen*, April 11, 1964.

107 **The fair organizers complained:** *Variety*, January 29, 1964.

107 **"I have long since been":** *Jackson Clarion Ledger*, January 21, 1964.

107 **"the greatest insult":** *Jackson Clarion Ledger*, January 24, 1964.

107 **"help destroy":** *Variety*, February 5, 1964.

107 **"We White":** *Jackson Clarion Ledger*, January 28, 1964.

108 **"There is no possibility":** *Variety*, January 29, 1964.

108 **With the loss of Hoss:** *Jackson Clarion Ledger*, January 21, 1964.

108 **An image of Roberts:** *TV Guide*, March 13, 1965; *Variety*, January 8, 1964; *Miami Herald*, July 28, 1963.

108 **"I think recent events":** *Long Beach Press-Telegram*, July 30, 1963.

108 **When they arrived:** *San Francisco Examiner*, July 28, 1963; *Calgary Herald*, July 29, 1963; *San Francisco Examiner*, July 28, 1963; *Calgary Herald*, July 29, 1963; *Mansfield News Journal*, July 28, 1963; *Calgary Herald*, July 29, 1963.

108 **Thirty members:** *Salt Lake Tribune*, August 2, 1963.

109 **"When God has drawn":** Kim Phillips-Fein, *Invisible Hands: The Businessmen's Crusade Against the New Deal* (New York: W. W. Norton, 2010), 228.

109 **"He was not a sissy":** Alan Crawford, *Thunder on the Right: The "New Right" and the Politics of Resentment* (New York: Pantheon Books, 1980), 159.

109 **"I wonder if it ever has":** *Saturday Evening Post,* April 10, 1965.

109 **In a run-down:** Club Peachtree Program, October 11, 1965, and January 22, 1968; *Atlanta Constitution,* April 1, 1967, and March 9, 1968.

109 **A folk trio from South Carolina:** *Windsor Star,* January 30, 1965.

110 **"And what, we ask":** *Salt Lake Tribune,* January 5, 1964.

110 **"Clad in black":** *Ventura County Star,* June 5, 1965.

110 **The Lions Club in Camarillo:** *Ventura County Star,* April 9, 1965, April 3, 1965, March 25, 1965, and March 12, 1965.

111 **Dr. Ted:** *Ventura County Star,* April 6, 1965.

111 **A reader from Ojai:** *Ventura County Star,* April 13, 1965.

111 **"I don't have":** Dave Gardner, *Brother Dave Gardner: Out Front,* comedy album, Tonka Records, 1970.

112 **Fans wondered:** Larry L. King, *The Old Man and Lesser Mortals* (New York: The Viking Press, 1974), 58.

112 **"sixty-odd appearances":** *Harper's,* September 1970.

112 **"Brother Dave rattled off":** King, *The Old Man,* 58.

112 **With his new wealth:** King, *The Old Man,* 60–61.

112 **"I got interested in":** *Harper's,* September 1970.

112 **Hunt felt anyone who collected:** King, *The Old Man,* 60–61.

112 **His former assistant:** John Curington with Mitchel Whitington *H.L. Hunt: Motive Opportunity; The Means by which H.L. Hunt Influenced the Assassination of JFK, King, Bobby & Hoffa* (Oklahoma City, OK: 23 House Publishing, 2018), 102.

113 **Larry L. King drove:** King, *The Old Man,* 55–69.

113 **The manager walked over:** *Harper's,* September 1970.

113 **"James Baldwin is":** King, *The Old Man,* 75.

113 **"Here's one":** *Harper's,* September 1970.

113 **The heckling started:** King, *The Old Man,* 67; *Harper's,* September 1970.

113 **"This here's a thought":** Dave Gardner, *The Very Best of Brother Dave Gardner,* comedy album, Landmark Productions, 1999.

113 **King saw a table:** King, *The Old Man,* 66.

114 **"I'm losing my ass":** King, *The Old Man,* 57.

114 **Asked about his drastic:** *Florida Today,* December 12, 1971.

114 **King joined Gardner at his home:** King, *The Old Man,* 71–73.

114 **Gardner's young son:** King, *The Old Man,* 58.

114 **He had released a vinyl record:** Allison Graham, Sharon Monteith, and Charles Reagan Wilson, eds., *The New Encyclopedia of Southern Culture: Media,* vol. 18 (Chapel Hill: University of North Carolina Press, 2011), 254.

115 **"focused chiefly on two issues":** *Variety,* June 12, 1968.

115 **"The real purpose of such enforced":** Gene Grove, *Inside the John Birch Society* (Greenwich, CT: Fawcett, 1961), 123.

115 **Showbiz was hypersensitive:** *Variety,* June 12, 1968.

115 **"I come into contact with a lot"**: *Livingston County Daily Press*, April 24, 1968.

115 **"pretended to be non-violent."**: Edward H. Miller, *A Conspiratorial Life: Robert Welch, the John Birch Society, and the Revolution of American Conservatism* (Chicago: University of Chicago Press, 2021), 266.

116 **"He usually spoke of non-violence"**: Neil Middleton, ed., *The I.F. Stone's Weekly Reader* (London: Penguin Books, 1973), 140.

116 **Georgia governor Lester:** *Atlanta Constitution*, April 26, 1968.

116 **Maddox called for a:** *Variety*, October 23, 1968.

116 **"These are the bands"**: Steve Randisi, *The Merv Griffin Show: The Inside Story* (Albany, GA: BearManor Media, 2018), 242.

116 **"Griffin Show Edits Out"**: *Abilene Reporter-News*, December 31, 1969.

116 **"I felt like an absolute jerk"**: *Variety*, December 31, 1969.

116 **Vice President Spiro Agnew:** Edith Efron, *The News Twisters* (Los Angeles: Nash Publishing, 1971), 134; Fred MacDonald, *Blacks and White TV: African Americans in Television Since 1948* (Chicago: Nelson-Hall Publishers, 1983), 151–152; Les Brown, *Television: The Business Behind the Box* (New York: Harcourt Brace Jovanovich, Inc., 1971), 231.

116 **"Spiro has a new show"**: *Variety*, November 26, 1969.

117 **In the weeks that followed:** Efron, *The News Twisters*, 138.

117 **"used to keep track of the hawks"**: Robert Metz, *CBS: Reflections in a Bloodshot Eye* (Chicago: Playboy Press, 1975), 369.

117 **"not sorry about it"**: Carl Rollyson, *A Real American Character: The Life of Walter Brennan* (Jackson: University Press of Mississippi, 2015), 200–201.

117 **"He feels strongly that there is a plot"**: *TV Guide*, March 30, 1968.

117 **"How can I do this"**: Rollyson, *A Real American*, 175.

117 **According to the American Party's platform:** *Ridgewood Sunday News*, October 8, 1972.

117 **"Walter showed me his bunker"**: John G. Stephens, *From My Three Sons to Major Dad: My Life as a TV Producer* (Lanham, MD: The Scarecrow Press, Inc., 2005), 73.

118 **Brennan even:** Rollyson, *A Real American*, 185–187.

118 **A survey published:** *Tampa Times*, June 5, 1968, and July 20, 1968.

118 **Latino actor Ray Martel:** *Variety*, March 19, 1969.

118 **"The bevy of girls"**: *TV Guide*, May 22, 1971.

119 **A number of programs:** *Los Angeles Times*, June 23, 1969.

119 **CBS promised:** *Los Angeles Times*, July 19, 1969.

119 **"Lots and lots of buildings"**: Budd Schulberg, *The Rise and Fall of the Watts Writers Workshop*, Burn Baby Burn, 1999, posted by EcoLogicalArt, August 16, 2009, https://www.youtube.com/watch?v=rC47F0mJ0Vk.

119 **"Nate Monaster and Stanley Shapiro were there"**: Charles Eric Johnson, interview by the author.

119 **"It was amazing,"**: Schulberg, *The Rise and Fall*.

120 **Harry Dolan graduated:** *Valley Times*, October 25, 1969; *Pasadena Independent Star News*, March 17, 1968.

120 **"First I planted two mics"**: *Mother Jones*, April 1977.

120 **"The Bureau had it burnt down":** Darthard Perry, *Like It Is with Gil Noble*, radio station WABC, November 2, 1980.

9

121 **"How do you think"; "obviously aimed at":** Linda Martin and Kerry Segrave, *Anti-Rock: The Opposition to Rock 'n' Roll* (New York: Da Capo Press, 1993), 163.

122 **"The McLendon radio stations":** *Billboard*, May 20, 1967.

122 **McLendon placed:** *Billboard*, April 8, 1967.

122 **Among the rejected songs:** *Billboard*, May 27, 1967.

122 **Major hits:** *Wilkes-Barre Times Leader*, May 20, 1967.

122 **Radio KNEL:** *Corpus Christi Caller Times*, June 11, 1967.

122 **McLendon stations demanded:** *Billboard*, May 27, 1967.

123 **"I think they oughta":** Donald T. Critchlow, *When Hollywood Was Right: How Movie Stas, Studio Moguls, and Big Business Remade American Politics* (New York: Cambridge University Press, 2013), 197.

123 **Violence followed screenings:** *Cedar Rapids Gazette*, September 22, 1968; *Variety*, August 21, 1968, and September 11, 1968; *Arizona Daily Star*, May 8, 1969.

124 **"Who knows, the words":** *Sikeston Daily Standard*, March 8, 1966.

124 **"If you didn't know him":** Marc Leepson, *Ballad of the Green Beret: The Life and Wars of Staff Sergeant Barry Sadler from the Vietnam War and Pop Stardom to Murder and an Unsolved, Violent Death* (Mechanicsburg, PA: Stackpole Books, 2017), 20.

124 **Years later his name:** Associated Press, June 3, 1979.

124 **At a screening in London:** *Arizona Republic*, October 24, 1967; *Variety*, November 1, 1967.

125 **"Talk shows take the refuse":** *Paducah Sun*, October 23, 1968.

125 **"As for the hippie-peaceniks":** *Montgomery Advertiser*, October 25, 1967.

125 **"The more I observe":** *Dayton Daily News*, August 29, 1970.

125 **Attitudes about:** John Billheimer, *Hitchcock and the Censors* (Lexington: University Press of Kentucky, 2019), 192.

126 **"Two of the greatest":** Sheilah Graham, *Confessions of a Hollywood Columnist* (New York: Bantam, 1970), 70–71.

126 **Actor Jeff Chandler:** *Variety*, August 27, 1952.

126 **Cardinal Francis Spellman:** Thomas R. Lindlof, *Hollywood Under Siege: Martin Scorsese, the Religious Right, and the Culture Wars* (Lexington: University Press of Kentucky, 2008), 28.

126 **The distributor of *The Miracle*:** Richard S. Randall, *Censorship of the Movies: The Social and Political Control of a Mass Medium* (Madison: The University of Wisconsin Press, 1968), 25–27.

127 **"Hollywood's Production Code":** *Variety*, December 28, 1955.

127 **Some film censorship:** *Variety*, April 13, 1959; *Birmingham News*, July 31, 1957; Donald Bogle, *Toms, Coons, Mulattoes, Mammies and Bucks: An Interpretive History of Blacks in American Films* (New York: Viking Press, 1973), 243; *Variety*, April 10, 1957.

127 **"Charles Coburn Joins":** *Bristol Herald Courier*, June 14, 1959.

127 **"Although *Tom Jones* ruptured":** Jack Vizzard, *See No Evil: Life Inside a Hollywood Censor* (New York: Simon & Schuster, 1970), 303.

128 **Stanley Kubrick's:** Stephen E. Kercher, *Revel with a Cause: Liberal Satire in Postwar America* (Chicago: University of Chicago Press, 2006), 340.

128 **Likewise, Ludwig von Mises:** *Arizona Republic*, September 2, 1964.

128 **That same year the:** Geoffrey Shurlock, *Life* magazine, January 15, 1965.

128 **The Catholic Legion of Decency was aghast:** Vizzard, *See No Evil*, 305.

128 **"They were just absolutely":** Robert Horton, ed., *Billy Wilder: Interviews* (Jackson: University Press of Mississippi, 2002), 154.

128 **Geoffrey Shurlock conceded:** Vizzard, *See No Evil*, 304–309.

128 **A projectionist at:** *Variety*, March 19, 1969, and August 11, 1969; *Tampa Tribune*, May 25, 1972; *Variety*, April 30, 1969, March 5, 1969, February 19, 1969, March 5, 1969, and September 18, 1968.

129 **A drive-in theater in Delaware:** *Wilmington Morning News*, March 19, 1970.

129 **"The local sheriff went into":** Allen Funt with Philip Reed, *Candidly, Allen Funt: A Million Smiles Later* (New York: Barricade Books, Inc., 1994), 156.

129 **Senator John L. Harmer of California:** George H. Murphy, comp., *Proposed Amendments to Constitution: Propositions and Proposed Laws*, voter information guide for 1972, California State Archives.

129 **"I am fed up with those":** *Boston Globe*, October 15, 1966.

129 **"As long as I am president":** Peter Biskind, *Easy Riders, Raging Bulls: How the Sex-Drugs-and-Rock 'n' Roll Generation Saved Hollywood* (New York: Simon & Schuster, 1998), 67.

129 **Someone asked director John Ford:** Critchlow, *When Hollywood Was Right*, 196.

129 **"I don't like to see the Hollywood bloodstream":** Randy Roberts and James S. Olson, *John Wayne: American* (New York: Simon & Schuster, 1995), 475.

130 **"I guess I'm a bit straitlaced":** *Reno Gazette Journal*, July 3, 1968.

130 **"whirlpool of filth and dirt"; "There is a different set of values today":** Horton, ed., *Billy Wilder*, 69–87.

130 **"I'm totally rattled":** Horton, ed., *Billy Wilder*, 69.

10

131 **"TV network programmers worry":** *Des Moines Register*, April 1, 1969.

131 **A racist letter to the editor:** *Corpus Christi Caller-Times*, June 10, 1964.

132 **Watermelon stereotypes:** *San Francisco Examiner*, October 7, 1980.

132 ***The Travels of Babar:*** *White Plains Journal News*, August 14, 2011.

132 **Friday night Tarzan:** *Variety*, March 27, 1974.

132 **Mexican stereotypes:** *York Dispatch*, December 10, 1969.

132 **The Frito-Lay brand:** *Lubbock Avalanche-Journal*, October 3, 1968; *Arizona Republic*, May 6, 1969.

132 **"tool of racist elites":** *Richmond Palladium-Item*, January 2, 1970.

132 **"carefully focus-grouped"**: *Lubbock Avalanche-Journal*, October 3, 1968.

132 **"Two of the major VHF"**: *Variety*, December 17, 1969.

133 **"It must be painful"**: *San Antonio Express*, September 19, 1968.

133 **"What's next?"**: *Independent Record*, August 3, 1969.

133 **"German, Irish"**: *Variety*, January 3, 1968.

133 **"The Mexican-American community"**: *Del Rio News*, April 5, 1971.

134 **"I started off in television"**: Bernie Kopell, interview by the author.

134 **"We are going to continue"**: *Bridgeport Post*, July 27, 1968.

134 **"The time of the Frito"**: *Monrovia Daily News-Post*, March 20, 1970.

134 **"People would come up to me"**: *Fort Lauderdale News*, July 8, 1970.

135 **"the worst theatrical"**; **"You'll notice"**: Richard Zoglin, *Hope: Entertainer of the Century* (New York: Simon & Schuster, 2014), 399–403.

135 **"Women lie"**: Mort Sahl, interview by Patricia Marx, radio station WNYC, March 24, 1964.

135 **"Chicks wrote in"**: Mort Sahl, *The Dick Cavett Show*, August 4, 1970.

136 **Sahl was booked:** James Curtis, *Last Man Standing: Mort Sahl and the Birth of Modern Comedy* (Jackson: University Press of Mississippi, 2017), 235–236.

137 **"Mort Sahl did in fact"**: Jinx Beers, *Memoirs of an Old Dyke* (Bloomington, IN: iUniverse, 2008), 171–172.

137 **"The best thing you can say"**: *Tampa Times*, May 30, 1970.

137 **Dr. David:** David Reuben, MD, *Everything You Always Wanted to Know About Sex: But Were Afraid to Ask* (New York: Bantam Books, 1969), 160–162.

137 **"The author's sudden"**: *Chicago Tribune*, January 15, 1971.

138 **Psychiatric meetings:** Ronald Bayer, *Homosexuality and American Psychiatry: The Politics of Diagnosis* (Princeton, NJ: Princeton University Press, 1987), 96–98.

138 **"Marcus Welby is a quack"**: Marc Stein, ed., *The Stonewall Riots: A Documentary History* (New York: New York University Press, 2019), 233.

138 **and staged a sit-in protest:** *Times*, February 17, 1973.

138 **Frank Blair was in the middle:** Stein, ed., *The Stonewall Riots*, 234.

139 **"NBC aired a segment"**: *Atlanta Constitution*, December 8, 1974.

139 **"Are we supposed to"**: *Corpus Christi Caller-Times*, December 29, 1974.

11

141 **"I don't think comedians"**: *Atlanta Constitution*, March 6, 1979.

141 **"Old, old, incredibly old"**: Harlan Ellison, *The Other Glass Teat* (New York: Pyramid Communications, 1975), 169.

141 **"I am tired"**: *St. Louis Post-Dispatch*, September 24, 1967.

142 **"Mr. Thomas has not been watching"**: Ellison, *The Other Glass Teat*, 184–185.

142 ***TV Guide* found a television:** *TV Guide*, November 28, 1959, A-5.

142 **"Most of those fellows just stand"**: *Quad City Times*, December 8, 1960.

142 **"Most of the new crop"**: Radio KPFK comedy panel with Groucho Marx, Steve Allen, Carl Reiner; April 2, 1962.

142 **"Only Jack Benny"**: *Detroit Free Press*, May 30, 1971.

142 **"Many of the young kids"**: *Fort Lauderdale News*, February 23, 1977.

142 **"I think most modern humor"**: *Los Angeles Times*, December 28, 1979.

142 **"So help me God"**: Jimmy Durante, interview by Larry Wilde, February 23, 1968.

142 **"I think it's instead of talent"**: Mort Sahl, *The Michael Jackson Show*, radio station KABC, May 20, 1983.

143 **"I don't believe in comedians"**: *Arizona Daily Star*, June 5, 1969.

143 **"They would probably be going yet"**: Bill Cassara, *Edgar Kennedy: Master of the Slow Burn* (Albany, GA: BearManor Media, 2017), 54.

143 **"In their communities"**: Brent E. Walker, *Mack Sennett's Fun Factory: A History and Filmography of His Studio and His Keystone and Mack Sennett Comedies, with Biographies of Players and Personnel* (Jefferson, NC: McFarland & Company Inc., 2013), 28.

143 **"In digging at the roots"**: *Chillicothe Constitution-Tribune*, September 15, 1923.

144 **"A high-ranking"**: *TV Guide*, January 19, 1963.

144 **"Episodic, and abounding"**: *Variety*, March 5, 1969.

144 **"The comedy team of Steve Rossi and Slappy White"**: Ronald L. Smith, *Goldmine Comedy Record Price Guide* (Iola, WI: Krause Publications, 1996), 293.

144 **"With the extremely difficult battle"**: *Los Angeles Evening Citizen News*, February 19, 1970.

145 **"I want to tell Chief Davis"**: *Los Angeles Evening Citizen News*, February 21, 1970.

145 **"I think piping dope"**: *Los Angeles Evening Citizen News*, March 21, 1970.

145 **The boundaries of what**: *Los Angeles Times*, July 30, 1972.

145 **"Both pilots tested"**: Metz, *CBS*, 332–333.

145 **"I felt we had to get"**: Metz, *CBS*, 333.

146 **"It had a laugh track"**: *Times Standard*, January 14, 1971.

146 **"nothing short of a"**: *St. Louis Post-Dispatch*, March 14, 1971.

146 **"tasteless intrusion"**: *Fort Lauderdale News*, March 14, 1974.

146 **"For some reason"**: *Edwardsville Intelligencer*, April 7, 1972.

146 **"Everywhere I go"**: *York Daily Record*, October 16, 1975.

146 **"I didn't think we'd get away with it"**: Carroll O'Connor, *The Vin Scully Show*, CBS, January 16, 1973.

146 **"I've seen Archie"**: Red Skelton, interview on KRTV, 1972, via Montana Historical Society, July 23, 2020.

147 **"The New Dick Van Dyke show is disgraceful"**: *St. Louis Post-Dispatch*, December 12, 1971.

147 **"Curiously, it was sex"**: *Camden Courier-Post*, March 26, 1975.

147 **In the face of the initial**: *Des Moines Tribune*, January 31, 1973.

148 **"The program treats"**: *Lincoln Star Sun*, February 11, 1973.

148 **"Anything that brings the UN"**: *Wisconsin Jewish Chronicle*, November 27, 1975.

148 **"the blood of Soviet"**: *Ogden Standard-Examiner*, June 20, 1973.

148 **"We had bomb threats"**: *Milwaukee Sentinel*, January 19, 1973.

148 **"Take this down carefully"**: *Los Angeles Times*, September 14, 1972.

148 **Manning was charged with**: *Arizona Republic*, January 10, 1973.

148 **Eight days later:** *Logansport Press*, January 18, 1973.

148 **threatening to murder Ralph Riskin:** *Long Beach Independent*, January 18, 1973.

149 **"We were gone and off":** Douglas S. Cramer, interview by the Archive of American Television, May 22, 2009.

149 **After the final:** *Los Angeles Times*, August 8, 1973.

149 **"undeniable malice":** L. Benjamin Rolsky, *The Rise and Fall of the Religious Left: Politics, Television, and Popular Culture in the 1970s and Beyond* (New York: Columbia University Press, 2019), 91–93.

149 **"I think Maude is abominable":** *Hartford Courant*, October 27, 1974.

149 **"I thought it was a wonderful idea":** *Entertainment Weekly*, October 15, 2018.

150 **"After screening tonight's episode":** Nancy T. Mihevc, et al., "The Censorship of *Maude*: A Case Study in the Social Construction of Reality," paper presented at the Annual Meeting of the International Communication Assn., April 1973.

150 **"Hear Cecil":** *The Messenger*, May 9, 1986.

150 **"jamming the minds":** *Minneapolis Star Tribune*, November 14, 1975.

150 **L. Brent Bozell Jr. founded a lobby:** George Thayer, *The Farther Shores of Politics: The American Political Fringe Today* (New York: Simon & Schuster, 1967), 293.

150 **"Times aren't necessarily":** *TV Guide*, September 1, 1973.

150 **"We conducted a poll":** *Broadcasting*, August 13, 1973; *Fort Lauderdale News*, November 30, 1973.

151 **"We are sick to death":** *Long Beach Independent*

151 **On average:** *Press-Telegram*, December 9, 1973.

151 **"no way I was going to":** Rolsky, *The Rise and Fall*, 83.

151 **"We want American families":** *Charlotte Observer*, August 20, 1976.

152 **"The creative people":** *Charlotte Observer*, September 12, 1976.

152 **Showrunners ran into problems:** *Charlotte Observer*, February 3, 1976; *Atlanta Constitution*, August 27, 1976.

152 **"It's the most ludicrous":** *Variety*, August 14, 1975.

152 **The sitcom *Welcome Back, Kotter*:** *Variety*, August 26, 1975.

152 **"We wanted to do one":** *Red Bank Daily Register*, May 9, 1977.

153 **Morality in Media:** *Boston Globe*, November 21, 1974.

153 **"prevent American culture":** *Utah Independent*, December 12, 1974.

153 **"We cannot guarantee":** George Carlin, interview by Bob Brown, *20/20*, ABC, 1998.

153 **After completing their:** *Fort Lauderdale News*, October 1, 1978.

153–54 **"Based on a Tampa":** *Tampa Bay Times*, August 27, 1973.

154 **Pryor was charged:** *York Dispatch*, August 8, 1974.

154 **Joan Rivers was playing:** FBI memorandum, January 16, 1974.

154 **"I would like to know":** *St. Louis Post-Dispatch*, November 16, 1975.

154–55 **"Saturday Night Live has gone too far":** *Arizona Republic*, April 19, 1980.

155 **A fundamentalist churchgoer:** *Passaic Herald-News*, June 27, 1980.

155 **The movement spread:** *Arizona Republic*, April 12, 1980.

155 **General Foods distanced themselves:** *Tennessean*, November 21, 1980.

155 **"Television, particularly the soap operas":** *Tampa Bay Times*, November 25, 1979.

155 **"I would like to know"**: *Indianapolis News*, April 10, 1976.

155 **The game show *Family Feud***: *Manitowoc Herald-Times*, August 15, 1982.

156 **"The diseases that could"**: *Philadelphia Daily News*, September 17, 1981.

156 **"Contestants, both male and female"**: *Pacific Daily News*, July 23, 1984.

156 **He mailed a monthly**: *Miami Herald*, March 4, 1978.

156 **The most committed**: *Hanford Sentinel*, January 26, 1980.

156 **Reverend Wildmon was**: *Charlotte Observer*, November 5, 1976; *Decatur Herald & Review*, November 28, 1976.

156 **Reverend Wildmon was**: *Hanford Sentinel*, January 26, 1980; *Decatur Herald & Review*, November 28, 1976.

156 **"There will be hard-core"**: *Miami Herald*, March 4, 1978.

157 **"With the rationale used"**: *Passaic Herald-News*, June 27, 1980.

157 **To protest their sponsorship**: *Marshall News Messenger*, June 18, 1978; *People*, November 27, 1978; *Louisville Courier-Journal*, July 11, 1978.

157 **"If you like the show"**: John Ritter, *E! True Hollywood Story*, December 27, 1998.

158 **Bryant became the face**: Crawford, *Thunder on the Right*, 52.

158 **"There are many things"**: Anita Bryant and Bob Green, *At Any Cost* (Old Tappan, NJ: Fleming H. Revell Company, 1978), 24.

158 **"There is no question"; "Gays should not"**: Bryant and Green, *At Any Cost*, 152.

158 **"The attempt by"**: Bryant and Green, *At Any Cost*, 35.

158 **"Anita Bryant was on television"**: Johnny Carson, *The Tonight Show Starring Johnny Carson*, June 10, 1977.

159 **"In recent months"**: *Ithaca Journal*, August 5, 1977.

159 **"It's fine for entertainers"**: Bryant and Green, *At Any Cost*, 62–63.

159 **"For me, in addition to all"**: Anita Bryant, *The Anita Bryant Story* (Fleming H. Revell Company, 1977), 21.

159 ***The New Laugh-In***: Bryant, *The Anita Bryant Story*, 36.

159 **Gay activists around the country**: Bryant and Green, *At Any Cost*, 61–62.

160 **"She is a lovely person"**: Bryant and Green, *At Any Cost*, 101–102.

160 **"I have been blacklisted"**: Bryant and Green, *At Any Cost*, 61.

160 **"Because of this"**: *National Inquirer*, July 1977.

160 **Executives met with the comedian**: *San Francisco Examiner*, April 21, 1978; Bryant and Green, *At Any Cost*, 70.

161 **"They made up all kinds of excuses"**: Associated Press, February 18, 2000.

161 **"I wanted to do a series"**: *Entertainment Weekly*, October 15, 2018.

161 **"ABC-TV is counting on our apathy"**: *World and Way*, October 13, 1977.

161 **A *Newsweek* story**: Josh Ozersky, *Archie Bunker's America: TV in an Era of Change 1968–1978* (Carbondale: Southern Illinois University Press, 2003), 11.

161 **"Action is needed"**: *Chippewa Herald-Telegram*, September 30, 1977.

161 **"What was difficult"**: Herb Jellinek, interview by the Archive of American Television, March 4, 2005.

162 **"The protests may not"**: *Entertainment Weekly*, October 15, 2018.

162 **According to comedian David Steinberg**: David Steinberg, *Inside Comedy: The Soul,*

Wit, and Bite of Comedy and Comedians of the Last Five Decades (New York: Alfred A. Knopf, 2021), 43–46.

162 **Richard Pryor already had a volatile:** Kevin Cook, *Flip: The Inside Story of TV's First Black Superstar* (New York: Viking, 2013), 158.

162 **Pryor appeared:** *Jet*, October 6, 1977; *Los Angeles Times*, September 20, 1977.

163 **"In this country of":** *Los Angeles Times*, September 25, 1977.

163 **"My guess is":** Steinberg, *Inside Comedy*, 43–46.

163 **Paul Lynde, the comic actor:** *Cincinnati Enquirer*, October 28, 1977.

164 **"Hey man, who ever told you":** *Munster Times*, October 28, 1977.

164 **Racism was a major discussion:** *Herald-Telegram*, January 29, 1977; *Hazleton Standard-Speaker*, January 28, 1977; John E. O'Connor, ed., *American History/American Television: Interpreting the Video Past* (New York: Ungar Pub. Co., 1983), 281; *Calgary Herald*, February 15, 1977; *Miami Herald*, September 13, 1977.

164 **Comedy legend Lucille Ball:** Lucille Ball, FBI file, Freedom of Information Act.

165 **Violence flared:** *Philadelphia Inquirer*, March 24, 1977; *Sacramento Bee*, March 9, 1977.

165 **"In nearly simultaneous":** *Wilkes-Barre Times Leader*, March 9, 1977.

165 **DC city councilman:** *Los Angeles Times*, March 9, 1977.

165 *Mohammad, Messenger of God* **was:** *Philadelphia Inquirer*, March 24, 1977; *Los Angeles Times*, March 9, 1977.

166 **"I feel very strongly":** *Los Angeles Times*, January 18, 1978.

166 **Shortly before 4:30 A.M.:** *Los Angeles Times*, June 15, 1978; *Philadelphia Daily News*, December 7, 1978.

166 **"Originally, we had the money":** Terry Gilliam, *Monty Python's Life of Brian*, audio commentary, November 16, 1999, Criterion Edition DVD.

166 **"Delfont had been approached":** Eric Idle, *Monty Python's Life of Brian*, audio commentary, November 16, 1999, Criterion Edition DVD.

167 **"It was the first scene":** Terry Jones, *Monty Python's Life of Brian*, audio commentary, November 16, 1999, Criterion Edition DVD.

167 **"The rabbis went away":** Eric Idle, *Always Look on the Bright Side of Life: A Sortabiography* (New York: Crown Archetype, 2018), 120.

167 **Organized evangelical groups:** *Sioux City Journal*, October 31, 1979.

167 **"The film held up":** *Alexandria Town Talk*, October 25, 1979.

167 **"There was no need":** Idle, *Always Look*, 121.

168 **"I would simply point out":** Malcolm Muggeridge, *Friday Night, Saturday Morning*, BBC2, November 9, 1979.

168 **"The area of life":** *Esquire*, April 1958.

168 *Life of Brian* **was banned:** Michael Palin, *Michael Palin: Diaries 1980–1988* (New York: St. Martin's Press, 2009), 11.

168 **And an advertising campaign:** The Secret Life of Brian, Channel 4 Television, 2007.

169 **"We were pilloried":** Gilliam, *Monty Python's Life of Brian*, audio commentary.

169 **"I was very surprised by the degree":** John Cleese, *Monty Python's Life of Brian*, audio commentary, November 16, 1999, Criterion Edition DVD.

169 **"One nice footnote":** Idle, *Always Look*, 121.

12

171 **Paul Weyrich caused:** *Racine Journal Times*, June 23, 1961.

171 **He marched with a sign:** *Racine Journal Times*, June 24, 1961.

171 **"Will someone ask the youngsters":** *Racine Journal Times*, June 24, 1961.

172 **"We condemn these tactics":** *Racine Journal Times*, June 23, 1961.

172 **"We have read and heard":** *Racine Journal Times*, June 27, 1961.

172 **"The Journal-Times attempted":** *Racine Journal Times*, June 30, 1961.

172 **His sharp tone led:** *Sheboygan Press*, May 12, 1962; *Madison Capital Times*, May 14, 1962; *Racine Journal Times Sunday Bulletin*, August 5, 1962, January 21, 1962, July 9, 1962, and October 23, 1961.

172 **"In my estimation his comment":** *Waukesha Daily Freeman*, May 25, 1965.

172 **"Paul Weyrich, WISN news":** *Waukesha Daily Freeman*, May 26, 1965.

173 **"I share your great concern":** *Waukesha Daily Freeman*, May 25, 1965.

173 **The few people who supported:** David Brock, *The Republican Noise Machine: Right-Wing Media and How It Corrupts Democracy* (New York: Crown Publishers, 2004), 82.

173 **"The Far Right has been":** John Harold Redekop, *The American Far Right: A Case Study of Billy James Hargis and Christian Crusade* (Grand Rapids, MI: William B. Eerdmans Publishing, 1968), 3–4; *Sacramento Bee*, May 26, 1968.

173 **"badly outmatched":** Alexander-Hertel Fernandez, *State Capture: How Conservative Activists, Big Businesses, and Wealthy Donors Reshaped the American States—and the Nation* (New York: Oxford University Press, 2019), 28.

173 **In 1973, Paul Weyrich met with Joseph Coors:** Brock, *The Republican Noise Machine*, 43–44; *Evansville Press*, December 29, 1975; Brock, *The Republican Noise Machine*, 44–45.

173 **"Pretending":** Lee Cokorinos, *The Assault on Diversity: An Organized Challenge to Racial and Gender Justice* (Oxford, UK: Rowan & Littlefield Publishers Inc, 2003), 6.

174 **As the book:** Fernandez, *State Capture*, 23.

174 **"In the world according to ALEC":** *The Nation*, July 12, 2011.

174 **Weyrich used a strategist:** Alan Crawford, *Thunder on the Right: The "New Right" and the Politics of Resentment* (New York: Pantheon Books, 1980), 12–13.

174 **Their team of lawyers:** Fernandez, *State Capture*, 32.

174 **Paul Weyrich established:** *Waterville Telegraph*, November 1, 1990.

174 **"to convert the politically dormant":** Brock, *The Republican Noise Machine*, 186–187.

174 **In 1974, a Texas school:** *Austin American Statesman*, October 2, 1974, and September 11, 1974.

174 **Norma Gabler, a housewife:** Russ Bellant, *The Coors Connection: How Coors Family Philanthopy Undermines Democratic Pluralism* (Boston: South End Press, 1991), 97; *Miami News*, April 30, 1983; Bellant, *The Coors Connection*, 96; *Miami News*, April 25, 1983; *Childress Index*, March 11, 1973; *Kilgore News Herald*, June 5, 197; *Wichita Falls Times-Record-News*, August 25, 1978; *Tyler Courier Times*, November 18, 1973; Crawford, *Thunder on the Right*, 157.

175 **"The only purpose"**: *Tyrone Daily Herald*, November 29, 1974.

175 **"The protest was publicly"**: Bellant, *The Coors Connection*, 3

176 **"Rise up in arms"**: *Miami News*, April 25, 1983.

176 **Weyrich brought:** Nina J. Easton, *Gang of Five: Leaders at the Center of the Conservative Crusade* (New York: Simon & Schuster, 2000), 84.

176 **"Weyrich proposed"**: Bellant, *The Coors Connection*, 17–18.

176 **"What is power?"**: Crawford, *Thunder on the Right*, 111.

176 **Paul Weyrich courted:** Page, *The Right to Lifers*, 171, 138.

176 **With Jerry Falwell as:** Crawford, *Thunder on the Right*, 160; Bellant, *The Coors Connection*, 18; Cokorinos, *The Assault on Diversity*, 23–24, 22.

177 **"He's just a Johnny-come-lately"**: Donald T. Critchlow, *When Hollywood Was Right: How Movie Stas, Studio Moguls, and Big Business Remade American Politics* (New York: Cambridge University Press, 2013), 178.

177 **Film noir:** Carl Rollyson, *Hollywood Enigma: Dana Andrews* (Jackson: University Press of Mississippi, 2012), 283.

177 **"I didn't know"**: Mary Kiersch, int., *Curtis Bernhardt: Interviewed by Mary Kiersch; A Directors Guild of America Oral History* (Metuchen, NJ: Scarecrow Press, 1986), 90.

177 **"He and Nancy were lunching"**: Sheilah Graham, *Confessions of a Hollywood Columnist* (New York: Bantam, 1970), 258–259.

177 **"This guy was thought to be a company man"**: Rod Serling, UCLA Lecture, November 11, 1966.

177 **"A few years after the TV release"**: Moe Howard, *Moe Howard and the 3 Stooges: The Pictorial Biography of the Wildest Trio in the History of American Entertainment* (New York: Citadel Press, 1977), 75.

178 **Vereen said ABC:** Associated Press, February 5, 2019.

178 **Meanwhile, Rich Little:** *Albany Democrat-Herald*, February 24, 1981.

178 **"Before we start anything"**: Rich Little, *The Tonight Show Starring Johnny Carson*, February 23, 1981.

178 **"He is probably the most"**: Johnny Carson, *The Tonight Show Starring Johnny Carson*, November 13, 1979.

178 *Saturday Night Live* **ridiculed:** Easton, *Gang of Five*, 147.

178 **"The same conservatism"**: *Alexandria Town Talk*, September 10, 1981.

179 **"I object to the networks"**: *Philadelphia Inquirer*, May 5, 1981.

179 **"I don't give a damn"**: *Weekly World News*, November 10, 1981.

179 **"An ignorant Bible-thumping"**: *Tampa Tribune*, October 2, 1982.

179 **The feud concerned:** *Tampa Tribune*, October 2, 1982.

179 **"Is it necessary"**: *Boston Globe*, July 10, 1981.

179 **"We were attacked by"**: Tony Randall, interview by the Archive of American Television, April 30, 1998.

179 **The Council for National Policy included:** Bellant, *The Coors Connection*, 38.

180 **"I am a conservative"**: Crawford, *Thunder on the Right*, 71.

180 **"Abortion is a private matter"**: *Clarksdale Press Register*, April 13, 1982.

180 **"The religious right scares the hell"**: Barry Goldwater, *20/20*, ABC, July 23, 1993.

180 **"Don't try to preach":** Barry Goldwater, *Crossfire*, CNN, 1988.

180 **"Isn't it interesting":** *60 Minutes*, CBS, September 21, 1980.

180 **Many politicians felt:** Timothy Stanley, *The Crusader: The Life and Tumultuous Times of Pat Buchanan* (New York: St. Martin's Press, 2012), 81.

180 **"If Ed Asner won't stop":** Douglass K. Daniel, *Lou Grant: The Making of TV's Top Newspaper Drama* (Syracuse, NY: Syracuse University Press, 1996), 142.

181 **Relying on information:** William J. Daugherty, *Executive Secrets: Covert Action and the Presidency* (Lexington: University Press of Kentucky, 2004), 254.

181 **"Today we want":** Daniel, *Lou Grant*, 132–133.

181 **"Every liberating force":** *Jackson Clarion-Ledger*, February 16, 1982.

181 **"I wish to state":** Ben Shapiro, *Primetime Propaganda: The True Hollywood Story of How the Left Took Over Your TV* (New York: Broadside Books, 2011), 185.

181 **"very dangerous man":** *LA Weekly*, July 4, 1985.

182 **"This letter was designed":** *Petoskey News-Review*, February 18, 1982.

182 **A campaign to cancel:** *Indiana Gazette*, January 27, 1981; *Hagerstown Morning Herald*, June 1, 1986; *Arizona Republic*, October 30, 1976; *Napa Valley Register*, February 24, 1982; Militarist Monitor, International Relations Center, January 1, 1991; *North Hills News Record*, March 2, 1982.

182 **"Ed Asner is a Communist":** *Edmonton Journal*, February 19, 1982.

182 **An anonymous phone call to SAG:** Daniel, *Lou Grant*, 137.

182 **One of the sponsors:** *Sioux City Journal*, July 2, 1982.

182 **"Asner's activities":** *Appleton Post-Crescent*, May 12, 1982.

182 **"Owning factories"; "The program was":** *Sioux City Journal*, July 2, 1982.

182 **"I regret the lack":** *Berkeley Gazette*, May 9, 1982.

183 **"From Miami to the Pacific":** *Miami News*, April 25, 1983.

183 **Citizens Organized for:** *Chico Enterprise Record*, September 27, 1987.

183 **Jerry Falwell and the Moral:** *Cincinnati Enquirer*, November 10, 1984.

183 **"Censorship always grows":** *Scranton Times-Tribune*, December 16, 1984.

183 **The Zion:** *Minneapolis Star*, November 30, 1979.

184 **Steve and Danny Peters came to prominence:** *Chicago Tribune*, October 11, 1980.

184 **The Peters Brothers claimed:** *Minneapolis Star*, November 26, 1980.

184 **"I believe that this is the largest":** *Minneapolis Star*, March 5, 1980.

184 **"I remember the day Danny":** *Lexington Herald*, February 21, 1981.

184 **The *Minneapolis Tribune* arranged:** *Minneapolis Star Tribune*, February 18, 1983.

185 **The Assembly of God Church in Keokuk:** *Des Moines Register*, March 3, 1981.

185 **"Rock n' roll stars stand for what's ungodly":** *Durham Herald-Sun*, May 9, 1981.

185 **In April 1983, the Santiam:** *Miami News*, April 25, 1983.

186 **"from Abba to Zappa":** *Lincoln Star*, October 13, 1981.

186 **"With the proliferation":** Frank Zappa, *Newsmagazine*, KCBS, May 18, 1984.

186 **"What the bill would require":** *Bellingham Herald*, May 24, 1982.

186 **"We have never done anything":** *Alexandria Town Talk*, May 3, 1982.

186 **Pastor Jim Brown:** *Chicago Tribune*, June 5, 1986.

13

187 **An organization called:** *Village Voice*, August 20, 2015.

187 **"You should be concerned":** *Fremont News-Messenger*, August 19, 1980.

188 **"To try and write something":** *South Bend Tribune*, March 12, 1980.

188 **"As a parent with two children":** *Lincoln Journal Star*, October 15, 1981.

188 **Police temporarily:** *Dayton Daily News*, August 24, 1979.

188 **A member of the Viletones:** *Edmonton Journal*, March 27, 1980; *Paterson Morning News*, March 6, 1979.

188 **Undercover police:** *Arizona Republic*, June 7, 1981; Associated Press, January 1981; *Springfield Leader*, January 23, 1981.

188 **Williams told the press:** *Lincoln Star Journal*, June 7, 1981; Associated Press, January 1981; *Fort Worth Star-Telegram*, February 4, 1981; *Santa Rosa Press Democrat*, June 4, 1981; Associated Press, January 1981.

188 **"Police told me they had seen me":** Wendy O. Williams, *Donahue*, June 1990.

188 **"sado-masochistic dance":** *Springfield Leader*, January 23, 1981.

188 **At the subsequent:** *Muncie Evening Press*, April 9, 1981; *Tucson Citizen*, June 11, 1981.

189 **A church leader from Hindman:** *Lexington Herald Leader*, May 2, 1984.

189 **Access to MTV:** *Tacoma News Tribune*, February 9, 1985.

189 **"There's a strong possibility":** Frank Zappa, Lincoln Christian University, April 7, 1986.

189 **"The whole business being so":** Frank Zappa, *Newsmagazine*, KCBS, May 18, 1984.

189 **"Around that time":** Tipper Gore, *Raising PG Kids in an X-Rated Society* (Nashville: Abingdon Press, 1987), 18.

190 **The PMRC included:** *Alternative Index*, September 14, 1991.

190 **The PMRC blamed:** *Hackensack Record*, October 6, 1985; Claude Chastanger, "The Parents' Music Resource Center: From Information to Censorship," *Popular Music* 18, no. 2, (Cambridge University Press, May 1999), 181; Gore, *Raising PG Kids*, 70–71.

190 **The PMRC suggested:** *Billings Gazette*, August 4, 1985.

190 **"This woman told me":** Gore, *Raising PG Kids*, 58–59.

190 **"The names of some":** Gore, *Raising PG Kids*, 49–50.

190 **Gore claimed the PMRC campaign:** James Davison Hunter, *Culture Wars: The Struggle Define America; Making Sense of the Battles over the Family, Art, Education, Law, and Politics* (New York: HarperCollins, 1991), 243; *Hackensack Record*, October 6, 1985.

191 **The PMRC expanded:** Gore, *Raising PG Kids*, 118, 140, 28.

191 **The PMRC was endorsed:** *Village Voice*, October 10, 1989.

191 **Other supplemental research:** *Village Voice*, August 20, 2015.

191 **Held in September 1985:** *Hackensack Record*, October 6, 1985.

191 **"drug oriented":** *Los Angeles Times*, December 12, 1972.

191 **An obscure pastor:** Gore, *Raising PG Kids*, 33.

191 **Ling set up a slideshow:** PMRC Senate hearing, C-SPAN, September 19, 1985.

191 **Frank Zappa said:** Gore, *Raising PG Kids*, 26.

191 **"No one has forced"**: *Record Labeling: Hearing Before the Committee on Commerce, Science, and Transportation*, 99th Cong. 1, September 19, 1985.

192 **Congresswoman Paula Hawkins**: *Record Labeling: Hearing Before the Committee on Commerce, Science, and Transportation*, 99th Cong. 1, September 19, 1985.

194 **"Now, it seems to"**: Frank Zappa, interview by Martin Perlich, October 12, 1988.

194 **"I think it's inherent"**: Frank Zappa, *Newsmagazine*, KCBS, May 18, 1984.

194 **The PMRC did not get everything**: *Hawaii Tribune-Herald*, February 27, 1997; Chastagner, "The Parents' Music Resource Center," 184–188.

195 **Reverend Don Wildmon returned**: University of Pennsylvania Law Review, "Advocacy group boycotting of network television advertisers and its effects on programming content," December 1991.

195 **including ALF; Murder, She Wrote**: *Albuquerque Journal*, July 15, 1993.

195 **"We are in the middle"**: *Scranton Times-Tribune*, December 26, 1985.

195 **A protest held in front of the Southland**: *Dayton Daily News*, September 3, 1985.

195 **Reverend Wildmon was busy**: *Moline Dispatch*, August 17, 1991; *Tampa Tribune*, June 21, 1989; *Jackson Clarion-Ledger*, January 16, 1988.

195 **"Are There Any Books Vile"**: *Arcadia Tribune*, December 16, 1962.

195–96 **"The Moral Majority picketed Gulf"**: *Boston Globe*, August 9, 1988.

196 **"This is Hollywood's darkest hour"**: Lindlof, *Hollywood Under Siege*, 220; *Sacramento Bee*, August 10, 1988.

196 **Falwell intended**: Lindlof, *Hollywood Under Siege*, 246.

196 **"Wasserman Fans"**: Lindlof, *Hollywood Under Siege*, 187–188.

196 **The Tabernacle**: *Sacramento Bee*, August 10, 1988.

196 **"the most perverted"**: *Great Falls Tribune*, August 7, 1988.

196 **MCA Universal's president**: Lindlof, *Hollywood Under Siege*, 191.

196 **"wave of anti-Semitism"**: Lindlof, *Hollywood Under Siege*, 190.

196 **"Of course, a sizable"**: Lindlof, *Hollywood Under Siege*, 201.

196 **Universal installed**: Lindlof, *Hollywood Under Siege*, 202.

196 **The FBI discovered**: Lindlof, *Hollywood Under Siege*, 204–205.

197 **"It was scary not only"**: Lindlof, *Hollywood Under Siege*, 204.

197 **Oscar-winning director Franco**: *Sacramento Bee*, August 10, 1988.

197 **"truly horrible and completely deranged"**: *Berkshire Eagle*, August 5, 1988.

197 **Ten years earlier**: *Asbury Park Press*, April 1, 1977.

197 **"I was in Los Angeles"**: Don Wildmon, *The Oprah Winfrey Show*, September 1988.

197 **A huge protest**: Lindlof, *Hollywood Under Siege*, 1–3.

197 **speech delivered by Dennis**: *The Los Angeles Times*, August 12, 1988.

197 **Theater operators in each city**: *The Sacramento Bee*, August 10, 1988.

197 **"I can recall areas"**: Lindlof, *Hollywood Under Siege*, 230–231.

197 **In Paris**: *The London Observer*, October 30, 1988.

198 **"The situation degraded"**: Lindlof, *Hollywood Under Siege*, 293.

198 **Pat Buchanan published**: Lindlof, *Hollywood Under Siege*, 196–197, 232, 12.

198 **Lutheran pastor**: Charles Bergstrom, *The Oprah Winfrey Show*, September 1988.

198 **"a narrow group"**: *Great Falls Tribune*, August 7, 1988.

14

199 **"Comedy has gotten"**: *Chicago Tribune*, March 16, 1984.

199 **In the 1980s:** Jean Maddern Pitrone, *Take It from the Big Mouth: The Life of Martha Raye* (Lexington: University Press of Kentucky, 1999), 178.

199 **She claimed:** *Baltimore Sun*, August 21, 1987; Maddern Pitrone, *Take It from the Big Mouth*, 183; *Twin Falls Times-News*, January 8, 1988.

200 **"I don't think show business"**: *Camden Courier-Post*, June 7, 1986.

200 **"Those four-letter words"**: *Christian Science Monitor*, May 16, 1984.

200 **"Is Buddy Hackett"**: *Cincinnati Enquirer*, August 25, 1969.

200 **"I don't use the"**: *Camden Courier-Post*, March 25, 1969.

200 **KTLA television personality:** Buddy Hackett, *Family Film Festival*, KTLA-TV, 1985.

201 **Bob Hope got in trouble:** Wesley Hyatt, *Bob Hope on TV: Thanks for the Video Memories* (Albany, GA: Bear Manor Media, 2017), 210.

201 **"Those who did not groan"**: *Los Angeles Times*, July 30, 1986.

201 **"Bob Hope did not speak"**: *Los Angeles Times*, August 9, 1986.

201 **Hope issued an apology:** Hyatt, *Bob Hope on TV*, 210.

201 **"In what appears to be a gallant"**: *Honolulu Advertiser*, August 16, 1986.

201 **Lyndon LaRouche was a perpetual:** Dennis King, *Lyndon LaRouche: And the New American Fascism* (New York: Doubleday, 1989), ix.

201 **"reintroducing and enforcing"**: Russ Bellant, *The Coors Connection: How Coors Family Philanthopy Undermines Democratic Pluralism* (Boston, MA: South End Press, 1991), 63.

201 **Dannemeyer was connected:** Thomas R. Lindlof, *Hollywood Under Siege: Martin Scorsese, the Religious Right, and the Culture Wars* (Lexington: University Press of Kentucky, 2008), 244.

202 **"How can you legislate poor taste"**: *San Francisco Examiner*, October 12, 1986.

203 **Murphy told a huge crowd:** *Manhattan Mercury*, May 19, 1985.

203 **"As the demonstrators lined the curb"**: *Palm Beach Post*, March 22, 1989.

203 **"Nearly a dozen"**: *St. Louis Post-Dispatch*, April 14, 1991.

203 **At a gig in Vancouver:** *Vancouver Sun*, March 9, 1991.

203 **The Associated Press reported on a scuffle:** *Victorville Daily Press*, May 17, 1989.

204 **"They say Sam's comedy is vanguard"**: *LA Weekly*, January 29, 1987.

204 **"I'm the one that's not threatened"**: Bobcat Goldthwait, appearing on CNN.com, April 5, 2012.

204 **"For years, primal-scream comedian"**: *People*, July 9, 1990.

204 **The all-comedy issue:** *LA Weekly*, January 29, 1987.

204 **Wearing a twenty-dollar:** Andrew Dice Clay with David Ritz, *The Filthy Truth* (New York: Simon & Schuster, 2014), 63–64.

204–5 **He got his first professional:** Clay with Ritz, *The Filthy Truth*, 91.

205 **"That character is too tough"**: Clay with Ritz, *The Filthy Truth*, 108–109.

205 **"I don't know what just"**: Clay with Ritz, *The Filthy Truth*, 186–187.

205 **"Andrew Dice Clay did not do this"**: *Southern Illinoisan*, September 8, 1989.

205 **"I felt that MTV"**: Clay with Ritz, *The Filthy Truth*, 220.

206 **"brownshirt humor"**: *Arizona Republic*, July 11, 1990.

206 **"to the worst instincts of humanity"**: *Alliance Times-Herald*, July 10, 1990.

206 **"I think that's just something"**: Bill Murray, *Larry King Live*, CNN, July 11, 1990.

206 **"What he needs is an act"**: *Modesto Bee*, August 2, 1990.

206 **"The thing that I find unusual"**: George Carlin, *Larry King Live*, CNN, July 20, 1999.

206 **"There is an undercurrent"**: Associated Press, May 18, 1990.

206 **"If you don't want to come"**: *Pottsville Republican*, February 16, 1991.

206 **"If the press didn't understand"**: Clay with Ritz, *The Filthy Truth*, 203.

207 **Protesters filled the lobby:** *Davenport Quad City Times*, May 14, 1990.

207 **Protests followed:** *Pottsville Republican*, February 16, 1991; *Philadelphia Daily News*, November 24, 1990.

207 **"obscenity laws in Texas were"**: *Fort Worth Star-Telegram*, August 16, 1990.

207 **and comedy team of Bowley & Wilson:** Associated Press, September 7, 1981.

207 **"We fear the possibility"**: *The Spokesman Review*, August 27, 1990.

207 **"Watching the way"**: *Sacramento Bee*, June 14, 1991.

207 **"creative philosophy"**: *Columbus Republic*, September 19, 1990.

207 **Despite his popularity:** Clay with Ritz, *The Filthy Truth*, 249–250.

207 **"I've created something so unique"**: *Hanford Sentinel*, August 27, 1990.

15

209 **"What radio does"**: Harrison B. Summers, ed., *Radio Censorship* (New York: Arno Press, 1971), 50.

209 **"to preserve our now vast"**: Michele Hilmes, ed., *Radio Reader: Essays in the Cultural History of Radio* (New York: Routledge, 2001), 29.

210 **"Should there ever be an attempt"**: Summers, ed., *Radio Censorship*, 242–252.

210 **"In theory if not always in practice"**: Robert J. Landry, *This Fascinating Radio Business* (New York: The Bobbs-Merrill Company, 1946), 99–100.

210 **A station owner in Long Island:** *Newsday*, December 2, 1947.

210 **There is a very real danger:** *Ventura County Star*, October 4, 1952; Lewis L. Gould, ed., *Watching Television Come of Age: The* New York Times *Reviews by Jack Gould* (Austin: University of Texas Press, 2004), 120–121.

210 **"I feel that if our constitutional"**: Merle Miller, *Plain Speaking: An Oral Biography of Harry. S. Truman* (New York: Berkley Publishing Corporation, 1974), 411.

211 **The Fairness Doctrine was amended again:** *TV Guide*, November 10, 1962; Nicole Hemmer, *Messengers of the Right: Conservative Media and the Transformation of American Politics* (Philadelphia: University of Pennsylvania Press, 2016), 114–115.

211 **"Liberals in the United States"**: Billy James Hargis, *Why I Fight for a Christian America* (Nashville: Thomas Nelson Inc., 1974), 88–89.

211 **"more often than not these forums"**: *Variety*, October 5, 1966.

211 **"What the people who run these programs"**: *Variety*, April 9, 1969.

211 **"Some say that corporate America"**: *Variety*, January 10, 1968.

212 **"One of the fantasies"**: Frank Zappa, *LA Live*, radio station KFI, October 30, 1988.

212 **"If you raise this bogeyman"**: Frank Zappa, *The Larry King Show*, Mutual Broadcasting System, June 6, 1989.

212 **"As disturbing as these racial stereotypes"**: *Orlando Sentinel*, January 23, 1988.

212 **"On his morning radio program"**: *Boston Globe*, December 19, 1987.

212 **Tom Barnard spoke:** *Minneapolis Star Tribune*, August 21, 1998; *Boston Globe*, December 19, 1987; *Minneapolis Star Tribune*, September 12, 1998.

213 **Florida shock jocks:** *Tampa Bay Times*, March 5, 1986.

214 **Tracht had joined:** *Eau Claire Leader-Telegram*, February 17, 1986.

214 **Speaking on Martin:** *Washington Post*, November 29, 1987; *Baltimore Sun*, May 5, 1989.

214 **Eighteen months later:** *Great Falls Tribune*, September 14, 1997.

214 **Limbaugh was hired:** *Sacramento Bee*, June 30, 1988.

215 **The station erected billboards:** *Sacramento Bee*, September 14, 1986.

215 **Premiere On Call told its clients:** *The Tablet*, February 11, 2011.

215 **According to journalist:** Jane Mayer, *Dark Money: The Hidden History of the Billionaires Behind the Rise of the Radical Right* (New York: Doubleday, 2016), 27–30.

215 **"As long as there is somebody"**: Frank Zappa, radio station WROQ, June 6, 1993.

215 **"I was invited by the Libertarian Party"**: Frank Zappa, radio station WLUP, November 7, 1988.

216 **"Their cause, they say, is liberty"**: Nancy MacLean, *Democracy in Chains: The Deep History of the Radical Right's Stealth Plan for America* (New York: Viking, 2017), xxviii.

16

217 **"The worst problems in my life"**: Luther Campbell and John R. Miller, *As Nasty As They Wanna Be: The Uncensored Story of Luther Campbell of the 2 Live Crew* (Kingston, Jamaica: Kingston Publishers, 1992), 68.

217 **"You had these leftover bigots"**: 2 Live Crew, Banned in the U.S.A. (Japan promo, NTSC laserdisc, 2000).

217 **Massive amounts of cash:** *Raleigh News & Observer*, October 29, 1972.

217 **"Dr. King's action-oriented Marxism"**: *Battle Creek Enquirer*, October 4, 1983.

218 **He claimed a holiday in his honor:** *Davenport Quad City Times*, October 4, 1983.

218 **Evan Mecham:** *Washington Post*, September 2, 1987; *Utah Daily Spectrum*, March 5, 1987; *Arizona Republic*, March 15, 1987; *Arizona Daily Sun*, March 25, 1987.

218 **"slavery hurt"**: *Arizona Republic*, March 26, 1987.

218 **They advocated budget cuts to PBS:** David Brock, *The Republican Noise Machine: Right-Wing Media and How It Corrupts Democracy* (New York: Crown Publishers, 2004), 76–77.

218 **as "Cultural Marxism"**: *The Somerset Daily American*, May 2, 1986.

218 **Pat Robertson promoted:** Jerry Falwell, interview by C-SPAN, August 29, 1985, https://www.c-span.org/video/?123662-1/south-africa.

218 **Congressman Dick:** *Nightline*, September 4, 1985.

218 **"front for South Africa's":** *Gettysburg Times*, July 17, 1995.

219 **Before he got into broadcasting:** Sara Diamond, *Spiritual Warfare: The Politics of the Christian Right* (Boston: South End Press, 1989), 13.

219 **"a socialist, anti-family":** *Times*, August 26, 1992.

219 **"Pat has made so many statements":** Barry Goldwater, *20/20*, ABC, July 23, 1993.

219 **"pollutes society"** *Wisconsin State Journal*, **March 25, 1990.**

219 **2 Live Crew were the undisputed:** Campbell and Miller, *As Nasty*, xi.

219 **"Our music is fun entertainment":** 2 Live Crew, *Banned in the U.S.A.*

219 **A judge halted sales:** Campbell and Miller, *As Nasty*, 130–131.

220 **"distributing obscene material":** *Fort Myers News-Press*, October 7, 1990.

220 **"Every year, if you notice it":** *Miami Herald*, March 17, 1990.

220 **"We are particularly offended":** Michael Medved, *Hollywood vs. America* (New York: Harper Perennial, 1992), 101.

220 **Cal Thomas, speaking for the Heritage Foundation:** *Quad City Times*, October 25, 1990.

220 **Police unions around the country:** *Sacramento Bee*, July 30, 1989; *Modesto Bee*, February 2, 1990.

221 **"We just wanted to show the kids":** *Village Voice*, August 20, 2015.

221 **"There were close to two hundred of us":** *Michigan Live*, August 27, 2015.

221 **A reporter with the *Village Voice*:** *Village Voice*, October 10, 1989.

221 **"I grew up threatened":** Ice-T, *Entertainment Tonight*, June 19, 1992.

222 **"I feel no shame for it":** *A Current Affair*, April 20, 1993.

222 **"The LAPD, they're a different breed":** *Salt Lake City Tribune*, January 5, 1993.

222 **"We want to educate the public":** *San Francisco Examiner*, July 16, 1992.

222 **"Ice-T didn't shoot":** *Fort Worth Star-Telegram*, June 9, 1992.

222 **The ironically named:** *Los Angeles Times*, July 2, 1992.

222 **"governors in all 50 states":** *Los Angeles Times*, July 26, 1992.

222 **"I have advised Colonel North":** *Los Angeles Times*, July 2, 1992.

223 **"It is laughable":** *Los Angeles Times*, July 26, 1992.

223 **"The album has been out":** Ice-T, interview by Fab 5 Freddy, *Yo! MTV Raps*, 1992.

223 **"That was just the funniest thing":** Ernie Cunnigan, "Ice-T controversy during the LA Riots," Mos-Def channel, posted November 29, 2013. https://www.youtube.com/watch?v=UxC3IU4BHV.

223 **"I've gotten a lot of angry":** Arsenio Hall, *The Arsenio Hall Show*, July 21, 1992.

223 **It was reported that:** Ice T, "Ice T / Body Count—Cop Killer Controversy," Ralph Viera Videos channel, published April 17, 2017, https://www.youtube.com/watch?v=AAouKLtnSFw.

224 **"I am going to make the request":** *Detroit Free Press*, July 29, 1992.

224 **"Over 70 percent of the people":** *Entertainment Tonight*, July 1992.

17

225 **"There was a time in radio"**: *Tucson Citizen*, October 25, 1990.

225 **Due to the "anti-family attitude" of:** *Lansing State Journal*, February 12, 1989.

226 **That year, the category:** The 43rd Annual Primetime Emmy Awards, August 25, 1991.

226 **Gottfried got big laughs:** *St. Lucie News Tribune*, August 27, 1991.

226 **"I was angry to no end"; "I could have gone":** *St. Louis Post Dispatch*, September 3, 1991.

226 **"juvenile addiction":** Michael Medved, *Hollywood vs. America* (New York: Harper Perennial, 1992), 119.

226 **"That was in bad taste":** *Allentown Morning Call*, September 20, 1991.

226 **"What gets me":** Judy Gold, *Yes, I Can Say That: When They Come for the Comedians, We Are All in Trouble* (New York: William Morrow and Company Inc., 2020), 164.

227 **Cosby criticized:** *Tampa Tribune*, April 13, 1991.

227 **"The mean-spirited and cruel":** *Fresno Bee*, August 25, 1990.

227 **"We need a nation closer":** *Modesto Bee*, January 28, 1992.

227 **William Bennett, a former:** *Kerrville Times*, May 17, 1990.

227 **"the dumbest thing I had ever seen":** *Detroit Free Press*, October 11, 1990.

227 **"This so-called comedy":** *Detroit Free Press*, September 30, 1990.

228 **"This gratuitous expression of violence":** *Los Angeles Times*, May 24, 1990.

228 **"To be proud of being an incompetent":** *Wilkes Barre Times Leader*, April 29, 1990.

228 **A school principal in Kentucky:** *Newark Advocate*, May 26, 1990.

228 **"I don't think Bart is helping us":** *Waterloo Courier*, September 25, 1990.

228 **"I believe the lawless":** Timothy Stanley, *The Crusader: The Life and Tumultuous Times of Pat Buchanan* (New York: St. Martin's Press, 2012), 204; *Wichita Eagle*, May 20, 1992.

229 **"appalled" him:** *Buffalo News*, May 24, 1992.

229 **David Letterman joked:** *Sioux Falls Argus Leader*, May 22, 1992.

229 **"He has never seen the whole show":** *Buffalo News*, May 24, 1992.

229 **Political observers from outside:** Gavin Esler, CNN, June 13, 1992.

229 **"Dan Quayle is":** Nikki Giovanni, International Correspondents, CNN, June 13, 1992.

229 **"Homeboy Shopping Network divided the staff":** David Peisner, *Homey Don't Play That!: The Story of* In Living Color *and the Black Comedy Revolution* (New York: Simon & Schuster, 2018), 125.

230 **"At one point, Fox brought":** Peisner, *Homey Don't Play That!*, 130–131.

230 **The sketch was:** Peisner, *Homey Don't Play That!*, 197.

230 **"The sketch is not a *bashing* sketch":** Damon Wayans, *Donahue*, November 1990.

230 **"All those stereotypes":** *Arizona Republic*, February 21, 1993.

231 **At the height of:** *Donahue*, November 1990.

231 **"not to do a sketch":** Peisner, *Homey Don't Play That!*, 155.

232 **"Comedy in the States"; "more attention":** *The er*, November 1, 1993.

233 ***Beavis and Butt-Head* apparel was banned in schools:** *South Bend Tribune*, October 10, 1993.

233 **"chainwide ban":** *Hawaii Tribune-Herald*, February 27, 1997.

233 **A factory worker:** *Lancaster Eagle-Gazette*, April 25, 1995.

233 **"The mother says":** *Dayton Daily News*, October 8, 1993.

233 **"I literally *never* saw the cartoon":** @BeavisnButtheadCollector, Instagram, June 7, 2019. https://beavisandbutthead.fandom.com/wiki/Fire_Controversy#:~:text=How%20 could%20I%3F,his%20side%20of%20the%20story.

234 **Screenwriter Joe Eszterhas:** *Los Angeles Times*, April 29, 1991.

234 **"disorderly conduct and harassment":** *Orlando Sentinel*, April 13, 1992.

234 **The action film *True Lies*:** Jack G. Shaheen, *Reel Bad Arabs: How Hollywood Vilifies a People* (Brooklyn: Olive Branch Press, 2001), 500; *Windsor Star*, July 27, 1994.

234 **Casey Kasem, the beloved:** Shaheen, *Reel Bad Arabs*, 503.

234 **Hollywood movies were banned:** *Variety*, October 17, 1994; Shaheen, *Reel Bad Arabs*, 188–189; 450–451.

235 **"nightmares of depravity.":** *Hawaii Tribune-Herald*, February 27, 1997.

235 **"the loony left":** Medved, *Hollywood vs. America*, 3.

235 **"When an industry attempts":** Medved, *Hollywood vs. America*, 29–33.

235 **"Not only did TV criminalize":** Burton Yale Pines with Timothy W. Lamer, *Out of Focus: Network Television and the American Economy* (Washington, DC: Regnery Publishing, Inc. Company, 1994), 28, 57.

235 **Reverend Wildmon purchased a page:** *Cedar Rapids Gazette*, July 11, 1993.

236 **"I've always had a problem":** *Baltimore Sun*, July 23, 1996.

236 **"We find it curious":** *Sunbury Daily Item*, June 15, 1996.

236 **The anti-Disney campaign continued:** *Indianapolis News*, April 17, 1997.

237 **When word got out:** *Indianapolis News*, April 17, 1997.

237 **Wendy's and JCPenney:** *Pittsburgh Post-Gazette*, April 30, 1997.

237 **Steve Allen disapproved:** Steve Allen, *Vulgarians at the Gate: Trash TV and Raunch Radio* (Amherst, NY: Prometheus Books, 2001), 86; 53.

237 **"in equal measure":** David Brock, *The Republican Noise Machine: Right-Wing Media and How It Corrupts Democracy* (New York: Crown Publishers, 2004), 93–95.

237 **Bozell ran an ad:** *Wilmington News Journal*, June 10, 1998.

238 **Steve Allen went on:** Allen, *Vulgarians at the Gate*, 93–94, 35, 51, 63–64, 108.

238 **"The producers,":** Allen, *Vulgarians at the Gate*, 35–36.

238 **But of the many things:** Allen, *Vulgarians at the Gate*, 237, 220.

238 **"Thank you for taking my call":** *Washington Journal*, C-SPAN, December 13, 2004.

18

239 **"[If the] public did not trust":** David Brock, *The Republican Noise Machine: Right-Wing Media and How It Corrupts Democracy* (New York: Crown Publishers, 2004), 107.

239 **In the late 1980s:** Institute for Cultural Conservatism, *Cultural Conservatism: Toward a New National Agenda* (Lanham, MD: Free Congress Foundation, 1987), 1–12.

239 **Lind delivered speeches:** Bill Lind, "Bill Lind Discussing the Spread of Cultural Marxism During It's [*sic*] Infancy as the Norm in 1998 YouTu [*sic*]," C-SPAN recording

from July 10, 1998, posted by Steps Towards Truth YouTube channel, July 18, 2017, https://www.youtube.com/watch?v=Mrx6xU_bwxM; Bill Lind, "College Campus Social and Political Issues," C-SPAN recording from July 10, 1998, https://www.c-span.org /video/?108496-1/college-campus-social-political-issues.

240 **"In fact, if we are going to rescue"**: Brock, *The Republican Noise Machine*, 197.

240 **"It is not our job"**: Nina J. Easton, *Gang of Five: Leaders at the Center of the Conservative Crusade* (New York: Simon & Schuster, 2000), 143–146.

240 **"corrupted academia"**: Jane Mayer, *Dark Money: The Hidden History of the Billionaires Behind the Rise of the Radical Right* (New York: Doubleday, 2016), 156, 364.

240 **"sought to slash their states'"**: Nancy MacLean, *Democracy in Chains: The Deep History of the Radical Right's Stealth Plan for America* (New York: Viking, 2017), 103.

240 **"a steady stream"**: Alexander-Hertel Fernandez, *State Capture: How Conservative Activists, Big Businesses, and Wealthy Donors Reshaped the American States—and the Nation* (New York: Oxford University Press, 2019), 162.

241 **"We learned that"**: Mayer, *Dark Money*, 364–365.

241 **NET was funded by**: Brock, *The Republican Noise Machine*, 196.

241 **"We will no longer allow"**: *Greenville News*, November 27, 1996.

241 **"Critical Theory is the basis"**: Bill Lind, "William S. Lind pushing his conspiracy of 'Cultural Marxism,'" posted by Sunny Mon YouTube channel, March 12, 2015, https://www.youtube.com/watch?v=ve6bulaiP3E.

241 **"Given how bad things have gotten"**: *Next Revolution*, July 8, 1999.

242 **"The violence of this political"**: *Baltimore Sun*, October 10, 2000.

242 **"I hadn't encountered anyone like"**: Timothy Stanley, *The Crusader: The Life and Tumultuous Times of Pat Buchanan* (New York: St. Martin's Press, 2012), 2.

242 **Buchanan believed**: Stanley, *The Crusader*, 18–19, 51, 52.

242 **"The African Americans"**: Stanley, *The Crusader*, 178.

242 **During his campaign**: Stanley, *The Crusader*, 177.

242 **And he blamed the**: Stanley, *The Crusader*, 203.

242 **"I will always be"**: Stanley, *The Crusader*, 182.

243 **"The Republicans wouldn't be content"**: Stanley, *The Crusader*, 5.

243 **Many Republicans objected**: Stanley, *The Crusader*, 286.

244 **"You don't build majorities"**: Stanley, *The Crusader*, 7.

244 **"What I don't like are the hairbrained"**: Harlan Ellison, *The Tom Snyder Show*, CNBC, June 30, 1994.

244 **"In news stories that day"**; **"While it may appear"**: Brock, *The Republican Noise Machine*, 61.

244 **Charles Koch and his "foundations" funded dozens of front groups**: MacLean, *Democracy in Chains*, xviii-xix.

244 **Every single one**: Mayer, *Dark Money*, 160.

245 **all of them were funded by the vast wealth**: Mayer, *Dark Money*, 151.

245 **"The news business has changed"**: Trudy Lieberman, *Slanting the Story: The Forces That Shape the News* (New York: W. W. Norton & Company, 2000), 8.

245 **FreedomWorks, one of the groups operated by Charles Koch:** Mayer, *Dark Money*, 183.

245 **Meyer said the purpose was:** Mayer, *Dark Money*, 83.

245 **"It doesn't take a rocket":** Brock, *The Republican Noise Machine*, 49.

246 **"They understand the propaganda potential,":** Lieberman, *Slanting the Story*, 5.

246 **Paul Weyrich warned his allies:** https://nationalcenter.org/ncppr/1999/02/16/letter-to-conservatives-by-paul-m-weyrich/.

246 **Someone once said:** George Will, "A Salute to Paul Weyrich," posted to YouTube, December 19, 2008.

247 **According to the president of a:** *Miami Herald*, April 1, 1999.

247 **"Racism, sexism and chauvinism":** *Intelligence Report*, August 15, 2003.

247 **"old White Citizens Council mailing lists":** *Berkshire Eagle*, January 15, 1999.

247 **He warned that the United States:** *Louisville Courier-Journal*, September 19, 2000.

247 **"We must take out country back":** Pat Buchanan, "Buchanan Vice President Announcement," C-SPAN recording from August 11, 2000, https://www.c-span.org/video/?158753-1/buchanan-vice-president-announcement.

247 **"He's anti-Semitic":** Donald Trump, *The Tonight Show with Jay Leno*, December 6, 1999.

248 **"Just so you know":** Chris Willman, *Rednecks & Bluenecks: The Politics of Country Music* (New York: W. W. Norton & Co., 2005), 25.

248 **"We've been overseas":** Willman, *Rednecks & Bluenecks*, 25.

248 **When the Dixie Chicks appeared in Greenville:** Willman, *Rednecks & Bluenecks*, xvi.

248 **"The phone just went":** Willman, *Rednecks & Bluenecks*, 26.

248 **Beck's radio program:** Willman, *Rednecks & Bluenecks*, 29.

248 **"Some of the biggest rallies":** *Chicago Tribune*, March 19, 2003.

249 **The music of the Dixie Chicks was banned:** Willman, *Rednecks & Bluenecks*, 27.

249 **"to be smashed by a tractor":** Willman, *Rednecks & Bluenecks*, 29.

249 **WDAF in Kansas City:** Willman, *Rednecks & Bluenecks*, 29–30.

249 **"How dare this first hippo":** Willman, *Rednecks & Bluenecks*, 31.

249 **Natalie Maines's aunt worked:** Willman, *Rednecks & Bluenecks*, 35, 41

249 **"I think it will go down in history":** Willman, *Rednecks & Bluenecks*, 44.

249 **"What a sickening disgrace":** Willman, *Rednecks & Bluenecks*, 31.

250 **"It's sinister to me":** Willman, *Rednecks & Bluenecks*, 32.

EPILOGUE

251 **"socially and racially reprehensible":** *Greenwood Index Journal*, April 17, 1982.

251 **"This activity has become":** *Oakland Tribune*, April 7, 1982.

251 **"They pay you for eight":** *Greenwood Index Journal*, April 17, 1982.

251 **"A city policeman whose":** *Baltimore Sun*, April 8, 1982.

252 **Officer Berger staged a night:** *Greenwood Index Journal*, April 17, 1982.

252 **"I would hate to think":** *Baltimore Sun*, February 27, 1982.

252 **Officer Berger kept:** *Baltimore Sun*, June 3, 1986, and May 3, 1984.

252 **"A city police department":** *Baltimore Sun*, May 3, 1984.

252 **"to protect its relations":** *Baltimore Sun*, December 29, 1985.

252 **The court ordered Officer Berger:** *Baltimore Sun*, September 26, 1991.

253 **"For them to be members":** *Palm Springs Desert Sun*, April 15, 1996.

253 **Now a senior citizen:** WJZ Television News, July 24, 2015.

INDEX

ISSED OFF THE STAGE

emarkable Demonstration at Theater in Gotham.

UST RESPECT THE IRISH

ree Hundred Irishmen Resent the Ridicule of Their Country.

AN-NA-GAEL ARE INVOLVED

DO NAUGHTY

the Good People of Gotham.

ill Dana 'Buries' Iis Jose Jimenez

ilwaukee Bans mos And Andy V Show

Audiences Nowadays,

ink Bombs, Fist Fights, 'How I Won the War'

ONDON (UPI) — Stink nbs exploded and a fight ke out last night in a Lon- theater during the screen- of the controversial British war film, "How I Won the

Controversial comic cancels Dallas show

☐ Andrew Dice Clay cites fear of arrest as reason

What Will These People Try to Ban Next?

There seems no limit to which some public agencies will go in racial matters, the latest example being the action of the New York City School Board in banning Mark Twain's "Huckleberry Finn" from the list of approved books for reading in various public school courses.

Ishtar upsets Arab group

WASHINGTON (AP) — An or- ganization of Arab-Americans is launching a protest against the movie Ishtar, condemning it as an affront to every Moslem.

Obscenities at gay rights benefit

Comedian stuns Hollywood

Too Thin Skinned, Comedian Claims

Editorials

France Outlaws Satire on Hitler

Are Americans Losing Our Sense of Humor?

Goebbels Bars Comedian

Werner Finck And Other Cabaret Actors Banned For Jokes About Nazism.

British Comedian Fi For Portraying H With a Jewish Ac

Raid on Mae West's Play Opens Broadway Clean-

Crusade Ordered by Mayor As Author and 55 A Of "Pleasure Man" Plead Not Guilty To Obscenity.

Danny Thomas Believes Audien Too Thin Skinne

Gottfried's masturbatio skit causes Emmy rift

Monologue shocks Emmys official

Negro Minister Protesting Minstrel Show in Anchora

Suburban Chief Disciplined for Anti-Negro Jokes

VIEWING TV

Dialect Comedy Bann By Television Taboos

OBSCENE VAUDEVI TO BE PROHIBIT

BBC Bans All Jokes About U. S. Soldier

Groucho Diagnose Our Ailing Comed

Miss. Theatres Give

laiming Charlie Chan a 'Racist,' Jerry Lewis the 'Hook' hinatown Residents Oppose Film Because of TV Cra